Writers and Politics in Germany, 1945–2008

Stuart Parkes

CAMDEN HOUSE
Rochester, New York

First published 2009
by Camden House

Camden House is an imprint of Boydell & Brewer Inc.
668 Mt. Hope Avenue, Rochester, NY 14620, USA
www.camden-house.com
and of Boydell & Brewer Limited
PO Box 9, Woodbridge, Suffolk IP12 3DF, UK
www.boydellandbrewer.com

ISBN-13: 978-1-57113-401-1
ISBN-10: 1-57113-401-8

Library of Congress Cataloging-in-Publication Data

Parkes, Stuart, 1943–
    Writers and politics in Germany, 1945–2008 / Stuart Parkes.
        p. cm. — (Studies in German literature, linguistics, and culture)
    Includes bibliographical references and index.
    ISBN-13: 978-1-57113-401-1 (hardcover : alk. paper)
    ISBN-10: 1-57113-401-8 (hardcover : alk. paper)
    1. Authors, German — 20th century — Political and social views.
    2. Authors, German — 21st century — Political and social views.
    3. German literature — 20th century — History and criticism.
    4. German literature — 21st century — History and criticism.
    5. Germany — Politics and government.   I. Title.   II. Series.

PT405.P3398 2009
830.9'35843087—dc22
                                                                2008046821

A catalogue record for this title is available from the British Library.

This publication is printed on acid-free paper.
Printed in the United States of America.

For Christy, Elise, Stefan, Gabrielle, William, Alastair, and Benjamin

Contents

Acknowledgments

I SHOULD LIKE TO THANK BY NAME Professor Arthur Williams (University of Bradford), Dr Ian King (London South Bank University), and Professor Julian Preece (University of Swansea) for their help and advice over many years. I also thank all those colleagues who have given me support since I took up my first lecturing appointment in 1971.

S. P.
October 2008

Abbreviations

THE FOLLOWING ABBREVIATIONS are used throughout to refer to frequently cited works. Full details are to be found in the bibliography.

FG   Frank Grützbach, ed., *Freies Geleit für Ulrike Meinhof. Ein Artikel und seine Folgen*

GDL   Ralf Schnell, *Geschichte der deutschsprachigen Literatur seit 1945*

KP   Manfred Jäger, *Kultur und Politik in der DDR 1945–1990*

M   Hans Werner Richter, ed., *Die Mauer oder Der 13. August*

TS   Günter Grass, *Aus dem Tagebuch einer Schnecke*

VLMS Klaus Wagenbach, ed., *Vaterland, Muttersprache*

Introduction

A 2004 COLLECTION OF ESSAYS, published under the auspices of the London Institute of Germanic Studies with the title *Politics in Literature,* has as its subtitle "Studies on a German Preoccupation."[1] This formulation undoubtedly implies that German writers have always been concerned, or even overconcerned, with matters political. In fact, given the course of German history, it might seem surprising if such a concern had not been evident. Nevertheless, any suggestion that writers' preoccupation with politics is uniquely German has to be questioned, for example by reference to France. The concept of committed literature (*littérature engagée*) was invented in France by Jean-Paul Sartre, as was the use of the term intellectual with reference to writers and others from the world of learning who take it upon themselves to intervene in political debates. The origins of this usage go back over a century to Emile Zola's essay "J'accuse," written at the time of the Dreyfus affair in 1898. For the quintessential British political author George Orwell, the significance of politics in literature is not a question of nationality but a consequence of the act of writing itself. In his 1946 essay "Why I Write," he claims that, "no book is genuinely free from political bias. The attitude that art should have nothing to do with politics is itself a political attitude."[2] If this is the case, then German literature is inevitably political. All that it might be possible to claim is that, to amend one of the best-known passages in Orwell's writing, some literatures are more political than others.

However, another note of caution is required if this is applied to German literature. In his lecture to an American audience at the Library of Congress in Washington in 1945 entitled *Germany and the Germans,* Thomas Mann, who had sought refuge from the Nazis in the United States, describes Germany as a nonpolitical country, where many (including writers) have often looked down on politics as an unsavory business and preferred abstract speculation or *Innerlichkeit* (inwardness).[3] That he too, in an earlier stage of his life, saw himself in that tradition is shown by the title of his *Betrachtungen eines Unpolitischen* (Reflections of a Nonpolitical Man, 1918).[4] In it he champions the German cause, seeing his country as representing the values of "culture" as opposed to France with its mere "civilization," based on the ideals of the Enlightenment and the subsequent Revolution. It is not necessary to be George Orwell to see this as a highly political stance. What it reflects, though, is a desire to keep a safe distance from the daily world of politics, especially the kinds of conflicts that are the essence of democratic politics.

This leads to another assumption often made about the relationship between the worlds of politics and literature in Germany: namely, that they have invariably been at loggerheads or at the least occupied distinct spaces without fruitful interchange. In this context, reference is again frequently made to France where, it is claimed, things are different. The popular writer Ulrich Wickert, for example, in his *Vom Glück, Franzose zu sein* (On the Good Fortune of Being French, 1999) refers to President de Gaulle's reported response during the May 1968 crisis to the suggestion that Jean-Paul Sartre should be arrested: "One does not imprison Voltaire."[5] Wickert goes on to suggest that literary aspirations on the part of German politicians would not be acceptable, even, he adds somewhat mysteriously, from Chancellor Gerhard Schröder. Here too some caution is necessary. A recent book on the relationship of federal chancellors to the arts suggests that, at least since the resignation of the first, Konrad Adenauer, all chancellors have taken an interest in cultural and artistic matters.[6] Helmut Schmidt, for instance, often seen as an arch-pragmatist and thus different from his predecessor, the more idealistic Willy Brandt, was greatly interested in modern art and a devotee of Henry Moore. More recently, Chancellor Schröder created a new government post: *Beauftragter der Bundesregierung für Angelegenheiten der Kultur und der Medien* (Delegate of the federal government for matters relating to arts and media). As will be seen in this volume, the GDR government did seek a close relationship with artists, a state of affairs to which many writers were not averse. Earlier, not all writers and intellectuals had been immune to the blandishments of National Socialism. The cases of the philosopher Heidegger, who accepted the post of Rector of Freiburg University in 1933, and of the poet Gottfried Benn, who welcomed the Nazi accession to power, are just two examples, although it should be pointed out that both quickly changed their stance.

This is not to say that the idea of a dichotomy between the world of the arts and that of politics is a myth. If that were the case, this book in its current form would be a senseless enterprise. Indeed, the distinction between the worlds of *Geist* (intellect) and *Macht* (power) is invariably taken as a given. Any reference linking the two attracts attention; hence, the title "Der Geist und die Macht" given to the review of the book on federal chancellors and the arts referred to above.[7] It is common in any treatment of the topic to refer back to a long history of disharmony, a tradition that will not be broken here, despite the provisos expressed above.

In this context it is usual to recall how in their *Xenien* of 1797 Goethe and Schiller pointed to the gap between Germany as a geopolitical and as a cultural entity by asking, "Deutschland, aber wo liegt es? Ich weiß das Land nicht zu finden. / Wo das Gelehrte beginnt, hört das Politische auf." (Germany, but where is it located? I do not know how to find the country. / Where learning begins, politics ends.)[8] They also suggested that Germans would be well occupied in making themselves better people rather than trying to form themselves into a nation. Accordingly, for the two greatest German writers, creating a political entity named Germany was not a priority. A slightly different topos concerning the phenomenon of Germany is found in the work of Heinrich Heine, whose two lines from the poem "Nachtgedanken" (Night Thoughts, 1844) are as well known as those of Goethe and Schiller: "Denke ich an Deutschland in der Nacht, / Da bin ich um den Schlaf gebracht" (If I think of Germany in the night / Then sleep quickly takes to flight).[9] In fact, unease about Germany was frequently expressed by writers well before the catastrophic events of the twentieth century. One of the most famous diatribes is contained in Friedrich Hölderlin's 1799 novel *Hyperion*. When the main character arrives in Germany, he describes the people as barbarians who cannot even be improved by religion, as they are incapable of any divine feeling.[10] Further, albeit less violent, examples of disquiet are to be found in some writers' reactions to the achievement of German unification in 1871. Ferdinand von Saar, for instance, in his poem "Germania," writes: "Ja, man fürchtet und preist weithin des Reiches Macht, / doch man beugt sich nicht mehr willig dem deutschen Geist" (Indeed the Reich's power is praised and feared far afield, / yet the German mind no longer gains willing acknowledgment).[11] The dichotomy between the realms of *Geist* and *Macht* could hardly be expressed more clearly and, what is more, the superiority of the intellectual realm implied more obviously. Such a standpoint has been widespread, although it has never gone unchallenged.

In this context, it is also relevant to mention the distinction made by the sociologist Max Weber in *Politik als Beruf* (Politics as a Profession, 1919) between *Gesinnungsethik* (ethic of conviction) and *Verantwortungsethik* (ethic of responsibility). Although he was talking about different kinds of politicians — those who followed their convictions without heed of the consequences as opposed to those who bore in mind the possible results of their actions — it is tempting to see intellectuals as giving priority to conviction, especially as they normally do not have the responsibility of office.[12]

If Weber shows skepticism about basing actions on intellectual conviction, his near contemporary Heinrich Mann took up a very different position, as he invariably championed the world of the intellect over that of the practicing politician. Unlike his brother Thomas, Heinrich was throughout his life a severe critic of the German authoritarian tradition, which he contrasted with France and its revolutionary achievements, and an unswerving champion of the world of intellect. Many of his ideas are set out in his 1910 essay "Geist und Tat" (Intellect and Deed). He speaks of power being the *Todfeind* (mortal enemy) of the world of the intellect,[13] while expressing confidence that the latter, which he links to the ideals of the French Revolution, will always triumph over authoritarianism. An even more pronounced championing of the world of the intellect is to be found in Mann's speech on the opening of the Prussian Academy of Arts in 1928:

> Wir nennen Geist die menschliche Fähigkeit, der Wahrheit nachzugehen ohne Rücksicht auf Nutzen oder Schaden, und Gerechtigkeit zu erstreben sogar wider praktische Vernunft. Der Staat hingegen vertritt die Menschennatur gerade so weit, als sie Vorteil sucht und sich seinetwegen auch mit dem Schlechten abfindet.[14]

> [We call intellect the ability to pursue truth regardless of weal and woe or to strive for justice even against the dictates of practical reason. The state, on the other hand, represents human nature just to the extent that it seeks advantage and for its own sake also accepts the bad.]

Whether this distinction was justified even in the admittedly less-than-perfect democracy of the Weimar Republic is open to question. What is entirely beyond doubt is that the next German state totally abused its power, dealing with its opponents from the world of the intellect who fell into its hands — and not just them — with unsurpassed brutality.

When the Nazis came to power in 1933, the Mann brothers were joined in exile by numerous fellow writers, for example, Bertolt Brecht and, not surprisingly, Jewish writers such as Lion Feuchtwanger and Arnold Zweig. They frequently saw themselves as representative of *das andere Deutschland* (the other Germany), at odds with Nazi barbarism. After the war, although they were not always honored as individuals, at least in the western zones, their ideal of a different kind of Germany, reinforced by the desire to prevent the country from ever again relapsing into authoritarian or worse rule, was important to later writers. At the same time, many postwar writers felt that their predecessors, in keeping with the tradition of *Innerlichkeit,* had not always taken sufficient interest in politics or had not fought strongly enough for the survival of the Weimar Republic, however flawed. The exasperated statement by the left-wing writer and journalist Kurt Tucholsky in a letter of 1926 in the light of increased censorship of the arts — "Diese Republik ist nicht die meine" (This republic is not mine) — is just one example of writers appearing to undermine the first attempt to create a democratic state on German soil.[15] Accordingly, the stage was set in 1945 for many writers to seek to overcome two perceived negative legacies: the historical forces that had led Germany to catastrophe and the tradition of the writer and intellectual who either turned his back on politics or too quickly became exasperated by its failure to live up to expectations.

This is the starting point for the present volume. While the first six chapters touch on some of the same ground as my 1986 book *Writers and Politics in West Germany,*[16] they also provide new insights from the past two decades as well as a number of changes. Each chapter begins with short sections on the political and literary developments during the period in question with the aim of providing basic background knowledge. The relationship between writers and politics in the GDR is also considered for the first time. Given the major event of unification in 1990 — a change that seemed highly unlikely in 1986 — it would have been unthinkable to omit reference to the other German state. In relation to the GDR, it is also important to stress that there was no public sphere for intellectual debate of the kind found in western democracies: that is to say, a variety of competing publication outlets, ranging from daily newspapers to specialist journals, in which different views could be put forward without the intrusion of state censorship. Accordingly, literary fiction often served as a way of expressing dissent, although this too was subject to censorship. In my previous book I largely used nonfictional writing as the basis of my examination of the topic. In the case of the GDR, given the state of affairs outlined above, this is impossible. I was arguably also over-restrictive in this regard in relation to the Federal Republic, since it is undoubtedly an oversimplification to equate nonfictional writing with the expression of deeply held convictions, and fiction with unreliability.

The second part of the book considers what has happened since the beginning of the unification process. After an intermezzo considering writers and the unification process and a brief introduction, which again outlines political and literary developments, there follow chapters on the major issues affecting intellectual life since unification. In this way, the history of the political activity of writers since 1945 is brought up to date. Additionally, more than sixty years after the end of the Second World War and nearly two decades after the unification of Germany, it does not seem too early to take stock in the hope of finding a response to at least two major questions: Have those writers who have intervened in political debates acted within the parameters of what can be expected from a public intellectual? And is the role of public intellectual still relevant in contemporary Germany? The author hopes that the conclusions drawn will encourage reflection on these questions, which he believes are relevant beyond the frontiers of Germany.

Notes

[1] Rüdiger Görner, ed., *Politics in Literature: Studies on a German Preoccupation from Kleist to Améry* (Munich: iudicium, 2004).

[2] George Orwell, "Why I Write," in *England Your England and Other Essays* (London: Secker and Warburg, 1954), 7–16, here 11.

[3] Thomas Mann, *Germany and the Germans* (Washington, DC: Library of Congress, 1945).

[4] Thomas Mann, *Betrachtungen eines Unpolitischen* (Frankfurt am Main: Fischer, 2001).

[5] See Ulrich Wickert, *Vom Glück, Franzose zu sein* (Hamburg: Hoffmann und Campe, 1999), 200.

[6] Norbert Seitz, *Die Kanzler und die Künste: Die Geschichte einer schweren Beziehung* (Munich: Siedler, 2005).

[7] Eckhard Fuhr, "Der Geist und die Macht," *Die Welt*, 12 February 2005. http://www.welt.de/date/2005/02/12/461986.html?prx=1. Consulted 23 February 2005.

[8] Quoted in: Hans Christoph Buch, *Tintenfisch 15. Thema Deutschland* (Berlin: Wagenbach, 1979), 30.

[9] Heinrich Heine, "Nachtgedanken," in *Historisch-Kritische Gesamtausgabe der Werke*, ed. Manfred Windfuhr (Hamburg: Hoffmann und Campe, vol. 2, 1983), 129–30, here 129.

[10] Friedrich Hölderlin, *Werke und Briefe*, ed. Friedrich Beißner, Jochen Schmidt, Frankfurt am Main: Insel, 1969,1: 433.

[11] See Helmut Lamprecht, ed., *Politische Gedichte vom Vormärz bis zur Gegenwart* (Bremen: Carl Schünemann Verlag, 1969), 221.

[12] Max Weber, *Politik als Beruf* (Stuttgart: Reclam, 1992).

[13] Heinrich Mann, "Geist und Tat," in *Essays* (Hamburg: Claasen, 1960), 7–14, here 13.

[14] Heinrich Mann, "Dichtkunst und Politik," in *Essays*, 299–315, here 299.

[15] Kurt Tucholsky, *Ausgewählte Briefe* (Reinbek: Rowohlt, 1962), 178.

[16] K. Stuart Parkes, *Writers and Politics in West Germany* (Beckenham: Croom Helm, 1986).

Part 1:
The Years of Division

1: The Aftermath of War and the New Beginning

Political Developments

THAT THIS ACCOUNT OF WRITERS AND POLITICS in Germany should commence at 1945 should not be regarded unthinkingly as a matter of course. Especially in the 1950s and 1960s, much public discourse in the Federal Republic of Germany referred to 1945 as *Stunde Null* (year zero), conveniently implying that everything started anew at that time and that, by implication, what had gone before had lost much, if not all, of its relevance. In the forty years existence of the German Democratic Republic, too, overlooking inconvenient facts of history was a frequent practice at an official level. Identification with the Soviet Union and its victory over Nazi Germany was so excessive that unofficially jokers coined the following gross distortion of historical fact: "The GDR won the Second World War alongside the Soviet Union," in this way humorously exposing the ludicrous implications of the approved historiography that denied any link between the GDR and the Nazi past. The degree of continuity between pre-1945 and postwar Germany will inevitably be a question that will recur throughout this book, in relation to both political and cultural developments. At this stage it is sufficient to point to the issue.

Despite this note of caution, the significance of 1945 is not to be denied. With Germany's unconditional surrender in May 1945, political power passed into the hands of the victorious Allies, each of which now administered a zone of occupation within the country. Plans for the future of defeated Germany had already been laid during the war. The Potsdam conference of July 1945 can be regarded as the last meeting of wartime Allies before the onset of the Cold War, and the agreement reached there the culmination of joint Allied planning for Germany's future. These plans — in particular the maintenance of Germany as a single unit, at least economically — crumbled in the face of increasing East-West tensions that manifested themselves in the subsequent division of Germany, the building of the Berlin Wall, and the apparently unceasing threat of nuclear war on Germany territory. This state of affairs only came to an end with the fall of the Berlin Wall in 1989 and German unity a year later.

Potsdam also envisaged the creation of a new democratic Germany that had broken with its fascist past. In all the zones of occupation, political life was to begin again within new parameters. The creation of new political parties, or the re-creation of political parties that had existed before the Nazi accession to power in 1933, was permitted sooner or later in all zones, as were newspapers and other media under Allied supervision. Political activity began at the local and regional level, with multi-party elections taking place in the federal states (*Länder*) as they were reconstituted after 1945. Another common feature between the zones was the policy of "denazification," whereby former members of the Nazi party were brought before tribunals to determine the extent of their involvement with the previous regime and, when judged appropriate, removed from positions of responsibility. Linked with this policy was the idea of "re-education," a process that had begun during the war among prisoners of war with the aim of turning the German people away from the poisonous ideology of National Socialism.

These superficial similarities between the zones, however, paled into insignificance before the increasing tensions between the allies, in particular the United States, and the Soviet Union. While maintaining officially a policy in favor of German unity, a stance that lasted into the 1950s, the Soviet Union began to take steps in its zone of occupation that were at the least consistent with the subsequent creation of a state based on the Soviet model, a model that had been initially rejected by the German communist party (Kommunistische Partei Deutschlands: KPD). In 1946 a merger was enforced between the KPD and the potentially stronger Social Democrats (Sozialdemokratische Partei Deutschlands: SPD) in the name of overcoming the previous disunity of the working class that, it was claimed with some justification, had aided Hitler's accession to power. The new party, the SED (Sozialistische Einheitspartei Deutschlands or Socialist Unity Party of Germany), was increasingly dominated by former communists and soon enjoyed a privileged position, becoming the leading force following the creation of a separate Eastern state. On the basis of a referendum held in the state of Saxony in 1946, which asked about the expropriation of war criminals, a large sector of industry was nationalized, while large agricultural holdings were divided among small farmers and landless laborers prior to moves in the next two decades toward collectivization. By contrast, in the western zones, most particularly the American zone, any movement toward extensive government ownership was resisted by the occupying power. Instead, as cooperation between the three western zones intensified, preparations were laid for a new economic order based on the market model, albeit tempered by social provisions. *Soziale Marktwirtschaft* (social market economy) was the name given to the system, under which the subsequent *Wirtschaftswunder* (economic miracle) was achieved. Accordingly, it was increasingly held up as an economic paragon, as the gap in prosperity between the two halves of Germany increased and the Federal Republic began to achieve a level of economic success that surpassed those of many of its Western neighbors.

In order to lay the foundations of this new economic order, a reform of the devalued currency, the Reichsmark, was decided upon in the western zones. With the introduction of the Deutsche Mark (D-Mark) in 1948, Germany became economically divided. The Soviet Union responded to this currency reform by blocking land access to West Berlin, which had also adopted the new currency, in the hope of forcing the city to become economically dependent on the Soviet zone. The western allies' answer was the Berlin Airlift, which supplied the city from June of 1948 to May of 1949 and increased their prestige with the population in all their zones. The way was open to the creation of a separate western state, and the Federal Republic of Germany came into being in the summer of 1949 following the adoption of a constitution that, to emphasize the supposedly provisional nature of the new state and the hope for the country's eventual unification, was given the name Basic Law (*Grundgesetz*). Following multi-party elections, the Christian Democrat Konrad Adenauer became federal chancellor at the head of a right-of-center coalition led by the chancellor's party, the Christlich-Demokratische Union (CDU) and its Bavarian sister party, the Christlich-Soziale Union (CSU), with the left-of-center Social Democrats consigned to opposition. The Soviet Union responded to these developments by the creation of the German Democratic Republic in the autumn of the same year. Although this too was theoretically a multi-party state with a constitution granting many democratic freedoms, it was from the outset very close to the Soviet system in that the major levers of power were in the hands of the SED.

Germany was to remain divided for forty years, with each German state identified with one of the major adversaries of the Cold War. As will be seen, this intra-German conflict and the very fact of division were to be at the center of intellectual discourse for much of this period.

Literary Developments

The assumption that 1945 represents a turning point in German literature has been as controversial as the idea of a political and historical caesura in that year, as embodied in the term "year zero." Debate has centered especially on the question of how far political and cultural developments represented a continuum in the years between 1930 and 1960, with some seeing this as a single period in cultural terms.[1] Whatever the truth in this claim, it nevertheless remains the case that the parameters of cultural production changed in 1945. Art was no longer subject to the requirement that it avoid anything perceived to be at odds with Nazi ideology, while anything that glorified German *Blut und Boden* (blood and soil) clearly did not find favor with the enemies of Nazism, who now held the power of censorship. The tradition of entertainment that was less political was able to continue under allied occupation, at least in the west. The best example is the area of film, where in the postwar years escapism predominated in the form of the *Heimatfilm* (homeland film), which presented sentimental stories of life in the German countryside as an embodiment of the rural idyll. Previously, the Nazi authorities had not been averse to comparable escapism, especially as life became harder during the war.

This is not to say that the idea of a new start was not in the air. In the field of literature, two terms, which are undoubtedly linked, are of particular importance, namely *Trümmerliteratur* and *Kahlschlagliteratur*. The first term (rubble literature) implies the presentation of the reality of Germany in the aftermath of war, in particular its cities, largely destroyed either by Allied bombing or ground fighting — the early works of Heinrich Böll are frequently cited as examples of this genre. The second has more to do with linguistic considerations. *Kahlschlag* is a word used in forestry to denote total deforestation through clear cutting, and in the aftermath of war, this term arose in response to the inflated ideological language of National Socialism. This, many felt, had to be cut away and replaced by a new language, where meaning would not be hidden by ideological obfuscation. The most quoted example of *Kahlschlagliteratur* is undoubtedly Günter Eich's 1947 poem "Inventur," which consists of an inventory of the few items in the possession of the poetic subject. Their limited nature also conjures up an era of deprivation, including the deprivation of freedom, as one can assume that this poetic subject is detained as a prisoner of war.[2]

By contrast, another poem of the same year, "Warum, wozu noch" (Why, To What End Still) by Herbert Lestiboudois, expresses the sense of a new, different literature in an extremely self-confident manner, claiming that the new poetry will be different from that of Goethe, Rilke, and Morgenstern, and that, "Es wird um nackte Tatbestände gehen" (It will be a case of bare facts).[3] Even if the tone is different, this concern with the concrete and factual does suggest a link with Eich.

Although both Böll and Eich went on to become leading West German writers, their acceptance by the general public was not instantaneous. At the start of the 1950s, there was little interest in the bare facts invoked by Lestiboudois — that is to say, in the depictions of the misery of the early postwar years. Accordingly, Böll's early novel *Der Engel schwieg* (The Angel Was Silent), completed by 1951, was not published at the time because the publisher believed there was no longer a market for a work set in war-ravaged Cologne; it appeared only posthumously. As early as 1947, Wolfgang Borchert gave his drama *Draußen vor der Tür* (The Man Outside), which shows the misadventures of a soldier returning home to a Hamburg in ruins, the subtitle, "Ein Stück, das kein Theater spielen und kein Publikum sehen will" (A Play That No Theater Wants to Perform and No Public Wants to See). In one scene, the returnee Beckmann is told by an impresario, who holds up Shirley Temple as a model, that his cabaret act is too serious. It consists of reflections on his own fate — the loss of his wife in his absence to another man and, when he finds another woman, the massive reproaches of her returning, one-legged husband, who had been under his command on the Russian front.

Since Borchert's play has established itself as a classic, the subtitle has ultimately proved to be incorrect. It is also true that there was a market for serious literature in the postwar era. Insofar as they dealt at all with contemporary issues, however, the works that enjoyed the best reception were those that eschewed realism in favor of an indirect, allegorical style. The best example is Hermann Kasack's *Die Stadt hinter dem Strom* (The City Beyond the River, 1947), where the city represents some kind of totalitarian state but is not immediately recognizable as Nazi Germany. What literary critic Ralf Schnell says specifically about the Christian writer Elisabeth Langgässer's aesthetic — namely, that it dissolves history into metaphysics (*GDL*, 94) — can be applied more widely. Generalized comments about the human condition were preferred to direct reference to the ills of the present and the recent past.

In this context, it is also important to say something about the fate of those authors who had left Germany during the years of National Socialism. Rather than being at the forefront of a revival of German culture after the years of barbarism, they found themselves largely ostracized, at least in the western zones. The situation was different in the Soviet zone, where especially, but not exclusively, communist writers were welcomed back and given important positions by the authorities. The poet Johannes R. Becher went on to become the GDR minister for culture, while Bertolt Brecht was given the facilities to found his celebrated Berliner Ensemble. Heinrich Mann, too, was on the point of leaving the Unites States for the GDR to become president of the Academy of Arts when he died. However fraught the relationships of Brecht and some of the other émigré figures may have been at times with Stalinist bureaucracy, they remained the dominant figures in GDR literary life during the early years of that state's existence. The importance attached in the Soviet Zone to the return of émigrés can be seen from remarks made by the novelist Günther Weisenborn, who held important political positions in the East until moving westwards in 1949. In a 1946 speech, he mentioned forty-five writers specifically, asking them all to return.[4] Significantly, he spoke of *das andere Deutschland,* a concept, as seen in the introduction, beloved of writers and intellectuals to invoke a Germany that had not succumbed to Nazism.

There was limited enthusiasm for this other Germany in the western zones, even if author and publisher Alfred Andersch stated that the only German literature worthy of the name produced between 1933 and 1945 had been written in exile.[5] One specific example of major conflict will be referred to in the next part of this chapter. Here it is sufficient to refer to comments made in 1951 by Alfred Döblin, the author of the 1929 modernist novel of the city, *Berlin Alexanderplatz,* who had returned to Germany to work in the French Zone. Neither the Social Democrats, whom he sees as no longer truly left-wing, nor his fellow writers, whom he describes as opportunists corrupted by Nazi ideology, escape his wrath.[6] It is small wonder that Döblin returned to France in 1953. In the immediate postwar period, it was indeed those who had stayed in Germany who dominated intellectual life, although they were increasingly challenged by a self-styled "young generation," as will be seen in the next section.

Writers and Politics

A Plethora of Periodicals

One of the most remarkable features of the immediate postwar period was the number of new periodicals that sprang up with the aim of contributing to the debate about the future of Germany. In itself, this was a sign that, as shown above, the immediate postwar period was a time of uncertainty and transition. Moreover, the same development occurred in all the zones of occupation. In many cases it is only necessary to look at the titles of these periodicals to gain a sense of what their intentions were. Such titles include *Neues Europa* (New Europe), *Die Wandlung* (Transformation) and *Die Besinnung* (Reflection). It was, at least for some, a time for serious reflection on the past, specifically the immediate past, and for planning the future. A number of these postwar periodicals went on to become an integral part of the political and cultural life in the two German states, for example *Merkur,* subtitled *Deutsche Zeitschrift für europäisches Denken* (German Periodical for European Thought) in the Federal Republic and the literary magazine *Sinn und Form* (Meaning and Form) in the GDR. In many cases, however, these magazines did not survive much beyond the currency reform, if they even lasted so long. The catalogue of an exhibition on postwar developments entitled *Als der Krieg zu Ende war* (When the War Was Over), held at the Deutsches Literaturarchiv at Marbach in 1973, notes the death of at least a dozen magazines in 1949 and 1950 alone. Two undoubtedly linked reasons can be adduced for this. One was the change of mood already referred to in connection with Heinrich Böll's *Der Engel schwieg.* The other was the availability of new, more desirable, consumer goods following the currency reform of 1948. In fact, it remains difficult to gauge the degree of enthusiasm for change and reflection in the postwar period; it is not clear, for instance, how many bought the new magazines for lack of anything better to purchase, given the shortages of the time. Nevertheless, it would be wrong to deny their significance entirely, however short-lived their existence or influence may have been.

Of course, not all the magazines and periodicals approached the new era in Germany from a similar point of view. Even where a common Christian inspiration can be noted, there were significant differences of emphasis. This can be shown by a comparison between *Die Gegenwart* (The Present), which started publication in Freiburg in the French zone, and *Frankfurter Hefte* (Frankfurt Journal), a publication that enjoyed an independent existence of almost forty years. What both magazines reflect is the significance of Christianity in the postwar period. Particularly the Protestant Church reflected on its role in the Third Reich and confessed its failings in the 1945 Stuttgart Declaration, while both major confessions sought to have a significant influence in the new Germany.

One word seems to characterize the early editions of *Die Gegenwart:* It seeks to look at the contemporary world from a *wahrhaftig* (truthful) standpoint, while in its discussion of the proclaimed "collective guilt" of the German people for the atrocities of National Socialism — as propounded by the Allies at the end of the war — it rejects a crude external condemnation of all things German in favor of a collective and individual examination of conscience by the German people themselves as the basis of a new beginning based on a spirit of absolute truthfulness. In common with other periodicals of the time, it is skeptical about political ideologies. This is obvious from a report on East Berlin dating from the autumn of 1949. Commenting on propaganda demanding the "r(R)ücksichtslose Ausrottung aller Agenten und Spione" (ruthless extermination of all agents and spies),[7] it notes that extermination is the method used by all systems that are incapable of converting people to their point of view. The viewpoints expressed are a forerunner of the totalitarianism theories of the 1950s and 1960s that equated Nazi and communist tyranny, and which surfaced again after unification in 1990. The economic ideas of *Die Gegenwart* — the need to reconcile true personal freedom with the well-being of the community — also seem a forerunner of the precepts of the social market economy. In its beginnings, however, the magazine is primarily concerned with moral renewal. The author Ernst Wiechert, who was imprisoned for a time in Buchenwald, is said to have saved his soul by describing these experiences in his *Der Totenwald* (The Forest of the Dead, 1946), part of which was reprinted in an early edition.[8]

While one of *Frankfurter Hefte*'s editors, Eugen Kogon, was also a prisoner at Buchenwald (his work portraying his experiences, *Der SS-Staat* (The SS State, 1946) remains a seminal text on life in the camps), the journal sought in contrast to encourage the creation of a new Germany based on what might be called Christian socialism. An essay in the third edition of the magazine by Kogon's co-editor Walter Dirks is significantly entitled "Abendland und Sozialismus" (The Occident and Socialism). The first term in German very much implies the western Christian tradition while the second implies the economic order of the Soviet Union. Dirks's demand that the two should permeate one another makes this clear and is reminiscent of other hopes of reconciliation between East and West expressed at the time.[9] Exactly what the *Frankfurter Hefte* meant by socialism — namely, the transfer into public ownership of key areas of the economy — was made clear in the same edition by Karl Heinrich Knappstein, while the link with Christianity is made clear in his call to Christians to be active in the movement toward socialism.[10] Far from being peripheral, this kind of thinking had a major influence on the CDU in that party's early years. Its 1947 Ahlen program, for instance, was distinctly anticapitalist in tone. However, other forces within the party held sway once it achieved power in 1949. Even Christian Democrats who were influenced by the social doctrines of the Catholic Church, which in any case fell far short of socialism, were destined to remain a minority within the party. As for the *Frankfurter Hefte*, it moved closer to the Social Democrats as that party became more attractive to Catholic voters after it abandoned Marxism in its 1959 Godesberg Program.

The one postwar periodical to have achieved almost legendary status is *Der Ruf* (The Call). The first publication of that name had appeared in Fort Kearney in the United States, where the Americans concentrated their efforts to re-educate German prisoners of war. It was the title's next manifestation in Munich in the years 1946 and 1947 under the editorship of Alfred Andersch and Hans Werner Richter that brought the magazine fame, even though only sixteen editions appeared before it was proscribed by the American authorities. Thereafter, the magazine continued in name under new editorship, but the golden era when it achieved a circulation of 100,000 was largely over. Part of the fame of the magazine rests on the subsequent careers of its editors. Andersch became both a leading writer and a key figure in the literary life of the Federal Republic in the 1950s and Richter founded the Gruppe 47, an association of mainly younger authors that came to be seen as almost synonymous with (West) German literature in the late 1950s and early 1960s. As will be seen, the Gruppe 47 also increasingly involved itself in the political development of the Federal Republic.

The link between these developments and *Der Ruf*'s self-image is visible in the magazine's subtitle, "Unabhängige Blätter für die junge Generation" (Independent Pages for the Young Generation). It saw itself, with some justification, as the circulation figures show, as the mouthpiece of those to whom National Socialism had denied any voice. The desire of this generation, or at least part of it, to make itself heard often expressed itself in condemnations of their elders. Another poem by Herbert Lestiboudois, entitled "Junge Generation" (Young Generation), sums up these feelings, and stresses a divide for which the term generation gap seems entirely inadequate:

Weit
Ist der Weg von uns zu euch!
Dazwischen liegt ein zertrümmertes Reich
Und liegen die Toten[11]

[Far
Is the way from us to you!
Between lies a destroyed empire in ruins
And lie the dead]

The older generation also often receives short shrift in *Der Ruf.* One example is the parody of a typical speech by the older Ernst Wiechert under the title, "500. Rede an die deutsche Jugend. Eine Parodie frei nach Ernst Wiechert" (500th Speech to German Youth. A Parody in the Style of Ernst Wiechert).[12] Wiechert's hopes for the future lay in a re-creation of the humanistic values of Goethe and Weimar Classicism, not in some kind of new start — a view that was unsurprisingly anathema to the young writers of *Der Ruf.*

What *Der Ruf* stood for is visible in a number of essays, but arguably most clearly in Alfred Andersch's "Das junge Europa formt sein Gesicht" (Young Europe Shapes Its Face). Here Andersch identifies German youth with their counterparts in other European countries, who are fighting for a different kind of world. The key concern, as in Knappstein's *Frankfurter Hefte* article, is the reconciliation of freedom and socialism. According to Andersch, the young generation desired economic justice, which can only be achieved through socialism, but at the same time displays "fanaticism" in its defense of freedom.[13] The use of the German word *Fanatismus,* which was beloved of the Nazis, seems ironical from someone claiming to speak for a new generation that identified itself with the desire, reflected in the term *Kahlschlag,* to rid the language of Nazi terminology. At the same time, it might offer a clue to the reason for the proscription of *Der Ruf* by the American authorities. Although it has never been possible to adduce an exact reason, the magazine was considered in some quarters to be excessively nationalistic. Certainly there is evidence that Richter himself thought that only Germans could forge their own future. His novel *Die Geschlagenen* (The Defeated, 1949) contains an interview between an American officer and a recently captured German soldier who bears close resemblance to Richter himself. Although the soldier, Gühler, claims to be opposed to Nazism, he is both unwilling to supply information about the positions of the German army and to concede a role to outsiders in post-Nazi Germany. There is to be no cooperation with what he deems to be foreign interests.[14] At the same time, there is an awareness in *Der Ruf* of the dangers of previous manifestations of German nationalism and, as the Gruppe 47 co-founder Heinz Friedrich states, of the need to escape from this kind of narrow nationalism.[15]

In fact, in many respects the magazine did not seek to be ideological. In his essay "Parteipolitik und Weltanschauung" (Party Politics and Worldviews), Richter condemns the tradition of German parties wanting to impose their particular worldview, something that inevitably led to tragedy.[16] Not surprisingly, dislike of parties is linked by Richter to the generational theme in another essay, "Warum schweigt die junge Generation?" (Why Does the Young Generation Stay Silent?), which attacks attempts to re-create German political life on the basis of what had existed before 1933.[17] He and many authors associated with the Gruppe 47 saw this as the case in the early years of the Federal Republic, not least after the septuagenarian Konrad Adenauer took power in 1949. At the same time, it has to be pointed out that this self-styled young generation was not without a past. Insofar as their writing career stretched back to the 1930s, some, including Andersch, had applied for membership to the Reichsschrifttumskammer, the Nazi association for writers, membership in which was a prerequisite for publication.

The Shadow of the Past

One of the first intellectual conflicts to break out in postwar Germany was over the issue of emigration during the Nazi period. Much of the controversy surrounded Thomas Mann, who had been a regular broadcaster from exile to Nazi Germany and whose novel *Doktor Faustus,* published in 1947, is at least in part a critical evaluation of the unhappy and problematical course of German history and culture. As pointed out in the introduction, Mann had already tried to explain the negative German attitude to politics to an American audience in his 1945 *Germany and the Germans* lecture at the Library of Congress.

The first major attack on Mann came from the writer Frank Thiess, who had remained in Germany during the years of National Socialism and had coined the phrase *innere Emigration* (internal Emigration) to describe the attitude of the people, among whom he numbered himself, who remained in Germany but nevertheless kept their distance from the Nazis. According to Thiess, this opposition from within was preferable to watching Germany's tragedy from the comfort of "den Logen und Parterreplätzen des Auslands" (the theater boxes and orchestra seats of abroad).[18] The material comforts this implies may have been true of the most famous, such as Mann and, for example, the Austrian Stefan Zweig, who enjoyed considerable royalties from the sales of their works abroad. Most, however, lived in considerable poverty, and suicide was not infrequent among exiles, with even Zweig choosing this course of action in 1942. Thiess's argument is also not helped by his use of abstract, idealistic language, which reaches its apotheosis in his reply about why he did not go into emigration. Unlike those watching from abroad, he says, he would if he survived gain so much "für meine geistige und menschliche Entwicklung" (for my mental and human development).

Moreover, he even claims to have emerged "reicher an Wissen und Erleben" (richer in knowledge and experience; *VLMS,* 47).

It is also important to consider the context in which Thiess's comments were made. They followed an open letter from another writer, Walter von Molo, urging Mann to return to Germany. When Mann refused and added that, as far as he was concerned, all books published in Germany between 1933 and 1945 carried a "Geruch von Blut und Schnade" (stench of blood and shame),[19] the stage was set for a vitriolic exchange, with Mann being accused by Thiess of hatred of Germany. This crude view of Mann persisted in certain quarters until his death. It can be found, for instance, in an article written in 1949 by the critic Friedrich Sieburg, despite the title "Frieden mit Thomas Mann" (Peace with Thomas Mann).[20] To be fair, the article is not entirely hostile to Mann but seeks rather to separate Mann the artist, whose genius is acknowledged, from Mann the political writer, who is dismissed out of hand. This attempt to separate the aesthetic from the political is typical of conservative literary circles at the time and persisted through the first decade of the existence of the Federal Republic. Sieburg — who, though not a convinced Nazi, himself had compromised with National Socialism by making anti-Semitic remarks while working as a journalist in occupied France — was arguably the leading literary critic in the 1950s, and when a new, more socially critical generation of writers associated with the Gruppe 47 including Günter Grass and Martin Walser emerged, he unsurprisingly reacted with unconcealed hostility.

Mann's reference to shame leads to the question of German guilt that has never been far below the surface since 1945. Another German émigré to the United States, the philosopher Hannah Arendt, had begun to discuss the subject even before the end of the war. However, unlike Mann, she did not see the evils to be linked with anything specifically German. Rejecting the idea that the Germans had been latent Nazis since the time of Tacitus, she suggests in a 1946 essay that shame at belonging to the human race is more appropriate than shame at being German. She sees the typical SS man as an ordinary husband and father, only interested in looking after his family and sacrificing all public virtues for this. This argument prefigures her comments on the trial of Adolf Eichmann in the early 1960s when her phrase "the banality of evil" became an accepted part of Holocaust-related discourse.[21] In Germany itself, as early as the winter semester of 1945/1946, the philosopher Karl Jaspers conducted a series of lectures on this topic at the University of Heidelberg. In them, he considers four kinds of guilt: criminal, political, moral and metaphysical. He also comes close to endorsing the concept of collective guilt that lay behind the Allied policy of re-education, by stressing that all individual Germans belong to the same political collective and must take responsibility for what happens in its name.[22] By contrast, others were not even prepared to contemplate any idea of guilt or responsibility. This applies especially to the writers of *Der Ruf*. Richter states baldly in his introduction to the collection of essays from the journal published in 1962 that they were against the idea of collective guilt and any dubious idea of re-education.[23] Another example of this stance can be found in Andersch's young Europe essay, where he singles out the young generation as being separated from older ones by its not having been responsible for Hitler.[24] This may have been true as far as the accession to power in 1933 was concerned; however, it ignores the fact that as soldiers and, in some cases, concentration camp guards, members of this generation committed many atrocities.

Not surprisingly, *Frankfurter Hefte* devotes much space to questions relating to the German past. In the very first edition, Kogon — while recognizing that the collective guilt theory and the idea of re-education, as practiced by the Allies, have not achieved their aims of changing the consciousness of the German people — asks individuals to look more at their own consciences. Taking the anti-Hitler conspirators of 20 July 1944 as models, he wants the Germans to judge themselves so that they need not fear any other judge.[25] Only in this way does he see any possibility of renewal in Germany. As this volume will show, the legacy of the Nazi past has remained an issue for writers and intellectuals long after the postwar period, with some of the most intense debate taking place after German unification.

The Fight for Unity

With the growing tensions between the Western allies and the Soviet Union, not to mention the de facto existence of four separate administrations in Germany, it soon became clear that, despite the provisions of the Potsdam Agreement, the future unity of Germany could not be taken for granted. Writers reacted to this situation by maintaining the ideal of a united country, while at the same time putting forward ideas for its future role within Europe.

Eastern writers, who were in harmony with official policy in their zone at that time, were very much to the fore in the campaign for unity. They inspired a congress of writers from all zones that was held in Berlin in 1947 under the auspices of the Kulturbund, the body set up in the Soviet Zone to encourage all forms of cultural activity. From this congress there emerged a number of manifestos stressing the importance of unity. Any loss of unity, it was claimed, would have a devastating effect on German culture. One manifesto refers to Heinrich Heine's comment, "Deutschland hat ewigen Bestand" (Germany has eternal existence) and proclaims a belief in the community of all those who speak the German language.[26] Apart from a gathering in Frankfurt to commemorate the hundredth anniversary of the 1848 revolution, this kind of all-German meeting was not to be repeated for more than three decades. In 1949 Thomas Mann did try to bridge the growing ideological divide by attending both the celebrations held in Frankfurt and Weimar to mark the bicentenary of Goethe's birth, but even a person of his stature could not hold back the tide of division.

How strong this tide was can be illustrated by the fate of the magazine *Ost und West* (East and West) that was founded in 1947 by Alfred Kantorowicz, a left-wing returnee from exile in the United States. His ambition was to create a publication for all the zones of occupation and incorporating a variety of views. Initially he did enjoy some success despite difficulties of distribution caused largely by the attitude of the American authorities. Subjects discussed included, as in *Der Ruf,* the situation of young people, with one nineteen-year-old reader, Gerhard Baumert, credibly attributing the disorientation of the young to the destruction of their false idol of National Socialism.[27] He sees as characteristic for his generation an uncertainty toward themselves and toward life. Unlike others of his age group, he calls upon the older generation, especially writers, to act as teachers to show the way toward humanity and freedom. By contrast, the Marburg student Käte Fuchs says that the young only require leadership to a certain degree; they must learn to take decisions themselves.[28] She sees as the main characteristic of young Germans the desire to escape from reality into a variety of worlds ranging from Rilke's mysticism to escapist cinema.

Despite the importance of such debates, *Ost und West* could not buck the trend. Circulation declined from a peak of seventy thousand to about five or six thousand and its demise was inevitable, with the growing division between the two parts of Germany no doubt contributing to the rapid loss of popularity. In fact, once division was established through the creation of two German states in 1949, pleas for unity took on an increasingly desperate tone. This can be illustrated by reference to the volume *Wir heißen Euch hoffen* (We Bid You Hope), which appeared in the West in 1951 but included contributors ranging from Walter von Molo to leading Eastern figures such as Johannes R. Becher and Rudolf Leonhard.

Both Becher and von Molo invoke the metaphor of the human body to portray the country as a unity. Becher in his poem "Deutschland, dich suchend" (Germany, Seeking You) speaks of an indivisible heart: "Und Deutschland war, wer jenes Trostwort fand / 'Man kann ein Herz nicht in zwei Teile spalten.'" (And Germany was the one who found this word of comfort: / "A heart cannot be split into two parts")[29] In his essay "Ja, wir wollen uns retten" (Yes, We Wish to Save Ourselves), von Molo too refers to the single heart, but extends the parallel with the body to other organs before moving into a mixture of banality and sub-Goethean rhetoric:

> Die Sonne geht nicht nur auf oder nur unter, sie geht ständig auf und unter, immer wechseln Tag und Nacht, dazu sind der Osten und der Westen nötig, sind sie in Einheit da. Der Wechsel ist das Dauernde, Naturgesetze der Einseitigkeit gibt es nicht.[30]

[The sun does not only go up or only down, it constantly goes up and down, day and night always succeed each other and for that both East and West are necessary; they exist in unity. What remains is change. There are no onesided laws of nature.]

Equally exaggerated rhetoric is found in Leonhard's poem "Unser Land" (Our Country), which begins with bold declarations and metaphorical exhortations to his fellow Germans:

> Deutschland ist keine Länder,
> Deutschland ist ein Land.
> Deutsche, zerreißt die Ränder,
> Deutsche, bindet die Bänder,
> Jeder mit seiner Hand.[31]
>
> [Germany is not some states,
> Germany is one land,
> Germans, tear up the borders,
> Germans, tie the bands,
> Each with his own hand.]

Given the crudity, for example, of the alliteration in the third line, it would be difficult to describe this as great poetry. Nevertheless, it would be presumptuous to dismiss this kind of outpouring as merely the expression of the official Eastern view. Much closer to official discourse is the comment about German unity as a precondition for peace made by the poet Anna Seghers at an international congress in Vienna in 1952 in which she contrasts the *Kriegstreiber* (warmongers) and the *Friedenskräfte der Welt* (forces for peace in the world).[32] This comment was made the same year as Stalin's offer of a united democratic but neutral Germany. The seriousness of the offer remains a bone of contention among historians, but the western rejection of it put an end to the Eastern pleas for unity in favor of concentration on the construction of a socialist GDR.

What Stalin appeared to offer in 1952 was in many ways close to what many writers and intellectuals had wished for in the postwar years. A united Germany, it was hoped by some, would act as a bridge between East and West. This was the title of an essay in *Der Ruf* by Hans Werner Richter, in which he speaks of a German society combining both Eastern and Western features pointing the way to the future of Europe and to the greatest possible degree of European unity.[33] The structures that were to emerge under the ideal of European unity or European cooperation, for example the European Community, were in fact entirely West European and were frequently seen by many, at least until 1989, as a barrier to German unity. Rather than integration with the West, as pursued by Adenauer, those fighting for unity saw some kind of neutrality as the only way forward. The various ideas are explained in a book by Rainer Dohse titled *Der Dritte Weg: Neutralitäts-bestrebungen in Westdeutschland zwischen 1945 und 1955* (The Third Way: The Struggle for Neutrality in West Germany Between 1945 and 1955).[34] Dohse distinguishes three types of movement. Firstly, he speaks of those, who, like Richter, sought to make Germany a bridge between East and West. His second category consists of those who hoped to make Germany into a *Brandmauer* (fire screen) between the two power blocs. In this scenario, Germany would have been a de-militarized zone, whereas, for the third group of people, the idea was for Germany to become a third force, armed and neutral rather than neutralized.

Space does not permit a detailed discussion of these ideas here. What is relevant in this context is the way that for all those seeking to preserve unity at this time, the way forward was seen as being negotiation with the Soviet Union rather than confrontation. This was in contrast with the *Politik der Stärke* (policy of strength) of the Adenauer government, which had the avowed aim of forcing concessions but was seen by many as only cementing division. Even the writer and journalist Paul Sethe, who favored Western integration, was clear on the need for negotiation with and concessions to the Soviet Union if German unity was to be achieved.[35]

However, such an understanding for the Soviet position was not common, not even among those who favored neutrality. Writing in *Frankfurter Hefte* in 1951, Walter Dirks was only willing to accept neutrality under strict conditions, including sovereignty and international guarantees.[36] Until that time, American protection would remain vital. The atmosphere engendered by the Cold War, which will be considered in the next chapter, was already casting a shadow.

Conclusion

There can be no doubt, in the light of what has been discussed above, that the immediate postwar period was a time of intense intellectual activity. What is much more open to debate, as mentioned above, is the nature of the reception of this activity. Despite the undoubted response among sections of the German population, there is reason to believe that many were not open to new ideas or interested in taking part in debates on the future of Germany. Even in *Der Ruf,* despite the self-confident tone of much of the writing (for example, when Andersch hails the new young Europe), there is also an awareness that the seed may be falling on stony ground. Richter's "Warum schweigt die junge Generation?" unsurprisingly lays much of the blame for the silence of the young generation at the door of the older generation, which is seeking refuge in the comforting shadow of the past.[37] By contrast, the young generation has had its existence ripped apart by war and can only find hope in "einem radikalen und absoluten Neuanfang" (an absolute and radical new beginning; 42). Ultimately, Richter is seeing his generation as victims, a view that is not without its dangers. The refusal to see the sufferings inflicted on others because of German suffering has frequently stood in the way of any honest appraisal of the Nazi past. Swiss writer Max Frisch, always a shrewd observer of developments in his neighboring country, criticizes this attitude in a unsent letter to a former German soldier who complained that someone like Frisch could never understand what he had been through. Frisch warns against bragging over the degree of misery suffered and speaks ironically of the Germans as the people who have suffered most on this earth — provided that the Jews, the Poles, the Greeks, and all the others are forgotten.[38]

There were undoubtedly also clear, objective reasons why young people, and many others as well, were indifferent to intellectual debates. Firstly, the majority of the population had to expend much of its energy on survival in a world marked by shortages of food and other material goods. Secondly, there was the question of what potential influence the ordinary person might have on political developments. The philosopher Hermann Nohl, in a 1947 essay, speaks, similarly to Richter, of young people being indifferent to politics, giving as one reason the realization by many that real political power lay in the hands of outside powers.[39] Whereas Nohl remains somewhat vague, Kantorowicz in *Ost und West* is more precise, speaking of Germany being an "object" rather than a "subject" in world politics.[40] In other words, the destiny of Germany lay in the hands of the victorious Allies whose disagreements created division and ideological opposition rather than the hoped-for single state incorporating both Eastern and Western elements.

It would also seem that these Allies, insofar as they spoke of collective guilt and the need for re-education and pursued a policy of denazification, met with more resistance than approval. For example, the Nuremberg trials were for many Germans *Siegerjustiz* (victor's justice). Many Germans retreated into a protective cocoon, which cut them off from the concerns of those fellow citizens like the writers of *Frankfurter Hefte* who did wish to engage with moral issues. Nevertheless, given the material deprivations of the time, it is perhaps surprising that there was any sort of renewal of intellectual activity in postwar Germany.

Notes

1 For a review of the debate, see Hans Dieter Schäfer, "Zur Periodisierung der deutschen Literatur seit 1930," in *Das gespaltene Bewußtsein. Über deutsche Kultur und Lebenswirklichkeit* (Munich: Hanser, 1981), 55–71.

2 Günter Eich, "Inventur" quoted with commentary in Deutschlandfunk, "Vergessener Rebell," http://www.dradio.de/dif/sendungen/buechermarkt/587156/. Consulted 28.04.2006.

[3] Herbert Lestiboudois, "Warum, wozu noch," in *Der Anfang,* ed. Paul E.H. Luth (Wiesbaden: Limes Verlag, 1947), 43–44, here 43.

[4] Günter Weisenborn, "Wir bitten um Eure Rückkehr," in *VLMS,* 43–45.

[5] Alfred Andersch, *Deutsche Literatur in der Entscheidung* (Karlsruhe: Verlag Volk und Zeit, [1947]), 7.

[6] Quoted in Bernhard Zeller, ed., *Als der Krieg zu Ende war* (Munich: Kosel Verlag, 1973), 255.

[7] Anon., "Alltag der Ostzone," *Die Gegenwart* 4:24 (1949): 6–7, here 6.

[8] The editors make this claim in a reply to a letter from a young person: "'Kein Mensch glaubt es,'" *Die Gegenwart* 1:2–3 (1946): 49–50.

[9] Walter Dirks, "Das Abendland und der Sozialismus," *Frankfurter Hefte* 1:3 (1946): 67–78, here 75.

[10] Karl Heinrich Knappstein, "Die Stunde der Sozialreform," *Frankfurter Hefte* 1:3 (1946): 1–3.

[11] Herbert Lestiboudois, "Junge Generation," in *Der Anfang,* ed. Luth, 46.

[12] Anon., "Rede an die deutsche Jugend. Eine Parodie frei nach Ernst Wiechert," in *Der Ruf. Unabhängige Blätter für die junge Generation,* ed. Hans A. Neunzig (Munich: Nymphenburger Verlagshandlung, 1976), 58–60.

[13] Alfred Andersch, "Das junge Europa formt sein Gesicht," in *Der Ruf,* ed. Hans Schwab-Felisch (Munich: DTV, 1962), 21–29, here 22.

[14] Hans Werner Richter, *Die Geschlagenen* (Munich: DTV, 1969), 125.

[15] Heinz Friedrich, "Nationalismus und Nationalismus," in *Der Ruf,* ed. Schwab-Felisch, 226–27.

[16] Hans Werner Richter, "Parteipolitik und Weltanschauung," in *Der Ruf,* ed. Schwab-Felisch, 83–88.

[17] Hans Werner Richter, "Warum schweigt die junge Generation?" in *Der Ruf,* ed. Schwab-Felisch, 29–33, esp. 32.

[18] Frank Thiess, quoted in *VLMS,* 47. As this volume consists frequently of short untitled extracts, it is not proposed always to refer to each item separately.

[19] Thomas Mann, "Offener Brief für Deutschland," in *VLMS,* pp. 47–48, here 48. Thiess's response is to be found on 49.

[20] Friedrich Sieburg, "Frieden mit Thomas Mann," *Die Gegenwart,* 4:14 (1949): 14–16.

[21] Hannah Arendt, "Organisierte Schuld," in *Bundesrepublikanisches Lesebuch,* ed. Hermann Glaser (Frankfurt am Main: Fischer, 1980), 227–35, esp. 234–35. Her comments on the Eichmann trial are found in Hannah Arendt, *Eichmann in Jerusalem* (Munich: Piper, 1986).

[22] Karl Jaspers, *Die Schuldfrage* (Munich, Zurich: Piper, 2nd ed., 1976), esp. 50–54.

[23] Hans Werner Richter, "Beim Wiederschen des 'Ruf,'" in *Der Ruf,* ed. Schwab-Felisch, 7–9, here 8.

[24] Alfred Andersch, "Das junge Europa," 25.

[25] Eugen Kogon, "Gericht und Gewissen," *Frankfurter Hefte,* 1/1 (1946): 25–37.

[26] See *VLMS*, 74.

[27] Gerhard Baumert, Letter to *Ost und West*, 1:4 (1947): 85–87.

[28] Käte Fuchs, "Suchende Jugend. Briefwechsel zwischen der Studentin Käte Fuchs und Alfred Kantorowicz," *Ost und West*, 2:2 (1948): 85–91, esp.85–87.

[29] Johannes R. Becher, "Deutschland, dich suchend," in *Wir heißen Euch hoffen*, ed. Georg Schwarz and Carl August Weber (Munich: Willi Weismann Verlag, 1951), 26.

[30] Walter von Molo, "Ja, wir wollen uns retten," in *Wir heißen Euch hoffen*, ed. Schwarz, 29–42, here 33.

[31] Rudolf Leonhard, "Unser Land," in *Wir heißen Euch hoffen*, ed. Schwarz, 43.

[32] Anna Seghers, "Appell an die deutschen Schriftsteller," in *VLMS*, 122.

[33] Hans Werner Richter, "Deutschland — Brücke zwischen Ost und West," in *Der Ruf*, ed. Schwab-Felisch, 46–49, here 49.

[34] Rainer Dohse, *Der Dritte Weg. Neutralitätsbestrebungen in Westdeutschland zwischen 1945 und 1955* (Hamburg: Holsten Verlag), 1974.

[35] Paul Sethe, quoted in *Westdeutsche Wiedervereinigungspolitik 1949–1961*, Hein Holink (Meisenheim am Glen: Verlag Anton Hain, 1978), 85.

[36] Walter Dirks, "Europa und die Neutralität," *Frankfurter Hefte*, 6:5 (1951): 305–8.

[37] Richter, "Warum schweigt die junge Generation?" 29. Further citations given in parentheses.

[38] Max Frisch, "Drei Entwürfe zu einem Brief nach Deutschland," in *Lesebuch*, ed. Glaser, 236–42, here 239.

[39] Hermann Nohl, "Die geistige Lage im gegenwärtigen Deutschland," in *Lesebuch*, ed. Glaser, 150–54, here 152.

[40] Alfred Kantorowicz, "Einführung," *Ost und West*, 1:1 (1947): 3–8, here 4.

2: The 1950s: The Deepening Division

Political Developments

IN THE FEDERAL REPUBLIC, the 1950s form the core of what is frequently referred to as the Adenauer Era. Having become Federal Chancellor at the age of 73, Konrad Adenauer remained in office for fourteen years, a record only surpassed in the 1980s and 1990s by his self-styled protégé Helmut Kohl. It was a time of unsurpassed electoral success for Adenauer's party, the CDU, and its Bavarian sister party the CSU, most especially in the federal elections of 1957, when for the only time in the history of the Federal Republic, a party (or, to be exact, two allied parties) managed to achieve an absolute majority of votes cast.

The major reason for this success was undoubtedly the economic miracle — the rapid recovery of the economy of the Federal Republic from wartime devastation and postwar uncertainties. The 1950s also saw the establishment of those features with which the post-1945 German economy has been most frequently identified: the independence of the Bundesbank (Central Bank), a degree of co-determination at both plant and company level (though this fell far short of trade union aspirations, outside of key mining and steel industries), along with generous social welfare provisions, not least for pensioners.

Although these developments undoubtedly improved the material conditions of the vast majority of the population and facilitated the integration of the *Heimatvertriebene* (Germans expelled from former German territories in the east) and those who had chosen to leave the German Democratic Republic, they did provoke critical comment. It appeared, as the American economist H. C. Wallich noted in 1955, that the German people were restricting themselves to "economic pursuits,"[1] while, according to many, society was undergoing a period of "restoration," a term coined by Walter Dirks that implied that traditional elites were re-establishing themselves despite their role in the national catastrophe of the Nazi era.[2] The figure most frequently cited was the top civil servant in the Federal Chancellor's Office, Hans Maria Globke, who, as a civil servant in the Nazi Ministry of the Interior, had co-written the commentary on the 1935 Nuremberg Laws that had in effect outlawed Jews from German society. A similar pattern was discerned in schools and universities, where teachers and professors from the Nazi era continued to hold sway; in the newly created army, into which former Wehrmacht officers were recruited; and in industry, where patterns of ownership remained largely unchanged despite the support given by swathes of business to the Nazis. At a social level, restoration meant for its opponents the maintenance of outdated conservative norms — for example, the prohibition of homosexuali ty and abortion, not to mention the classification of adultery as a criminal offense. Needless to say, the church, in particular the Catholic Church, enjoyed considerable influence within the CDU/CSU at this time.

Despite these controversial issues, many of which will be considered later in this chapter, changes were taking place. In particular, the Federal Republic was being integrated into the Western system of alliances that developed alongside the Cold War. It was a founding member of the European Coal and Steel Community in 1951, which developed into the European Economic Community with the Rome Treaties of 1957, and it also became a member of the North Atlantic Treaty Organization (NATO) in 1955. The process of reconciliation with the former *Erbfeind* (hereditary enemy) France had begun, while compensation for Nazi persecution of Jews was paid to the new state of Israel. However, little or no progress was made in relations with the East, although a visit to the Soviet Union in 1955 by Adenauer did lead to diplomatic relations and the return of the last German prisoners of war. In general the Adenauer government remained strongly anticommunist, something which was also seen as part of the restoration insofar as it continued the tradition established by Joseph Goebbels, who had cast Nazi Germany in the role of defender of European values against barbarian hordes from the east. The opposition Social Democrats, who spent most of the decade in the political wilderness, undoubtedly suffered as a result of this anticommunism, not least in the 1953 elections when the CDU based its campaign on the claim that all forms of socialism led to Moscow.

If the Federal Republic was being westernized in the 1950s, then the German Democratic Republic represents its mirror image — namely, the integration of that state into the Soviet bloc. Whereas initially, as one historian claims, the GDR may have been Stalin's "ungeliebtes Kind" (unloved child)[3]— since his ideal would have been a single but neutral German state — the rejection of his 1952 offer of unification led the Soviet Union set to introduce, or to allow the East German communists to introduce, the Soviet model. Initially, this led to protests, in particular the strikes and demonstrations of June 1953 against the imposition of higher work norms. When these events threatened the survival of the state, Soviet troops intervened, setting the unhappy precedent for what was to happen in Hungary in 1956 and Czechoslovakia in 1968.

If the 1950s were the Adenauer era in the West, then the same period in the East was increasingly the Ulbricht era. During the course of the decade, the man who had spent the war years in the Soviet Union and survived

Stalin's purges managed to rid himself of rivals within the SED (particularly after the 1953 uprising), quell the upsurge of reformist ideas emanating from Hungary in 1956, and attain the most significant offices of state and party. In particular, after the death of Wilhelm Pieck in 1960, the office of president was abolished and replaced by the Staatsrat (Council of State), of which Ulbricht himself became chairman. Given his ideological rigidity and that of his counterpart Adenauer in the West, it is small wonder that, except in the area of trade, intra-German relations remained frosty, as indeed did East-West relations in general.

At the same time, some economic progress was being made in the East, although the major effort was put into the development of industry at the expense of housing and the consumer. Despite the euphoria, at least in official circles, engendered by such events as the launch of the Soviet Sputnik in 1957, many East Germans remained discontented with their standard of living and the lack of intellectual freedom. The result was a steady flow of refugees to the more prosperous Federal Republic, a country where the majority of citizens felt content in the path it had chosen as the beacon of anticommunism and partner of the United States.

Literary Developments

Insofar as the West Germans, as noted above, were concentrating largely on enjoying the material improvements brought about by the economic miracle to the exclusion of everything else, literature was arguably an area that suffered. Ralf Schnell speaks of a population in the thrall of the economic miracle (*GDL*, 247), noting as well that this had a particularly debilitating effect on the theater, as critical drama was the last thing a public willing to accept the seamier side of the Adenauer era wished to be confronted with (*GDL*, 278).

Part of this seamier side was the Adenauer administration's disregard, at best, of writers and intellectuals who challenged official policies, and, at worst, its propensity to attack them with any available weapons. Two examples of this will suffice. When in 1957 eighteen atomic scientists protested against the prospect of the Bundeswehr acquiring nuclear weapons, Adenauer curtly commented that the gentlemen in question lacked the knowledge to pass judgment (*VLMS*, 140). This in turn prompted the writer and journalist Kurt Hiller to attack Adenauer for the lack of any relationship to the world of science (*VLMS*, 140). Three years later there appeared an anonymous "red book," published under the title *Verschwörung gegen die Freiheit. Die Kommunistische Untergrundarbeit in der Bundesrepublik* (Conspiracy Against Freedom. Underground Communist Activity in the Federal Republic), listing 452 university teachers, writers, and artists who were to be classed as communist; in whose publication, it is generally assumed the Adenauer government was involved. By then, however, writers had achieved a new status. The year 1959 can be regarded, in fact, as the literary equivalent of the economic miracle, with the appearance of Günter Grass's *Die Blechtrommel* (The Tin Drum), Heinrich Böll's *Billard um halbzehn* (Billiards at Half-past Nine) and Uwe Johnson's *Mutmaßungen über Jakob* (Speculations about Jacob). The extent to which the Adenauer government had overplayed its hand can be seen in the ironic plea by Hans Magnus Enzensberger, another writer emerging at this time, to be included in the list of communist shame. He speaks of being "erbarmungslos ausgestrichen" (mercilessly excluded).[4]

In fact, the names most associated with West German literature had emerged by the end of the 1950s. Alongside Böll, Enzensberger, Grass, and Johnson, Martin Walser had already published two works, the collection of stories *Ein Flugzeug über dem Haus und andere Geschichten* (An Airplane over the House and Other Stories, 1955), one of which won him the prize of the Gruppe 47, and his first novel *Ehen in Philippsburg* (The Gadarene Club, 1957).

What had been taking place in the literary life of the Federal Republic in the 1950s was its gradual opening to Western modernism. Both Böll and Johnson, in the works mentioned above, make use of features that are associated with modernist writing. *Billard um halbzehn* owes a great deal to the French *nouveau roman,* while Johnson's title clearly encapsulates the idea of the no-longer-omniscient narrator. In a sense, what was happening in the literary and intellectual worlds ran parallel to political developments, even if the circles most associated with the Adenauer government rejected anything that could be called decadent or perverse. In short, just as the Federal Republic was developing its specific political and economic identity, it was also developing its own intellectual and literary identity. Stressing the importance of the role played by Alfred Andersch, literary historian Rhys Williams has spoken of the invention of West German literature.[5] At the same time, what has been called the intellectual foundation of the Federal Republic was taking place, with the critical theory associated with the Frankfurt School and the returned émigrés Theodor W. Adorno and Max Horkheimer playing an increasing role, although its influence on intellectual life only reached its peak in the 1960s.[6]

If the 1950s were a period of transition for literature, the process itself was often difficult. There was much to be overcome before a self-confident critical literature could establish itself — specifically, what Adorno called German ideology, the tendency to take refuge in visions of a perfect, conflict-free world. In his work *Jargon der Eigentlichkeit* (Jargon of Authenticity, 1964), Adorno quoted the poet of the internal emigration, Werner Bergengruen, from a collection that appeared in 1950: "Was aus Schmerzen kam, war Vorübergang. / Und mein Ohr vernahm nichts als Lobgesang" (What came from pain, was transitory. / And my heart heard nothing but songs of praise). Not surprisingly, given his personal background, Adorno shows his horror that such a thing could be written only a few years after the Holocaust.[7] Adorno also takes exception to the stance of the philosopher Otto Friedrich Bollnow, who in 1956 published a work entitled *Neue Geborgenheit* (New Sense of Well-being). By the end of the decade, however, the influence of such voices that sought refuge in dubious idyllic visions from both the reality of the present and the horrors of the recent past was very much on the wane.

What happened in the Federal Republic in the 1950s in the area of literature was mirrored in the GDR, although in this case it was less a case of individual literary works establishing a new literary identity than of attempts from above to create a distinct GDR literature. Once again 1959 was a key year. In April of that year, a conference was held in the industrial town of Bitterfeld — incidentally, a place whose name was to become synonymous with the worst environmental pollution in the GDR — at which two ideals were proclaimed: firstly, that workers should take up their pens and write — the phrase *Greif zur Feder, Kumpel* (Grab your pen, mate) emerged as a slogan of exhortation — and secondly, that professional writers should acquaint themselves with the working world and reflect their experiences in their work. The attempt to create a cultural identity in the GDR through the *Bitterfelder Weg* (The Bitterfeld Way) did bear fruit in works that appeared in the 1960s, although the hopes of cultural functionaries were not always fully fulfilled.

Bitterfeld was also the culmination of efforts throughout the decade to promote literature based on the Soviet model with once again the link with political and economic developments being clearly apparent. In the first years of the GDR's existence, war was declared on formalism — in other words, modernism, which was seen as a product of capitalist decadence. Insofar as culture in the western part of Germany was being influenced by outside forces, it was claimed that the GDR was keeping to German traditions. Thus, Viennese waltzes could be seen by cultural functionaries as a better basis for modern dance music than American jazz (*KP*, 39). However, the influence of the Soviet model was such that Socialist Realism, which had been proclaimed in the Soviet Union in the 1930s, became the required literary form. At the same time, writers such as Johannes R. Becher and Erich Weinert produced verse that sang the praises of the Party or Stalin or both.[8] A cultural divide between the two parts of Germany had replaced the optimism of the initial postwar period.

Writers and Politics

Division

As has been seen above, the 1950s was a time when Germany became increasingly divided: at a political level through the consolidation of two separate states and at the cultural level with the dissemination of modernist ideas in the West and the adoption at an official level of Marxism-Leninism and Socialist Realism in the East. Although much of this chapter will be devoted to protest, at least in the West, against political developments, it is important to remember that many aspects of what was happening in politics were mirrored elsewhere. In certain writing of the time, Jost Hermand has even seen a crusading zeal, referring, for example, to utopian works by such writers as Curt Riess and Edwin Erich Dwinger that present the downfall of communism.[9] If these writers are now largely forgotten, many other figures of greater stature — for example, leading members of the Frankfurt School — clearly identified with the West against the Soviet model.[10]

As early as 1950, the divisions between intellectuals were apparent with the holding of a *Kongreß für kulturelle Freiheit* (Congress for Cultural Freedom) in West Berlin in June of that year. This was organized by the American Melvyn J. Lasky of the magazine *Der Monat,* the German equivalent of the respected British *Encounter,* and equally, it transpired later, a beneficiary of CIA funding. The congress produced a manifesto that, although partly pacifistic in tone, clearly contains, with its stress on the right of individuals to form and express their own opinions, negative allusions to developments in the GDR (*VLMS,* 96). Those present at the conference included many who could not be classed as unrepentant cold warriors, for example, Eugen Kogon and Luise Rinser as well as foreign guests such as A. J. Ayer. Nevertheless, Johannes R. Becher was moved to speak of "Handlanger der Kriegshetzer" (lackeys of warmongers), "eine Bande internationaler Hochstapler" (a gang of international confidence tricksters) and "literarisch getarnte Gangster" (gangsters under a veneer of literature).[11] This led, a little later, to *Der Monat* hitting back at Becher in a series of articles by authors such as Stefan Andres and Rudolf Hagelstange, not to mention in an open letter from Becher's son John, who was living in London at the time. Although he speaks of filial love and an understanding of his father's ideals, he concludes that the reality of communism is "eine Finsternis, die aufs neue Europa bedroht" (a darkness that threatens Europe anew).[12]

Conflicts at a personal level were replicated at the institutional level, for instance with the German section of the International PEN Club splitting in 1951 and the foundation of a GDR branch. For a brief period, there were even three associations in Germany, with the Deutsches Penzentrum zwischen Ost und West (German PEN Club Between East and West) trying to maintain links between writers from both parts of the divided country. As it turned out, writers from the two German states increasingly lived in different worlds. Occasionally, an Eastern writer such as Johannes Bobrowski, who would go on to win the Gruppe 47 prize in 1962, would attend the group's gatherings, and other meetings between intellectuals would take place, as in Hamburg in 1961, an event that turned largely into a dialogue of the deaf.[13]

However, there were no quasi-official contacts until the 1980s debates about the threat from new nuclear weapons, and when unification came, it was not easy to re-create unified institutions, as the example of the PEN clubs shows. A single body for the whole of united Germany was only established again in 1998.

Individuals, too, were faced with choices about which part of Germany they wished to live in. As with other parts of society, the main movement was from East to West. Those making the change included some who had been relatively important figures in the East, as with the novelist Günther Weisenborn who, as referred to in the previous chapter, had acted for a brief period as a small-town mayor under the Soviet occupation. The movement was, however, not only in one direction. Among those choosing the East was the young dramatist Peter Hacks, who left Munich for the GDR in 1955. Despite all the efforts described in the previous chapter to maintain unity, it is fair to say that the Cold War alienation between the two German states also had a major effect on the world of culture.

The Campaign against Re-armament

One issue on which a large number of both Eastern and Western writers could agree was that of the creation of an army in the Federal Republic, preparations for which began in the early 1950s. That such a development should occur so soon after the physical and moral defeat of the Wehrmacht and in a period in which pacifism was the order of the day caused a shock not only among writers, but among large sections of the population, who reacted to the plans with the slogan *ohne mich* (count me out). As for writers and other intellectuals, they reacted both individually and collectively.

An important publication in this context is the volume *Worte wider Waffen* (Words Against Weapons, 1951), which contains a variety of contributions in both prose and verse from both well-known writers such as Brecht and Hans Henny Jahnn, and others who are now largely forgotten, such as Johannes von Tralow, a writer who had flirted with National Socialism but settled in the GDR. In his afterword, Tralow launched an extremely direct — if not to say crude — attack on the hypocrisy of those in favor of re-armament:

> Ihr drittes Wort ist "christlich," und sie denken dabei an fette Rüstungsdividenden, Schmuck für die Frau, Spitzenwäsche für die Töchter, und neiderweckende Mätressen für die Herren Söhne und sich selber.[14]

> [Their every third word is "Christian," and, at the same time, they are thinking of fat profits from armaments, jewellery for their wife, lace lingerie for their daughters and envy-provoking mistresses for their dear sons and themselves.]

If this kind of polemic can be readily associated with Marxist anticapitalism coupled with skepticism about the misuse of religion, then other contributors write from a clear Christian standpoint. Herbert Adam von Eyck, for example, while admitting that the New Testament does not say explicitly that war is inadmissible, states that the destructive capacity of modern weapons makes war impossible.[15] Another Christian writer, Rüdiger Syberberg, even attempts to reconcile Christianity with Eastern atheism, which, it is claimed, at least shows the passion of religious faith.[16]

One other contributor, Reinhold Schneider, can be seen as the leading Christian opponent of re-armament among writers. He too expresses his concern about modern (including nuclear) weapons, seeing their use as sinful and in no way to be compared with the concept of, in the words of his title, "Das Schwert der Apostel" (The Apostles' Sword), as used, for example, in Paul's letter to the Romans.[17] His active commitment to the cause of peace lasted from the end of the war until his death in 1958, during which time he frequently attracted criticism from the official Catholic Church and found himself excluded from the broadcasting media. As early as the autumn of 1945 he expressed his ideal for humanity in a new peaceful era, saying that it was people at peace with themselves and possessing God's peace who should take responsibility for the future.[18] Schneider, whose work enjoyed a major renaissance in the 1980s at a time of major concern about the increasing arms race, was a co-founder of the Notgemeinschaft für den Frieden Europas (Emergency Association for Peace in Europe), along with the theologian Helmut Gollwitzer and the politician Gustav Heinemann, who had resigned from the Adenauer government over the issue of re-armament and subsequently, as a member of the SPD, became federal president from 1969 to 1974. Both signed the *Deutsches Manifest,* which resulted from a gathering in the Frankfurt Paulskirche in 1955 (*VLMS,* 129–30). The manifesto, also signed by, among others, Walter Dirks and the Christian writer Albrecht Goes, attacked the Paris Treaties of 1954 that paved the way for a West German army (Bundeswehr), and demanded negotiations to create a unified German state rather than the creation of opposing military blocs.

As it turned out, all the protests failed to prevent the creation of a West German army in late 1955, and its incorporation into NATO. By contrast, campaigns against the arming of the Bundeswehr with nuclear weapons were successful, although this was undoubtedly due as much, if not more, to international opinion as to domestic protest. Nevertheless, the protests were significant and widespread. Moreover, the arguably major proponent of equipping the new army with nuclear weapons, Bavarian politician and defense minister at the time Franz Josef Strauß, became the bête noire of intellectuals for the next three decades.

Concern over the nuclear issue was again expressed both individually and collectively. In 1958 Hans Werner Richter founded the Komitee gegen

Atomrüstung (Committee Against Nuclear Armament) and was also involved with other antinuclear organizations such as Kampf dem Atomtod (Struggle Against Atomic Death), which initially was close to the opposition SPD. A variety of resolutions emerged at this time with the signatories including Paul Schallück, Heinrich Böll, Martin Walser, and even politically more conservative writers such as the popular novelist Hans Habe (*VLMS*, 144–45). A co-signatory of these resolutions, Hans Henny Jahnn, was among the most vocal of the critics of nuclear weapons. In his seminal essay of 1956 "Der Mensch im Atomzeitalter" (Man in the Atomic Era), he points to the dangers both of war and of a society dominated by technology to the detriment of all other considerations. This leads him to express ecological concerns, which prove that environmentalism in the Federal Republic is older than the 1970s and 1980s. He writes, for instance, that the idea of the disappearance of thousands of animal species with man left in control of the world would be unthinkable.[19] On the specific question of nuclear weapons, in a 1958 essay, he rejects the idea that nuclear war could be justified on any grounds, even on the ideal of liberty as propounded by Western powers, stating that people like himself who desire individual freedom cannot risk the death of millions for their ideal.[20]

Although the antiatomic movement lost momentum in the early 1960s, not least when the SPD withdrew its support as part of the modernization process associated with its Godesberg Program of 1959, its significance, along with that of the campaign against re-armament, should not be underestimated. Not only were such campaigns to recur in the 1980s, when a new kind of atomic threat was perceived, but also military issues have remained highly controversial throughout the history of the Federal Republic, both before and after unification.

Writers and the New Federal Republic

Re-armament is a major theme in two political novels that appeared in the 1950s: Günther Weisenborn's *Auf Sand gebaut* (Built on Sand, 1956) and Wolfgang Koeppen's *Das Treibhaus* (The Hothouse, 1953). In fact, these two are arguably the only two substantial political novels of the pre-unification Federal Republic, if the term is narrowed to apply only to works set largely in the political world of Bonn. Of the two, Koeppen's work has undoubtedly stood the test of time better, with the metaphor of the title remaining in public consciousness as an apt encapsulation of the atmosphere of an unnatural and frenzied world.

Koeppen's main figure is Keetenheuve, an opposition member of parliament who in many respects seems much more a disenchanted intellectual than a typical politician. Although he is willing to confront a visitor to the Bundestag who, using Nazi terminology, regards parliament as a *Quasselbude* (waffling shop), he too is disillusioned with politics because of the policy of re-armament. This disillusionment extends to his own party, as its leadership, specifically Knurrewahn (who seems based on the postwar SPD leader Kurt Schumacher), is willing to accept a new army in principle, believing that it can be made subject to democratic control. For Keetenheuve, the military tradition is like a malignant tumor; what is more, in his view the history of the Weimar Republic shows that the army can easily become a state within a state.[21] Despite the offer of a sinecure from the government in the form of an ambassadorship, he makes a passionate speech in the parliamentary debate on re-armament. Finally, knowing his efforts are doomed to failure, he commits suicide. The idea of the military mentality as a creeping sickness is also present in Weisenborn's novel. His main figure, like Keetenheuve, is also an opposition politician who can be classed as an intellectual. His main worry is that the whole of society will be permeated by the dubious values of the military, believing, for instance, that the military ethos will come to dominate both the school and the workplace.[22] It goes without saying that this never happened, as any normally observant visitor to a German school in the 1960s and later could testify.

It was not solely the possible militarization of society that concerned writers and intellectuals. It was the whole gamut of measures that led to the term "restoration" being increasingly used to describe the atmosphere of the time. One measure that understandably perturbed authors was the plan, announced in the first year of the existence of the Federal Republic, to restrain artistic freedom by more or less reintroducing the *Schund- und Schmutz-gesetz* (law against trash and filth) of the Weimar Republic. This 1926 law, which purported to protect young people against pornography and other dangerous material, had always been seen by writers as part of that state's extensive censorship apparatus. As early as 18 November 1949 the PEN club protested the planned new law, while a year later Stefan Andres saw in it a measure to facilitate silencing "die verantwortlichsten Stimmen der Nation" (the most responsible voices of the nation).[23] Regardless, a law was passed in 1952, albeit under the new name *Gesetz über den Vertrieb jugendgefährden-der Schriften* (law on the distribution of writing that might endanger young people). Similar steps were also taken in the area of film. As the Eastern writer Daniela Dahn points out, censorship was not restricted to the GDR.[24]

Writers' anger over the possibility of the limitation of their own freedom was compounded by their awareness of the freedom apparently being enjoyed by those formerly closely associated with the Nazi régime. Erich Kästner, for example, was horrified at the way that the Nazi film maker Veit Harlan, who was responsible for the notoriously anti-Semitic *Jud Süß* (The Jew Süss), was not only able to resume his career but also see his work protected by the authorities when there were student demonstrations against his first postwar film in 1952. Kästner noted that the only people regarded as being out of step were those who were called by their conscience to protest

in the name of humanity against "eine derartige Gerechtigkeit und ihre sicht-
baren, wie unabsehbaren Folgen" (such a justice and its visible as well as its
unpredictable consequences).[25] Harlan had, it should be noted, escaped any
judicial punishment for his previous activities.

Whether it was one of the consequences of the kind Kästner feared or
not, writers were deeply shocked when on Christmas Eve 1959 a Jewish
cemetery in Cologne was desecrated with anti-Semitic slogans. For Stefan
Andres, there was a link with the continuing prominence of so many former
Nazis, those he called "prominente Mitkämpfer, Mitarbeiter und Mitläufer
des seligen Führers" (prominent comrades-in-arms and associates of the late
Führer and those who went along with him; *VLMS*, 179). Walter Jens also
saw a link with re-armament, saying that those who seek missile bases so
soon after Hitler's war should not be surprised by what had happened
(*VLMS*, 180). Although despicable in itself, this act of anti-Semitism did
have the effect of increasing writers' concern about social and political issues
and may well have contributed to greater political commitment of the type
shown in the next chapter. That, in some cases, such vandalism was apparently instigated by the GDR in order to besmirch the name of the Federal
Republic has only become known since unification.

The other major issue that concerned writers in the 1950s was the economic miracle. A particularly vituperative essay, which appeared in the magazine *Die Kultur* in 1958, is Rudolf Hagelstange's "Endstation Kühlschrank.
Mass und Vernunft frieren ein" (A Desire Named Refrigerator. Restraint and
Sense Congeal). In it he attacks the mentality of the age from a standpoint
akin to the cultural pessimism of Oswald Spengler, proclaiming his despair at
the attitudes of a majority that seems to have no higher aspirations than the
possession of a refrigerator. He complains:

> Es wäre blasse Illusion, an den Geist zu appellieren, Moral zu predigen
> . . . Eine Generation . . . ist mit Verantwortung, Geist und ethischem An-
> spruch nicht vor dem Ofen hervorzulocken, an dem sie sich wärmt und
> genüßlich und selbstzufrieden der Ruhe pflegt. Ihr Schlachtfeld ist die
> Wirtschaft, ihr Heldentod der Herzinfarkt. Sie kämpft um Kühlschränke,
> Volks- oder kospspieligere Wagen, um Sommervillen, um Auslands-
> aufträge.[26]

> [It would be a worthless delusion to appeal to the intellect, to preach
> morality. A generation . . . cannot be enticed away from the fire, at which
> it warms itself and cultivates tranquillity in enjoyment and self-satisfac-
> tion, by responsibility, intellect, and moral demands. Its battlefield is the
> economy, its heroic death, the heart attack. It fights for refrigerators, for
> Volkswagens and more expensive vehicles, for summer residences and
> foreign orders.]

In invoking traditional heroism of the type demanded just over a decade previously, this attack on his fellow West Germans is highly dubious, being redolent of a questionable kind of intellectual snobbery.

More appealing is the attitude taken up by the novelist Paul Schallück in a collection of essays entitled *Zum Beispiel* (For Example, 1962). The first three essays, originally dating from the mid 50s, dealt with qualities that are seen as characteristic for the Germans of the time — hence the use of the word *deutsch* in each title. In "Von deutscher Tüchtigkeit" (On German Efficiency), he turns to economic matters, warning his fellow-countrymen against having no other interests, thus echoing the concerns of Wallich above. The essentially moral basis of his criticism is visible in his attack on the pursuit of economic success at the expense of such virtues as kindness, solidarity, and mercy.[27] As a corollary to this way of thinking solely in economic terms, Schallück sees a desire to suppress all thoughts of the past. This is the topic of the second essay in the collection, "Von deutscher Vergeßlichkeit" (On German Forgetfulness). Here, he speaks of the hopes of the immediate postwar era being replaced by a feeling of "Leere, der Herzenskälte, des rein materiellen Wohlbefindens" (emptiness, of coldness of heart, of purely material well-being).[28] According to Schallück, this is an injustice to all the victims of the war, from those who died in bombing raids to the victims of concentration camps. Not only does he see moral dangers in this, he also fears that what has been suppressed about the past could return in a virulent and dangerous form. In the third essay, "Von deutscher Resignation," he links the unwillingness to talk about the past with a passive, resigned state of mind that ignores anything that is potentially controversial. This, in turn, is harmful to democracy, which requires the active participation of the citizen, as well as controversy, something that adds piquancy to life and helps to make it worthwhile.[29]

Schallück's essays are an example of an individual trying to cajole his readers toward more democratic ways of thinking. A more concerted effort, at least for a time, to strengthen the Federal Republic's fledgling democracy was undertaken by Hans Werner Richter in the form of the Grünwalder Kreis (Grünwald Circle), which existed from 1956 to 1958. Concerned that democracy lacked firm foundations in the Federal Republic, Richter hoped for a "Demokratisierung in unserer Demokratie" (democratization in our democracy).[30] To this end, he convened the first meeting of the Kreis in 1956, hoping to bring together a coalition of democratic forces. However, the organization foundered for a number of reasons. Richter was unwilling to invest in clear organizational structures, hoping to use the same form of management or lack of it that he employed with the Gruppe 47. There was also the lack of any clear program, a result of the all-inclusiveness the Kreis aimed for and of Richter's distrust of professional politicians. It was only in the 1960s and 1970s, when writers were more willing to associate with political parties, that more sustained political involvement occurred.

Developments in the GDR

The efforts of the SED to establish both political and cultural hegemony in the GDR on the basis of the Soviet model in the 1950s did not pass without resistance. Less than four years after its creation, the very existence of the GDR was challenged by the events of June 1953 when, as mentioned above, workers in a number of cities, following the example of Berlin building workers, went on strike and took part in demonstrations that were relatively quickly crushed by the intervention of Soviet armed forces. In general, however, writers and intellectuals did not openly show solidarity with the uprising, and the more orthodox expressed their disgust at workers attacking their own socialist state. The poet (or perhaps more accurately, versifier) Kurt Barthel, who published under the name Kuba and was at the time secretary of the writers association, even titled his article on the workers' behavior, "Wie ich mich schäme" (How Ashamed I Am). (*VLMS,* 119–20). This provoked a memorable response in free verse by Brecht that concluded by turning Kuba's championing of the party against the people into the rhetorical question: "Wäre es da / Nicht doch einfacher, die Regierung / Löste das Volk auf und / Wählte ein anderes?" (Wouldn't it after all / be easier, if the government / dissolved the people and / elected a new one?; *VLMS,* 120). This reaction was, however, kept under wraps, and publicly, Brecht expressed his solidarity with the SED — a stance that was later seen by Günter Grass, in his play *Die Plebejer proben den Aufstand* (The Plebeians Rehearse the Uprising, 1966), as within the tragic tradition of German authors. The official line of the GDR authorities was that the disturbances had been provoked by Western agitators, a claim that enjoyed some sympathy among intellectuals. This idea of Western interference was still present in Stefan Heym's novel *Fünf Tage im Juni* (Five Days in June, 1974), which nevertheless was also critical of SED party policy.

Three years later, the shoe was on the other foot. Some intellectuals, inspired by the liberalization that was taking place in Hungary and the condemnation of Stalin by his successor Kruschev during the XX Congress of the Soviet Communist Party, began to question the rigidities of the cultural policies of the SED. There was, however, little or no support from other parts of the population. What followed were arrests, show trials, and terms of imprisonment for many of those who had demanded change. One of the principal victims was the head of the Aufbau publishing house, Walter Janka. His account of the events of 1956 and 1957 entitled *Schwierigkeiten mit der Wahrheit* (Difficulties with the Truth) attracted considerable attention when it could finally be published in the autumn of 1989. A major topos is the silence of GDR writers when confronted with persecution, both generally and specifically in the case of his own arrest and trial. Particular attention is given to the cases of Johannes R. Becher and Anna Sehgers, at that time the doyenne of GDR authors. In the case of Becher, Janka acknowledges that Becher did make a stand against Hitler, although he never publicly condemned Stalin despite his knowledge of the crimes committed by him. Janka also makes the general point that great writers are even greater if they protest against injustice.[31] As for Seghers, she was present during the trial and, although Janka notes that she did not join in the stage-managed condemnations, he points out that she was one of the few writers with enough status to have not risked persecution if she had shown a little courage and spoken out against what was going on (91). Sadly, in the 1950s, when GDR writers did speak, it was in many cases to give over-fulsome praise to the state or its symbols. The claim to omniscience contained in the chorus of the song "Lied der Partei" (Song of the Party) by the relatively minor writer Louis Fürnberg — "Die Partei, die Partei, sie hat immer recht" (The party, the party is always right) — was accepted by many writers, at least in public.[32]

Conclusion

As the above has shown, the 1950s were not the easiest of times for writers and intellectuals in Germany. In the Federal Republic, there was frequently a considerable gulf between them and both government and people. It might even be possible to turn Brecht's quip about the desirability of creating a new people against them. Certainly there have been those who, in retrospect, have been critical of a perceived arrogance among writers that set them apart from their fellow citizens. Writing two decades later in a volume with the curious title *Die zornigen alten Männer* (The Angry Old Men, 1979), the concentration camp survivor Jean Améry, who was shortly after to commit suicide, mocked his own and colleagues' attitudes in an essay entitled "In den Wind gesprochen" (Spoken into the Wind). He claims that in the first years of the Federal Republic, the Left lived in a dream world on many issues, while the ordinary people had a much-greater grasp of reality on such questions as Berlin. He speaks of unforgivable arrogance and "eine noch unverzeihlichere Blindheit gegenüber den Sehnsüchten, Hoffnungen und Ängsten der Mitmenschen" (an even more unforgivable blindness toward the longings, hopes, and fears of our fellow men).[33] This he sees as having been particularly true of the economic sphere, where the pleasure at enjoying the good things in life was dismissed as alienation (265).

More recent criticism of the political attitudes of writers, and especially those associated with the Gruppe 47, has centered on the accusation that they lacked a radical edge. Literary historian Sabine Cofalla speaks of a complementary opposition, that is to say, an opposition that came from within the system, adding that the group was characterized by pragmatism at the expense of political vision.[34] One specific claim has been the lack of any clear break with the Nazi past, with Klaus Briegleb even seeing the group as anti-Semitic.[35] The poet Paul Celan, for example, was given a very cold reception on the one occasion he attended a Gruppe 47 meeting, even suffering the indignity of being compared to Goebbels. Although the Gruppe 47 and Richter in particular are not above criticism for this and other reasons — as shown above, their efforts to influence political developments were somewhat desultory — one wonders how more radical social criticism would have been received, given the overall conservative climate of the age.

It is this climate, as much as writers' own failings, that must be seen as a major factor contributing to the lack of impact by critical writers in the 1950s. In both parts of Germany, authoritarian leaders (albeit with democratic legitimacy in the case of the Federal Republic), kept a tight grip on power. Dissidence was met with a severe response in the GDR, as has been seen from the example of Walter Janka, with persecution and imprisonment. Clearly, this was not the case in the Federal Republic, although the use of different kinds of blunt instruments has been well illustrated in this chapter. By the end of the decade, however, these were beginning to lose much of their efficacy, a development that continued in the 1960s.

Notes

[1] H.C. Wallich, *Mainsprings of the German Revival* (New Haven: Yale UP, 1955), 20.

[2] See Albrecht Clemens et al., *Die intellektuelle Gründung der Bundesrepublik* (Frankfurt am Main: Campus, 2000), 133.

[3] Wilfried Loth, *Stalins ungeliebtes Kind: Warum Stalin die DDR nicht wollte* (Berlin: Rowohlt, 1994).

[4] Hans Magnus Enzensberger, "Beschwerde," in *VLMS*, 181–82, here 181.

[5] Rhys W. Williams, "Inventing West German Literature: Alfred Andersch and the Gruppe 47," in *The Gruppe 47 Fifty Years on: A Re-appraisal of Its Literary and Political Significance*, ed. Stuart Parkes and John J. White (Amsterdam and Atlanta: Rodopi, 1999), 69–88.

[6] See note 2.

[7] Theodor W. Adorno, *Jargon der Eigentlichkeit* (Frankfurt am Main: Suhrkamp, 3rd ed. 1967), 23.

[8] See *KP* 34/46 for examples of two such poems.

[9] Jost Hermand, "Streit in den fünfiziger Jahren," in *Kontroversen, alte und neue. Akten des VII Germanistentages*, ed. Albrecht Schöne (Tübingen: Max Niemeyer Verlag, 1986), 207–11, here 210.

[10] See, for example, Clemens, *Die intellektuelle Gründung der Bundesrepublik*, 136.

[11] Johannes R. Becher, "Die Sprache des Friedens," *Der Monat* 3:29 (1950/51): 488–89, here 488.

[12] John T. Becher, "John T. Becher schrieb an seinen Vater," *Der Monat* 3:29 (1950/51): 488–89, here 489.

[13] The Hamburg debates are reproduced in *Schriftsteller Ja-Sager oder Nein-Sager. Das Hamburger Streitgespräch deutscher Autoren aus Ost und West* (Hamburg: Rütten und Loening, 1961).

[14] Johannes von Tralow, "Nachwort," in *Worte wider Waffen,* ed. Georg Schwarz and Johannes von Tralow (Munich: Willi Weismann Verlag, 1951), 107–9, here 107.

[15] Herbert Adam von Eyck, "Der Hauptmann von Kapharnaum," in *Worte,* ed. Schwarz, 95–99.

[16] Rüdiger Syberberg, "Gedanken zur Zeit," in *Worte,* ed. Schwarz, 33–36.

[17] Reinhold Schneider, "Das Schwert der Apostel," in *Worte,* ed. Schwarz, 37–42.

[18] Reinhold Schneider, "Gedanken des Friedens," in *Schwert und Friede,* Reinhold Schneider (Frankfurt am Main: Suhrkamp, 1987), 246–47, here 247.

[19] Hans Henny Jahnn, "Der Mensch im Atomzeitalter," in *Das Hans Henny Jahn Lesebuch,* ed. Uwe Schweikert (Hamburg: Hoffmann und Campe, 1984), 69–83, here 81.

[20] Hans Henny Jahnn, "Der Abgrund," in *VLMS,* 147.

[21] Wolfgang Koeppen, *Das Treibhaus* (Frankfurt am Main: Suhrkamp, 1982), 81.

[22] Weisenborn, Günther, *Auf Sand gebaut* (Vienna, Munich, Basle: Desch, 1956), 184.

[23] Stefan Andres, "Warum nicht ein anderes Gesetz," in *VLMS,* 92–93, here 92.

[24] For examples of Western censorship, see Daniela Dahn, *Wenn und aber* (Reinbek: Rowohlt, 2002), 134–58, esp. 149–58.

[25] Erich Kästner, "Offener Brief an Freiburger Studenten," in *VLMS,* 110–11, here 110.

[26] Rudolf Hagelstange, "Endstation Kühlschrank. Maß und Vernunft frieren ein," *Die Kultur* 16:112 (1958): 1–2, here 2.

[27] Paul Schallück, "Von deutscher Tüchtigkeit," in *Zum Beispiel,* Paul Schallück (Frankfurt am Main: Europäische Verlagsanstalt, 1962), 7–11, here 9.

[28] Paul Schallück, "Von deutscher Vergeßlichkeit," in *Zum Beispiel,* Schallück, 12–16, here 14.

[29] Paul Schallück, "Von deutscher Resignation," in *Zum Beispiel,* Schallück, 17–26, here 19.

[30] Hans Werner Richter, quoted in Sabine Cofalla, *Der soziale Sinn Hans Werner Richters* (Berlin: Weidler, 1997), 97.

[31] Walter Janka, *Schwierigkeiten mit der Wahrheit* (Reinbek: Rowohlt, 1989), 10–11. Further citations given in parentheses.

[32] The full text of the song can be found on the following Web site: http://www.dhm.de/lemo/html/dokumente/JahreDesAufbausInOstUndWest_liedtextSEDLied/index.html. Consulted 14.08.2006.

[33] Jean Améry, "In den Wind gesprochen," in *Die zornigen alten Männer,* ed. Axel Eggebrecht (Reinbek: Rowohlt, 1979), 258–79, here 266. Further citations given in parentheses.

[34] Cofalla, *Der soziale Sinn,* 114.

[35] Klaus Briegleb, *Mißachtung und Tabu* (Berlin and Vienna: Philo, 2003).

3: The 1960s: Taking Sides

Political Developments

IN THE FEDERAL REPUBLIC AT LEAST, the 1960s were a time of major change in both the political and cultural fields. In the world of politics, the Adenauer government still held sway at the beginning of the decade, whereas at its end, power lay for the first time in the hands of an SPD-led government under Willy Brandt. Although it could have been foreseen in 1960 that the Adenauer era was approaching its close (the patriarch attained the age of eighty-four in that year), it was not just a matter of the inevitable passing of time leading to new constellations of power. Various significant events, many of which attracted considerable attention from writers and intellectuals, helped bring about the many changes that occurred during the decade.

In August 1961, the division of Germany was sealed by the construction of the Berlin Wall. This act by the GDR authorities with Soviet backing seemed to many to be tangible proof that the reunification policy of the Adenauer government, to force concessions from the East through a "policy of strength," had failed. The result was that the CDU/CSU was punished in the autumn elections, the big winner being the CDU's frequent coalition partner, the liberal Freie Demokratische Partei (Free Democrats, or FDP), which increased its share of the vote from 7.7 to 12.8 per cent, not least by having conducted an anti-Adenauer campaign. As it turned out, the FDP did accept membership in a new coalition with the CDU, albeit with the understanding that the octogenarian would retire after two years. However, before this period elapsed, there was a major crisis: the Spiegel Affair of 1962. *Spiegel* magazine had long been critical of the government, in particular the CSU Defense Minister Franz Josef Strauß. When an article was published criticizing the state of preparedness of the Bundeswehr, the offices of the magazine were raided and the editor Rudolf Augstein, along with the journalist Conrad Ahlers, who was in Spain at the time, arrested. When it became clear that Strauß had had a hand in these events, the FDP ministers left the government and forced his resignation.

Although the CDU/CSU was undoubtedly weakened by these events, the eventual resignation of Adenauer in 1963 did not bring about cataclysmic change. His successor Ludwig Erhard was popular with the general public as "father of the economic miracle," even if he was held in something near contempt by his predecessor. Thus, the CDU made up some lost ground in the 1965 election, only for a renewed crisis to surface in 1966 when the first (although by later standards minor) economic problems hit the Federal Republic. The result was a Grand Coalition between the CDU/CSU and the SPD, which, since agreeing to its Godesberg Program, had been trying to convince the electorate it was fit to govern at national level. The performance of its ministers in the post-1966 coalition, not least that of economics minister Karl Schiller, proved their case to enough people for there to be a change of government in 1969. This change was also made possible by the new stance of the FDP, which under Walter Scheel, who became Brandt's foreign minister, was now willing to join up with the Social Democrats and force the CDU/CSU into opposition.

While the 1960s saw major political changes in the Federal Republic, this was much less the case in the GDR, although the significance of the Berlin Wall for its population, which could no longer even consider moving to the West, should not be underestimated. Ulbricht maintained his grip on power; what is more, he did not face major challenges of the kind that he had in the 1950s. This was despite a number of developments that can be viewed as major setbacks for the East German state. The decade began with a degree of confidence. Following the first Sputnik in 1957, the Soviet Union had begun to speak of overtaking the West. This was echoed in the GDR, where the Seven Year Plan of 1958 announced similar ambitions. Eventually, the plan had to be abandoned, and the "New Economic System," which operated from 1963 and gave economic actors more autonomy, was modified in 1967. This return to relative rigidity in the economic sphere was complemented in the sphere of foreign affairs in 1968 when GDR troops took part in the Soviet-led invasion of Czechoslovakia. It was only in the following decade, to a large extent because of the challenges presented by the Brandt government's *Ostpolitik* (policy toward the East), that there was a degree of change in the GDR.

Literary Developments

The changes that took place in the cultural life of the Federal Republic in the 1960s were at least as radical as those in the world of politics. The previous decade had seen the emergence of a distinct literature emanating from the new state, but by the end of the 1960s, any sense of achievement was thrown into doubt by what was trumpeted as the "death of literature." The debate over this — in hindsight much-exaggerated — death will be discussed separately in the next chapter, as it relates very much to the political developments of the time, specifically, the student movement.

The early years of the decade were marked by a certain continuity. Günter Grass, for instance, consolidated his reputation with two further works largely set in his native Danzig — *Katz und Maus* (Cat and Mouse, 1961) and *Hundejahre* (Dog Years, 1963) — that, together with *Die Blechtrommel*, became known as the Danzig Trilogy. New, substantial prose works by Uwe Johnson, Heinrich Böll, and not least Martin Walser, who also turned to writing plays in an effort to revitalize German theater after Brecht, confirmed their places in the new literature. The Gruppe 47 came increasingly to be regarded as almost synonymous with the literature of the Federal Republic, especially by its detractors, one of whom, the CDU politician Josef-Hermann Dufhues, infamously compared it with the Reichsschrifttumskammer. By the end of the decade, however, the group was in essence no more. Following the annual 1967 gathering, which was interrupted by student demonstrators, Richter ceased to convene any more regular meetings.

It was not just outside influences, but also internal political differences that helped to bring about the end of the Gruppe 47. The 1960s did see a politicization of literature, not least in the area of theater, where documentary drama occupied an increasingly significant position. Plays were created on the basis of documents or other authentic material to make political statements. One striking example is Peter Weiss's play *Die Ermittlung* (The Investigation, 1965), which deals with the trial of Auschwitz guards that took place in Frankfurt between 1963 and 1965. Here the aim is not only to evoke the horrors of the camp on the basis of official records, but also to proclaim a link between the camp and the workings of capitalism. Whereas Weiss seeks to retain a clear aesthetic dimension in his work — for example, in his use of free verse — others saw the potential political effect of a piece of writing as the sole criterion to be considered, hence the increasing use of the phrase "death of literature" toward the end of the decade.

In the GDR, the 1960s saw the emergence of many of the writers most associated with the literature of that country. This is not the place to discuss in detail whether there ever was a separate GDR literature or whether it always remained possible to speak of a single German literature; what can be said is that, beginning in the 1960s, a significant number of writers began to tackle themes relating to developments in the GDR. How far this was due to Bitterfeld, or just to a change of generations of the kind that occurred in the Federal Republic in the late 1950s, can only be surmised. A number of newcomers did concern themselves with industrial themes, not least Christa Wolf in her first major work *Der geteilte Himmel* (The Divided Sky, 1963), where the heroine's experiences as a student working in a railway rolling stock works form a major part of the novel, or in Erik Neutsch's *Spur der Steine* (Trail of Stones, 1964), set on the site of a major building project. Wolf (born 1929) and Neutsch (1931) can be seen as belonging to the same generation as Grass, Walser, and Enzensberger in the Federal Republic, as can also

Hermann Kant (born 1926), whose novel *Die Aula* (The Great Hall, 1965) portrays the state's efforts to extend higher education to the working class. What unites these authors also is their identification, albeit to differing degrees, with socialism and the GDR. This did not mean, however, that they and other colleagues did not have to face difficult political questions during the decade, as will be seen below.

Writers and Politics

Identification with the Federal Republic

GDR literature, as noted above, was marked in the 1960s by greater identification of writers with that state, and a similar process was occurring in the Federal Republic in the early years of the decade. One reason for this was undoubtedly the realization that hopes for a rapid return to a single German state were evaporating, as was confirmed by the building of the Berlin Wall. This led to a willingness to engage more closely with the Federal Republic and to consider new forms of political activity, not least because the kinds of protest that had marked the 1950s had apparently been so unsuccessful. Moreover, there were greater opportunities for writers to engage with left-wing politics thanks to the SPD's Godesberg Program. On the one hand, this program disappointed some on the Left because it accepted much that leftists disliked about the Federal Republic, including its membership of the Western military alliance; on the other, it opened the party up beyond its traditional working-class base. Finally, there was the realization that an era was coming to an end. The inevitable changes referred to in the first part of this chapter offered writers the opportunity to comment on political issues.

A volume that appeared at the beginning of the decade and that rapidly achieved high sales caught the new mood with its title *Ich lebe in der Bundesrepublik* (I Live in the Federal Republic). In his brief introduction, the editor Wolfgang Weyrauch begins with a declaration that, given the volume's title, amounts to a statement of identification with the Federal Republic, even if he does not use political terminology: "Ich liebe meine Heimat. Weil ich sie liebe, sorge ich um sie" (I love my homeland. Because I love it, I worry about it.)[1] He concludes by expressing his hope that the Federal Republic might become "ein Modell des Maßes, der Vernunft und einer friedlichen Ordnung" (a model of moderation, reason, and a peaceful order; 9). As for the need for intellectuals to play a part in such a development, this was the subject of Martin Walser's contribution: "Skizze zu einem Vorwurf" (Sketch for a Reproach). He castigates his fellow writers for enjoying a reasonably comfortable existence characterized by self-satisfaction based on their literary abilities. In this situation, any invitation by state or society to cooperate would cause only embarrassment, even if the democracy of the Federal Republic deserves more support than any other kind of state.[2]

Walser's call was in fact taken up, albeit somewhat reluctantly and arguably only by implication, by Hans Magnus Enzensberger in his piece "Schimpfend unter Palmen" (Cursing under Palm Trees). This took the form of a letter to the book's editor — with the place of writing given as Lanuvio near Rome — consisting of a contrast between the pleasures of life in Italy and the horrors of affluent Germany. For instance, in the city of Düsseldorf, the coffee houses with their outmoded décor and their whipped cream are said to teach "Fürchten vor der Ewigkeit der Hölle" (fear of the eternity of hell).[3] More seriously, Enzensberger goes on to criticize the policy of rearmament in the Federal Republic, before totally damning the way people live in Germany. The two German states are equated in the remarkable aphorism: "In den beiden streitigen Haufen Deutschland leben teilweise Leute teilweise" (On the two disputing piles known as Germany, partial people lead partial lives; 30). There follows as the final comment the bald statement that the author does not live in the Federal Republic (31). However, the main body of the text is followed by a postscript which takes back the last sentence quoted above, albeit with the proviso of only partially (31). Equally, the stance adopted in the main letter is seen as only being possible for a limited period. In essence, Enzensberger is admitting to having returned, however reluctantly, to the German fold.

In his contribution "Wahn" (Delusion), Wolfgang Koeppen also shows scant enthusiasm for the Federal Republic. Although he acknowledges that he lives comfortably and that great economic progress has been made, he shows his concern about how the past has been forgotten and about what the future might hold: "Man leugnet was war, man ahnt nicht, was sein wird." (What was is denied; there is no sense of what will be.)[4] At the same time, there is a degree of identification not just with the Federal Republic as a state, but also with Germany, with Koeppen stressing he would not want to be anything else but a German writer (36). There are similar split feelings in the Austrian Kasimir Edschmid's essay "Aus meinem Notizbuch" (From My Notebook), although here the positive predominates. He says of the Federal Republic that it is a decent embodiment of the idea of Germany. Nevertheless he finishes with a critical comment on some, if not all, Germans: "Der deutsche Weltmann . . . der alte Typ war nicht gerade angenehm. Vor dem neuen graut es mich." (The German man of the world . . . the old type was not exactly pleasant. I have a horror of the new one.)[5]

One essay stood out in Weyrauch's collection, that of Johannes Gaitanides, which amounts to a criticism of the attitudes of German intellectuals during the 1950s. Entitled "Von der Ohnmacht unserer Literatur" (On the Impotence of Our Literature), it castigates writers for their blanket condemnation of all aspects of the Federal Republic, their total lack of self-criticism, and their ignoring of such achievements as increased social security, the integration of so many refugees into society, and the reconciliation with the Western powers. These criticisms are made from a conservative standpoint, as is indicated by both the somewhat archaic style and the content of this comment about history. According to Gaitanides, history consists of a fabric, woven simultaneously by unchanging laws and laws of change.[6] Given the change of direction among writers that *Ich lebe in der Bundesrepublik* reveals, these criticisms are less valid than they might have been earlier. Writing in 1979, the academic Helmut Koopmann even claimed that the volume represented the zenith of writers' identification with the Federal Republic.[7] While exaggerated, this claim did underline the differences between the 1960s and the previous decade.

Events and Protest

As was seen in the previous chapter, there were many protests by writers and intellectuals in the 1950s. This continued into the 1960s but with the difference that some of these protests met with a greater degree of success. Clearly, it would be a crude and inappropriate yardstick if the political activity of writers were to be judged by some criterion of success, however this might be measured. Nevertheless, the fact that, at times, writers' protests no longer reflected an almost complete isolation from other social forces is another change worth noting.

One example of a successful protest against the policies of the Adenauer government was that directed against the plan for a centralized second television channel. Since 1945, the broadcasting media, along with education, had been organized on a regional level as a reaction against their misuse during the Nazi period under the direction of Goebbels's Ministry of Propaganda. When the first television channel opened in the Federal Republic, it was based on a cooperative model between the various regional broadcasters. It was this pattern that Adenauer intended to break in 1960. Twenty-one authors, mainly associated with the Gruppe 47 and including Heinrich Böll, Günter Grass, and Hans Werner Richter, expressed their opposition to what they saw as a plan to make the new television station a tool of the Federal Government.[8] As it turned out, the Federal Constitutional Court deemed the proposed station unconstitutional because it violated the individual states' supremacy in the area of broadcasting.

Another issue, on which writers found themselves on the side that eventually prevailed, was the Spiegel Affair of 1962, referred to at the beginning of this chapter. By coincidence, when the affair broke, the Gruppe 47 was meeting in Berlin. Not only did it issue a resolution condemning Strauß and demanding his resignation, it also maintained that in an era when wars were no longer to be contemplated, it was a duty for journalists to betray "so-called" military secrets.[9] This stance meant that some writers, notably Günter

Grass, did not sign the resolution, but many other prominent names, including Hans Magnus Enzensberger, Uwe Johnson, and Martin Walser, did.

In addition to reacting to certain events, writers in the 1960s turned their attention to what might be called the *Lebenslügen* (life-lies) of the Federal Republic, particularly in the area of reunification policy. As mentioned above, the Adenauer government had always maintained that the way to achieve German reunification was to strengthen the Federal Republic's Western alliances and thus force the East into concessions. This policy of strength, however, was seen by opponents — who in any case doubted whether the Catholic Rhinelander Adenauer was at all interested in the traditionally Protestant East — as having the opposite effect. For them, the building of the Berlin Wall was final confirmation that Adenauer's policy had been misguided.

As has been seen in the two previous chapters, in the postwar years writers and intellectuals were never short of ideas about how the division of Germany might be overcome. Increasingly the idea was accepted that some kind of negotiations between the two German states would be necessary, an idea that was anathema to Adenauer. Stefan Andres, for example, in his speech on the occasion of the Easter 1960 antinuclear march, spoke of meeting the other side with justice and with trust, although he acknowledged a degree of risk (*VLMS*, 157). In July 1961, shortly before the building of the Berlin Wall, Rudolf Augstein expressed his fears that Berlin might be lost if no compromises were agreed with the East (*VLMS*, 183). When the city was to all intents and purposes divided a month later, writers and intellectuals quickly took sides.

Although Adenauer's policy had failed, his intellectual followers lost no time in attacking those who had advocated a different approach. The Berlin writer Wolf Jobst Siedler, for instance, maintained that those who favored dialogue with the East were suffering from foolish delusions. Clichés such as "talking is better than shooting," as proclaimed on both sides, were based, according to Siedler, on "der einigermaßen rührenden Überzeugung, daß irgendwelche Beziehungen zwischen der eigenen Gesprächigkeit und der Erhaltung des Weltfriedens bestehen" (the somewhat touching assumption that there is some kind of relationship between one's own loquaciousness and world peace).[10] Moreover, according to Siedler, insofar as Western writers favored dialogue with their colleagues in the East, they were ignoring the point that the latter were loyal servants of the régime. Rudolf Krämer-Badoni did not mince his words either when he accused many of his colleagues of being *Dummköpfe* (fools) and *Feiglinge* (cowards), accusing them of only being willing to criticize the Federal Republic but not the other German state over the building of the Wall.[11] Heinrich Böll made an adequate response on both points. He pointed out that, following the building of the Wall, dialogue had become inevitable, but would now take place on less favorable terms than before. The start of such dialogue at the end of the decade under Chancellor Brandt would appear to prove the point. As for Krämer-Badoni's attack, Böll noted that it was odd that those who now asked writers to speak out had previously desired their silence on matters of the day (*M*, 132–34).

In fact, writers did anything but keep silent. Two writers associated with the Gruppe 47, Wolfdietrich Schnurre and Günter Grass, both resident in West Berlin, reacted particularly forcefully. In an open letter to the president of the GDR Writers Union, Anna Seghers, Grass compared the GDR to a concentration camp and Ulbricht to a camp commandant (*M*, 62–64). In another open letter to the East German Writers Union, Grass and Schnurre called on their Eastern counterparts either to express condemnation of the Wall or condone its construction (*M*, 65–66). Schnurre, especially, did not leave it at that. In a speech in September 1961, he recalled some of the brutal incidents following the building of the Wall, spoke of writers as the "Gewissen der Nation" (conscience of the nation) — incidentally, a rare example of a writer accepting this epithet — and called on East German authors to follow their consciences.[12] A month later he resigned from the PEN club because of what he deemed to be the lethargy of the West German section and the inhumanity of the East German one. However, it was also possible to react less emotionally. Twenty-three writers, mainly associated with the Gruppe 47 and, it must be said, including Grass and Schnurre, deferentially called on the United Nations to turn their attention to the situation in Germany and even to consider moving its headquarters to Berlin (*M*, 123–26).

In view of the strident tones of the debate, it was no surprise that Hans Magnus Enzensberger, speaking of statements on both sides that were "erpresserisch, dumm und rüde" (blackmailing, stupid, and crude), impatiently pointed out that similar tones were being adopted by the West German Right and the hardline East Germans.[13] Enzensberger's increasing exasperation with the German question surfaced most clearly in 1967 with the publication of a collection of essays under the ironic title *Deutschland, Deutschland unter anderm* (Germany, Germany Among Other Things). The first essay, which had originally appeared in English in *Encounter* with the title "Am I a German?" takes exception to stereotyping by nationality and describes nations as an "illusion," albeit one that continues to be influential.[14] The essay "Versuch, von der deutschen Frage Abschied zu nehmen" (Attempt to Take Leave of the German Question), is a particularly vitriolic attack on the Federal Republic's official policies and its self-importance. In its final section, Enzensberger scornfully dismisses German self-aggrandizement:

> "Wir sind wieder wer in der Welt," soll in Bonn jemand behauptet haben. Irgendein Bundeskanzler wird es gewesen sein. Wir sind wieder

wer, wir gelten wieder was, ungefähr wie auf dem Jahrmarkt das Kalb mit zwei Köpfen.[15]

[We are something again in the world," somebody in Bonn is supposed to have claimed. It will have been some Federal Chancellor or other. We are somebody again, we count again, about as much as the two-headed calf on the fairground.]

Despite the brilliance of this withering irony, it has to be pointed out that Enzensberger was only partially right. Germany did not count enough for either superpower to risk nuclear war; on the other hand, it remained at the center of world politics until the end of the Cold War in 1989/1990.

In 1962 Hans Werner Richter edited a volume with the title *Bestands-aufnahme* (Taking Stock). In this collection of essays, writers, academics and journalists addressed themselves to a variety of familiar topics, including the consequences of war and the role of religion in society. Although the volume did not reflect a single viewpoint, it did draw attention to the variety of concerns prevalent in the Adenauer era. There were doubts, for instance, about the inequalities produced by the economic miracle and the rigidity of Adenauer's foreign policy. All in all, the book showed the growing feeling of the 1960s that the Federal Republic was in need of modernization if it were to face up to the problems of the future. This modernization, it was felt, was hindered by a large number of almost taboo subjects, ranging from the unquestioning championing of the market economy to anticommunism. At the end of his essay "Vorurteile und Tabus" (Prejudices and Taboos), Paul Schallück lists a number of these. He suggests, for instance, that the use of the word "so-called" or of inverted commas in connection with the name German Democratic Republic shows that the other German state is a taboo, while the CDU slogan "no experiments" renders all discussion of the internal order of the Federal Republic equally taboo.[16] What was becoming increasingly clear was that writers were increasingly willing to challenge what they saw as an atrophied society and seek change.

Electoral Involvement

By the beginning of the 1960s, Martin Walser was not only willing, as seen above, to criticize fellow intellectuals' refusal to engage with society. He also took the lead in instigating their involvement in the key event within democratic politics — namely the electoral process. In the period before the 1961 federal election, he edited a volume *Die Alternative oder Brauchen wir eine neue Regierung?* (The Alternative, or Do We Need a New Government?), in which twenty writers endorsed the Social Democratic Party. Although the SPD's new chancellor candidate, Willy Brandt, invited the contributors to a meeting in Bonn, the initiative came largely from writers themselves and Walser in particular. The "homelessness" or *ohne mich* attitude of the 1950s had been replaced by a degree of identification with a political party, great enough at least to advocate a vote for the Social Democrats in preference to the Christian Democrats of Chancellor Adenauer.

This is not to say that the book consisted of an enconium for the SPD of the kind that is normally found in political parties' own election literature. In fact, the general impression conveyed is one of considerable skepticism toward the post-Godesberg SPD as it sought to move toward the middle ground of West German politics. How much such skepticism was justified from a left-wing standpoint can be seen from the party's willingness after the election to enter into a coalition with the Christian Democrats when the strengthened Free Democrats began to impose conditions for a new coalition. The doubts about the SPD are even visible in the editor's contribution, with Walser speaking of the party having made sacrifices to the most vulgar anticommunism.[17] Comparable doubts are to be found in many more of the contributions. The poet Peter Rühmkorf says he is loaning his vote to the SPD only with the greatest misgivings,[18] while the novelist and librettist Heinz von Cramer reproaches the party, even in opposition, for having taken the path of least resistance and conformity in the search for popularity at any price.[19] In the case of Hans Magnus Enzensberger, the reader of his typically robust comments is left wondering how the writer of the following could recommend the SPD at all:

> Es gibt bei uns zulande eine Partei, die heißt sozial und demokratisch und ist in der Opposition. Sie biedert sich bei ihren Feinden an, sie ist zahm, sie apportiert und macht Männchen. Ein Anblick, der nicht eben erhaben, ein Anblick, der salzlos, langweilig, medioker ist.[20]
>
> [There is in our country a party that is called democratic and social and is in opposition. It ingratiates itself with its enemies, it is tame, it retrieves and begs like a dog. A sight that admittedly is not what might be called elevating, a sight that is unsavory, boring, mediocre.]

The only reason that Enzensberger can advance for voting SPD is that it is the lesser of two evils. This is, in fact, a common refrain throughout the book. Equally unreflective of great enthusiasm for the alternative government is the argument put forward by both the novelist Siegfried Lenz and the journalist Erich Kuby — namely, the slogan "it is time for a change." Kuby even goes so far as to say that he would probably be saying the same thing if the SPD had been in office for twelve years.[21] In general, it is relatively hard to find much positive endorsement of the SPD in *Die Alternative*. Gerhard Schoenberner praises its plans for a more democratic society and a more flexible foreign policy,[22] while Siegfried Lenz does manage to congratulate some of its leading figures for not separating politics from the idea of justice.[23] Indeed, it is in terms of personalities that much of the support is given, the sympathy toward the figure of Brandt being particularly noticeable. Hans Werner Richter, for instance, states baldly that, just as he prefers Kennedy to Eisenhower, "so ist mir der junge demokratische Willy Brandt als Kanzler der Bundesrepublik sympathischer als der autokratische Urgroßvater Konrad Adenauer" (similarly I find the young, democratic Willy Brandt preferable as chancellor of the Federal Republic to the autocratic great-grandfather Konrad Adenauer.)[24] Apart from the two adjectives democratic and autocratic, the argument here is based solely on the dubious premise of age.

Rather than committed support for the Social Democrats, it is the condemnation of the Christian Democrat government of Adenauer and the kind of society it has engendered that is the most marked feature of Walser's volume. Here again, personalities loom large — not just Adenauer himself, but the then-up-and-coming Franz Josef Strauß. In 1961, a good year before his fall over the Spiegel Affair, many of the contributors to *Die Alternative* saw the minister of defense with his strongly pro-nuclear policy as the natural successor to Adenauer. Such a contingency made them fear not just for the survival of democracy in the Federal Republic, but also for peace itself, undoubtedly an overstatement given the limited sovereignty of the Federal Republic at this time. The literary critic Franz Schonauer sees Strauß as greedy for power,[25] while Walser, after referring to his scenarios for nuclear war, calls him the "Alptraum von Bayern, der uns gegen alles verteidigen kann, nur nicht gegen sich selbst" (nightmare from Bavaria, who can defend us against anything, except himself).[26] Beyond the question of personalities, the criticisms directed against the CDU are to some extent the familiar ones from the 1950s — for example, the failure to engage with the Nazi past and the blind anticommunism encouraged by the government. The most repeated complaint is probably that the CDU has created a society concerned only with material well-being and whose atrophied authoritarianism represents a threat to democracy. Particularly singled out for criticism also is the phenomenon of "clericalism."

This term refers to the power of the church, — the Catholic Church specifically — to impose its conservative tenets on society through its links with the Christian Democrats. The radical Catholic writer Carl Amery, in his essay "Eine kleine Utopie" (A Small Utopia), calls for the separation of church and state, which is still, unlike France, not entirely the case in the Federal Republic,[27] while Heinz von Cramer attacks the Catholic Church for supporting dictatorships and the CDU government for letting itself be used in the interests of the church.[28] The writer on religious affairs, Gerhard Szczesny, attacks the hypocrisy bred by the way advancement in society depends on paying lip service to Christianity. His essay is a plea for the establishment of a Humanist Union to preserve the rights of all citizens regardless of their religious convictions — something that duly took place before the end of 1961.

One of the criticisms referred to above is also found more than once in Walser's volume: namely, the need for the Federal Republic to modernize and overcome taboos. Whereas Axel Eggebrecht once more specifically highlights the refusal to have anything to do with communist countries,[29] Gerhard Szczesny comes up with a whole range of areas where he considers radical change to be necessary. These include, besides limiting the power and influence of the church, greater emphasis on human rights, more freedom for the press and the arts, and enhanced educational opportunities for all.[30] Specifically, Inge Aicher-Scholl, sister of the Munich students Hans and Sophie Scholl martyred by the Nazis, expresses her fear — one that became increasingly current in the 1960s when the term *Bildungskatastrophe* (educational disaster) entered the language — that the Federal Republic was falling behind because the education system was being neglected in favor of private affluence and consumption.[31]

Despite the many arguably justified criticisms of West German society in *Die Alternative*, it is hard to believe it played a great part in the increase of the popular vote gained by the SPD, which in any case was not sufficient to dent the hegemonic position of the CDU. Its at times lukewarm support for the party would no doubt have today's spin doctors running for their smelling salts. Some contributors even wrote that they did not believe the SPD could win, hoping only that that the party would gain the third of the votes necessary to block constitutional changes that might threaten the democratic substance of the state. At least this hope was fulfilled. Nevertheless, for all its amateurishness, *Die Alternative* is a likeable collection. The contributions are marked by an honesty and openness that one should expect from critical writers. Historically, it remains interesting as the first example of systematic support to be given to a party by a significant number of writers and intellectuals.

By the time of the next federal election in 1965, the parameters had changed, at least at an individual level. In the world of literature, the leading light of 1961, Martin Walser, was no longer willing to commit himself to the SPD, which in his view had moved too far to the right. As for politics, both the major targets of earlier intellectual protest, Adenauer and Strauß, were no longer playing a front-line role. Nevertheless, the new chancellor, Ludwig Erhard, quickly proved himself unpopular with intellectuals when he described the Federal Republic as a "formierte Gesellschaft," a term that implied both that dynamic change was not the order of the day and that there were no longer significant class differences within society either. On the other side, Hans Werner Richter took up the cudgels and edited a pre-election volume, the title of which referred back to 1961 but propounded the need for change in a much more emphatic way.

Plädoyer für eine neue Regierung oder Keine Alternative (Plea for a New Government, or No Alternative, 1965) also sought to be more professional in that it was closer to conventional election literature. The first section comprises a series of portraits of leading Social Democrats, thus reflecting a new emphasis on personalities. Besides replicating in part the methods of professional image builders, this part of the book reflects an even more nonideological stance — apart from a general espousal of change and progress — than was already prevalent at this time. In his introduction, Richter sums up this conception of politics, arguing that because change is now so rapid, ideas and policies quickly become outdated. The only solution is to elect new people who are open to new initiatives.[32] Other contributions not specifically about individual politicians reflect this outlook. In his model of a possible politician, Jürgen Becker (still an up-and-coming writer at the time) approves of a nonparty type characterized by cool pragmatism.[33] Peter Härtling in his portrait of the critical intellectuals of the Federal Republic sees the use of such labels as "conservative" or "socialist" as increasingly irrelevant, preferring to see intellectuals' criticisms in the traditions of *Der Ruf* primarily in terms of generational conflict, in which the young generation is united in its rejection of past taboos. He adds, with reference to these younger people, that the election of President Kennedy provided a point of identification.[34] (Such a statement now appears particularly ironic in the light of the criticisms of the United States that came to the fore later in the decade.) However one reacts to the concentration on personality in this part of *Plädoyer für eine neue Regierung,* it must be pointed out that one portrait at least is largely negative. That is the one by Rudolf Augstein, the editor of *Der Spiegel,* of Herbert Wehner. Wehner was the SPD politician usually associated with the party's change of direction as encapsulated in the Godesberg Program, and was later instrumental in forcing the resignation of Chancellor Brandt in 1974. Adopting a standpoint one might readily associate with idealistic intellectuals, Augstein portrays him as an unprincipled tactician willing to pay almost any price to bring his party into government.[35]

After its series of portraits, Richter's collection has a section providing a view from abroad given by German writers living in various countries. The substance of Reinhard Lettau's argument, entitled in English "It's time for a change," is that the SPD enjoys greater confidence in the United States than the CDU.[36] While this may have been true of the intellectual circles in which Lettau no doubt mixed, one wonders nevertheless how widespread such a feeling was. The poet Erich Fried provides a similar message from Great Britain, even using as evidence an English acquaintance who at home supports the Conservative Party.[37] That such "home thoughts from abroad" are included and were no doubt considered helpful to the Social Democrat cause is a reflection of West German political culture at the time. Respect for opinions held in other countries reflected the wish to be seen in a positive light following the horrors of the past. Thus, when neo-Nazism appeared to be gaining ground in the late 1960s with the electoral success of the National Democratic Party, one constantly advanced argument was that the party had to be resisted because of the bad image it gave the Federal Republic abroad. One might have thought that the party's policies offered sufficient grounds for opposition.

In contrast to the reports from the countries allied to the Federal Republic, the other two contributions from outside were less sympathetic to the SPD. Robert Havemann, the East German dissident who never lost his belief in Marxism, reflects on the division of Germany in a way, as Richter concedes in his introduction, that might well harm the SPD.[38] Peter Weiss, whose major play *Marat Sade* (to give it its short title) had been first performed in 1964, writes from Sweden to make a more general criticism of the affluent society of the Federal Republic, adding that the country's general atmosphere has always made it impossible for him to return to the land he left in face of Nazi racial persecution. His specific attitude to the Social Democrats, too, can hardly be classed as positive given his claim that there is scant difference between the arguments of the Christian and Social Democrats.[39]

The third and final section of Richter's volume was a more varied selection of essays, many of which were very much in keeping with both the concerns of the time and arguably the concerns of intellectuals in general. Hans Schwab-Felisch criticizes the cultural policy of the government abroad, which is seen as excessively restrictive. Taking up the aforementioned idea that the Federal Republic was facing an educational disaster, the publisher Klaus Wagenbach demands expansion and reform, while the scientist Robert Jungk stresses in general terms the need to confront the future. These contributions underline the general message of the book — the need for a new broom in the shape of the Social Democrats to sweep Germany out of its inertia toward the challenges of the future. The general tone is therefore not surprisingly more bland than that of its predecessor in 1961. Whether, because of this, it contributed more positively to the electoral progress made by the SPD — still, however, not enough for the party to be able to form a government — must remain in the nature of things a matter for speculation.

The above comments do not mean that controversy was entirely forsaken for positive election propaganda. Two articles in *Plädoyer für eine neue Regierung* deserve special mention for their radical stance. Ulrich Sonnemann takes the German judicial tradition severely to task in his long essay "Vom Preis des Unrechts und der Rentabilität des Rechts" (The Price of Injustice and the Value of Justice). He concentrates particularly on the role of the judiciary in the Third Reich, pointing out that no judge had ever been convicted for his activities at that time because of the prevailing positivistic view that they were merely administering the law of the day. He finds it particularly ironic that the Federal Republic honors the memory of those who conspired against Nazism in the July 1944 bomb plot, while retaining the services of their judicial persecutors. Furthermore, Sonnemann connect this judicial tradition with a wider, much more dangerous German custom of excessive respect toward authority and toward what he calls "den Nimbus der Institutionen" (the halo of institutions).[40] Rather than relying on the external authority, citizens should seek to revalorize political and human spontaneity (168). On a less speculative level, Rolf Hochhuth used his portrait of the trade union leader Otto Brenner to attack the unequal distribution of wealth in the Federal Republic. This essay with the, at the time, distinctly unfashionable title *Klassenkampf* (Class Struggle), provoked the most notorious of all Christian Democrat expressions of anger toward critical writers when Ludwig Erhard dubbed Hochhuth a "Pinscher" rather than a poet, a crude insult in both its canine meaning and in the figurative sense of pipsqueak.

Hochhuth's title itself was clearly a provocation in the face of Erhard's categorization of the Federal Republic as a nonantagonistic *formierte Gesellschaft*. At the same time, when looked at more closely, Hochhuth's article reveals itself as being anything but a plea for Marxist revolution, despite its title. In fact, at most times during his long political involvement, he has been closer to the liberal Free Democrats than to any idea of socialism. What he is asking for here is a broader distribution of wealth throughout the population. In fact, he sees this as the most effective bulwark against communism, as more people would have much more to lose in any change of system. The present tendency toward concentration, on the other hand, would render a takeover by the state a much more feasible proposition. Coupled with this economic argument, Hochhuth's essay reveals the moral concern that underlies all his writing. As an example of this, the following statement could hardly be more direct and forceful:

> Dieser Staat zahlt Kriegsverbrechern und Justizmördern, die das Verstecken eines vom Gas bedrohten Judenkindes mit Guillotine bestraften, im Monat vierzehnhundert Mark, ja mehr. Acht-, neunmal soviel wie er den Eltern oder der verwitweten Mutter zweier Söhne, die gefallen sind.[41]

> [This state pays war criminals and judicial murderers, who punished the concealment of a Jewish child threatened with the gas chamber by the guillotine, 1400 Marks per month, even more. Eight or nine times as much as the parents or widowed mother of two sons killed in the war.]

Even where on other occasions his political claims and arguments appear eccentric, it is impossible to deny either Hochhuth's moral courage or the power of his polemics.

Writers' involvement in the Federal Election of 1965 went beyond the publication of a single book. In West Berlin, a number of mainly young writers and intellectuals established a Wahlkontor deutscher Schriftsteller (Election office of German writers) to help the SPD. The main aims of this office were to coin slogans and to write or improve the speeches of the party's politicians. In charge nominally was Klaus Wagenbach, and other writers involved — who incidentally were paid for their efforts — included Nicolas Born, Günter Herburger, and Peter Schneider.[42] One person associated with the group, Gudrun Ensslin, was to achieve notoriety later as a terrorist. She, like many others in the *Wahlkontor,* soon tired of the SPD's gradualist approach.

The 1965 election campaign was also remarkable in that it was the first time that Günter Grass entered the lists as a full-blooded campaigner for the SPD. Besides contributing to Richter's volume with a tribute to his political hero, Willy Brandt, he undertook a barnstorming tour of the Federal Republic. Independently — as the extremely cautious hierarchy of the SPD was at pains to point out, given his controversial reputation — but not without contact with party politicians, Grass traveled the country seeking support for the party, choosing towns and areas where the Social Democrats were weak. Expenses were defrayed by an admission charge, and surpluses were to be used to provide libraries for the Bundeswehr and for a competition for a more appropriate school reader for the subject of German.

The texts of the four standard speeches delivered by Grass during his two tours — he spoke in all on fifty-two occasions — are contained in the first collected volume of his political writing *Über das Selbstverständliche* (Concernng the Obvious, 1968, translated as *Speak Out,* 1969).[43] They are "Es steht zur Wahl" (The Issue), which seeks to follow the example of Walt Whitman in praising democracy; "Loblied auf Willy" (Song in Praise of Willy), the title of which is self-explanatory; "Was ist des Deutschen Vaterland?" (What Is the German's Fatherland?)— the title refers back to a poem written by Ernst Moritz Arndt during a period of national ferment at the beginning of the nineteenth century — which asks, at a time when the mainstream political parties were unwilling to contemplate this, the German people to accept the loss of the former eastern territories and his own birthplace, the former Free City of Danzig; and finally, "Des Kaisers neue Kleider"(The Emperor's New Clothes), which is a fierce attack on Ludwig Erhard and his government. As the last three titles have literary nuances and the first speech is based on the model of Whitman, it was plain that Grass the writer of fiction was still very much present within his political activity. Indeed, in "Es steht zur Wahl," he characterizes himself as a storyteller and admits by implication in a series of rhetorical questions, that he is not the typical political expert: "Wer spricht hier und zu wem? Ein Geschichtenerzähler. Jemand, der immerzu sagt: Es war einmal." (Who is speaking and to whom? A storyteller. A man who is always saying: Once upon a time).[44] This speech is marked by frequent anecdotal references to different types of voters (one is reminded of characters in a novel), while throughout all the four there are endless stylistic flourishes, as in the following comment on the electoral promises of political parties:

Denn in einem Wald gleichmäßig einfallloser Wahlplakate irren wir,
gleich Hänsel und Gretel rat- und weglos umher. Überall werden uns
Knusperhäuschen versprochen. Im Märchenton warden uns Zufrieden-
heit und Sicherheit verheißen.[45]

[For in a forest of equally uninspired election posters we are wandering
like Hansel and Gretel without path or guide. Everywhere gingerbread
houses are promised us. In the tones of a Children's Hour storyteller we
are promised satisfaction and security.]

Here the literary rhetoric is amusing and appropriate; doubts arise, however,
when he himself lapses, albeit ironically, into the tone of the professional ad-
vertiser by concluding his encomium on Brandt with the slogan adapted
from Esso "Pack einen Willy in den Tank" (Put a Willy in your tank).[46]

Although Grass speaks of elections not being clear-cut affairs offering
black and white choices, a considerable portion of his four campaign speeches
is devoted to blistering attacks on the Christian Democrats. These reach
their climax in "Des Kaisers neue Kleider," in which the perceived political
bankruptcy of the Erhard government is illustrated by reference to the
Andersen fairy tale. Criticizing the government's performance, Grass speaks
of only cigar smoke and vacuous language to hide a nakedness marked by a
lack of planning and rationality.[47] Whatever the validity of the criticisms,
which incidentally reflected a widespread 1960s belief in progress based on
planning, these comments again showed Grass's literary talents. Elsewhere in
the speech, he is simply vitriolic, as when he castigates the then–minister of
health Frau Schwarzkopf, who is accused in general terms of neglecting the
nation's health and is specifically condemned for the Erhard government's
outright rejection of abortion. Arguing, it might be claimed, in the manner
of later anti-abortionists, he accuses Schwarzkopf of having failed "auf mörde-
rische Weise" (in a murderous manner; 55). Insofar as Grass is speaking of a
minor, now largely forgotten minister, his tone appears exaggerated and mis-
placed, reflecting a tendency to dwell too exclusively on personalities. In
fact, one impression of the four election speeches of 1965 is that they are often stronger on polemics and rhetoric than on argument and policies.

Nevertheless, it would be wrong to dismiss Grass's intervention in the
1965 election outright. As some of the above quotations show, his contribution was anything but boring. Nor was he entirely a dilettante on policy matters. His frankness on the question of the former German territories in the
east, something the SPD prevaricated over in 1965, was to be vindicated
when the Federal Republic accepted Poland's postwar frontiers as part of the
Brandt government's *Ostpolitik*. The willingness to speak in areas where the
Social Democrats were woefully weak brought their cause notice in places
where, without the personality of Grass, it might have been ignored. Moreover, the reactions of the CDU and its supporters in such strongholds

revealed something about the hidebound attitudes of at least sections of that party. In the Lower Saxony town of Cloppenburg, where a 60 percent vote for the CDU was often the norm, the local party issued a statement following Grass's visit that thanked the residents for not letting themselves be provoked, seeming to imply that the good people there had withstood something akin to an alien invasion.[48] Most important of all was that Grass had actually participated directly in the democratic process and added a new dimension to the political commitment of West German writers. However skeptical critics or some fellow writers might have been or might have become over Grass's public appearances, this first entry into the political arena should, in the context of its time, be seen as a bold step.

Following the SPD's failure to achieve its targets in 1965, Grass turned on at least some of his fellow writers for not following his example of direct involvement in politics and, specifically, for not supporting the SPD. In his speech "Rede über das Selbstverständliche" (Speech on the Self-Evident), delivered in Darmstadt on 9 October of that year on the occasion of his being awarded the Georg Büchner Prize, he demanded of certain colleagues why they had not followed his example during the election campaign. He mentioned Heinrich Böll and Alfred Andersch by name, while the speech also contained implicit references to Enzensberger.[49] What Grass's speech showed was that intellectual opinion was increasingly divided, with many moving to the left of the Social Democrats, a development that will be considered in the following chapter.

Grass, however, has remained loyal to social democracy and his conception of the role of the writer in society, even if he has been at times unhappy with certain developments, not least the Grand Coalition of 1966 under the chancellorship of a former member of the Nazi party, Kurt Georg Kiesinger, which he described as a "miese Ehe" (miserable marriage).[50] The late 1960s and early 1970s arguably represent the period when his work has been most dominated by political concerns. The novel *Örtlich betäubt* (Local Anaesthetic, 1969) and the play *Davor* (Before, 1969) have linked subject matter relating to the student movement, while the volume of poetry *Ausgefragt* (Interrogated, 1968) contains several political poems. If the play *Die Plebejer proben den Aufstand* is not strictly contemporary in that it is set at the time of the East German workers uprising of 1953, it nevertheless takes up one of Grass's key topics: the role of the artist in society. Finally, *Aus dem Tagebuch einer Schnecke* (From the Diary of a Snail, 1972), a work that contains both fictional and nonfictional elements, encapsulates much of Grass's political thinking at this particular time.

Grass's commitment to political activity in the 1960s was based on his view of the writer as citizen. He rejected any idea of writers being inhabitants of an ivory tower or Mount Parnassus, preferring to stress their prime role as citizens of their countries. The already mentioned speech "Rede über das Selbstverständliche" refers to a lack of this kind of tradition in Germany, asking rhetorically, "Was muß in diesem Land Schlimmes geschehen, damit ein gelehrter Kopf für wenige Stunden von seinen Papieren abläßt und hier, heute und jetzt Partei ergreift?" (What disaster must befall this country before a scholar will look up from his papers for a few hours and take a position, here, now and today?)[51] It is entirely in keeping with this view that he should also refuse any idealization of the writer as the "conscience of the nation" (68) and equally reject the much-vaunted German dichotomy between intellect and power. The same point is made in one of his 1965 election speeches, where he says that writers do not pay their taxes and vote on some Mount Parnassus "zwischen Musen und Weihrauch" (between muses and incense) but in the society of the Federal Republic.[52] A year later, however, speaking at Princeton, he did make a distinction between the two worlds, but only in relation to the writer's activities. Seeing a difference between traditional literature and politics, he stated: "das Gedicht kennt keine Kompromisse, wir aber leben von Kompromissen" (the poem knows no compromises, but we live by compromise).[53]

It was this pragmatic view that led Grass to reject the student movement and take his political involvement a step further in the election campaign of 1969. He was a co-founder in that year of the Sozialdemokratische Wählerinitiative (Social democratic voters' movement), the aim of which was to provide a framework for citizens who were not necessarily party members to show their support for the SPD. One aim was to promote dialogue between the party and its voters, another to put forward rational arguments in favor of the SPD with the aim of attracting the votes of nontraditional supporters.

Rather than producing a book, the Wählerinitiative chose smaller-size publications, of which the most important was the glossy magazine *Dafür* (In Favor), which appeared twice. The role played by Grass was visible not only in the title, which recalled his recent play, but also in the organization's logo designed by him, a cock crowing the quasi-phonetic version of the initials SPD "Es-Pe-De." The layout was intended to be appealing and modern with the text reinforced by numerous photographs. Even so, the first edition contains the time-honored reluctant endorsement of the party, this time by Hans Werner Richter, who says that two years earlier he would not have voted for the party because of the Grand Coalition, but concludes that there is no practical alternative, as small left-wing parties, however likeable, can never gain sufficient support to have any influence. Nevertheless, he shows scant enthusiasm for the party, stressing that there is much to criticize.[54] In general, however, this tone is rare. The aim of *Dafür*, especially the second edition, was, according to Grass, to appeal directly to the voter. To this end, this second edition grouped around a series of issues, including transport, education, and justice, where the SPD promised major improvements. The most notable coup was an article by Heinrich Böll, "Offener

Brief an eine deutsche Katholikin" (Open Letter to a German Catholic Lady). Although Böll's letter does not contain any exhortation to vote for the Social Democrats — 1972 was the first occasion on which he committed himself — its publication in such a context must have given added prestige to the Social Democrat cause. Although it is impossible in the nature of things to quantify the success of the Wählerinitiative, either through its publications or the speeches made by its prominent members, who included the novelists Siegfried Lenz and Peter Härtling along with the Swabian regional writer Thaddäus Troll, it may well have helped to secure an election result in 1969 that made a change of government possible. The model convinced supporters of other parties to follow the example, with both the Free Democrats and the Christian Democrats making use of it in the 1970s, although by the mid-1980s the idea seemed to have largely run out of steam. How far it contributed to a higher level of political understanding is, however, another question. Writing in the magazine *Das Parlament* shortly after the election of 1972, Heidrun Abromeit and Klaus Burkhardt see a danger of such voters' action groups becoming solely an additional source of party propaganda and hence just another way of manipulating the electorate, particularly by exploiting the aura surrounding the famous.[55] They also criticize the general level of argument that did little to make the citizen more politically aware. If the voters' groups of the other parties are left aside — it is, however, worthy of note that the Free Democrats enjoyed for a time the support not only of Rolf Hochhuth but also of the novelist Walter Kempowski — these criticisms do have some substance in relation to the Sozialdemokratische Wählerinitiative, even if it never paid its supporters, as some other parties apparently did. A letter from Brandt's office, for instance, dated 1 September 1972, suggests that the Wählerinitiative adopt the slogan "Wähler für Willy Brandt" (Voters for Willy Brandt), something that was indeed taken up and can hardly be called sophisticated political argument. On the other hand, it would be extremely harsh to condemn the efforts made by a writer like Günter Grass to pursue his deeply held political feelings, something he did through the Wählerinitiative over a considerable period of time.

Grass's experiences with the Wählerinitiative during the 1969 campaign formed a major part of his *Aus dem Tagebuch einer Schnecke*. More generally, it could be seen as an expression of his political credo at this time. His staring point is a belief in reason as the core ideal of the Enlightenment. From this basis he embraces the idea of progress, albeit slow progress as indicated by the metaphor of the snail in the book's title. This sets him against both the reactionary Right and the student movement with its clamor for revolutionary change. Frequently, Grass stresses the similarity between the two extremes, often at the level of personal insult. Thus, a young woman decried as an "APO-Jungfrau" (extra-parlimentary opposition party virgin) has the look of a mini-Goebbels (*TS*, 184). At this time the Right was represented by Kiesinger, who, according to Grass, pinned his hopes on people forgetting about his past. The writer, however, is "jemand, der gegen die verstreich-ende Zeit schreibt" (someone who writes against the passage of time; *TS*, 98). As for the Left, Grass sets out his stall against both the students and orthodox communism. In a passage addressed directly to his children — indeed within the narrative they figure as the addressees of his words — he warns them against doctrines that promise utopian solutions. As these doc-trines do this "um jeden Preis" (at any price), he will remain an implacable opponent (*TS*, 100).

In the same passage, he also sees a propensity among Germans to put theory before reality. This mistrust of Germans, based on the experience of the Nazi past, resurfaces in Grass's comments at the time of unification, as will be seen later. How far it has remained justified is a key question in rela-tion to Grass's political writing. He, as with all writers most associated with the Gruppe 47, can be criticized for a lack of radical vision. Nevertheless, as with the political dimension of the Gruppe 47 in general, it is reasonable to point out that Grass and those writers whose support for the SPD has been considered in this chapter were embracing the only practical force for change in a society that needed to progress from the rigidities of the Adenauer era.

The Sixties in the GDR

The 1960s undoubtedly posed many challenges to writers in the GDR. Like Western writers in the 1950s, they were, arguably, having to respond to events rather than seeking to shape them in the way their Western counter-parts were hoping to do through, for example, their involvement in elec-tions. One such challenge was undoubtedly the building of the Berlin Wall. In addition to the event itself, there was the gauntlet, referred to above, thrown down by Grass and Schnurre. Not surprisingly, they did not, publicly at least, take one of the options offered to them — namely, to criticize the actions of their state. It is true that Stephan Hermlin admitted that he had not expressed "freudige Zustimmung" (joyful approval; *M*, 67) because of his belief in the free movement of people and ideas, but he did speak of his "un-eingeschränke ernste Zustimmung" (unlimited earnest approval; *M*, 67). Other writers rehearsed the official GDR arguments with Franz Fühmann — for instance, claiming that the true division of Berlin took place in 1948 with the introduction of the D-Mark in West Berlin and the establishment of a separate city government (*VLMS*, 187). Similar tones were adopted by the Writers Association in a communiqué that repeated the official claim that the GDR had saved peace in Germany (*VLMS*, 188).

In his book on literature and politics in the GDR, Werner Mittenzwei speaks of subdued approval, based in part on the unwillingness to be seen as giving succor to ideological opponents.[56] A short story with the telling title

"Am Ende der Jugend" (At the End of Youth) by Klaus Schlesinger, whose relationship with the GDR, became increasingly strained over the years, would appear to capture the mood. The narrator's friend uses a remaining gap in the not-yet-fully-sealed border between the two parts of Berlin to cross to the western part of the city. The narrator does not follow suit, mentioning in this order: his wife's pregnancy, the inevitable gloating of certain unpleasant acquaintances, and the propaganda triumphs this would give the Western media. His feeling, though, is not one of triumph; he moves back slowly eastwards "krebsartig" (crab-like).[57] Moreover, the priority given to the personal does not imply positive political identification with the GDR.

Schlesinger's fictional narrator has a choice, unlike the majority of GDR citizens after the construction of the Wall, including the majority of writers. Some of these hoped that the new clear situation would enable improvements in all aspects of life. At the end of Wolf's *Der geteilte Himmel*, for example, an ideal of socialism, where the truth would have top priority, is advanced. Insofar that, as noted above, a new generation of writers came to the fore and were allowed to publish books that raised important social issues, there were grounds for hope. Additionally, at the international level within the socialist bloc, there was a sense of change. In the Czech town of Liblice in 1963 there took place an international conference on the relevance of Kafka, who had been seen in the Stalin era as a representative of modernist decadence. Now the issue was how far his work was relevant to the socialist countries in their present state of development. At the same time, within the GDR the period after the building of the Wall was marked by repressive measures in some areas. In 1962 the poet Peter Huchel, who had stayed in Germany during the Nazi era and did not have a history of Marxist-Leninist commitment prior to the establishment of the GDR, was dismissed from his post as editor of the prestigious journal *Sinn und Form*, which until that point had aspired to reach a wide audience in both parts of Germany. Thereafter Huchel lived in isolation until he was allowed to leave for the Federal Republic in 1971. The early sixties also saw the departure of two renowned Marxist scholars, the literary scholar Hans Mayer and the philosopher Ernst Bloch, who saw no future for his undogmatic Marxism in the GDR.

That there were good reasons not to stay in the GDR became all too apparent at the end of 1965. During the eleventh plenary session of the Central Committee of the SED, the party's top brass inveighed against what they saw as negative developments in the world of culture. The case for the prosecution was made by Erich Honecker, who attacked not only what he saw as antisocialist tendencies in the arts but also, in what might be classed as an fit of "Victorian values," those works that offended against standards of ethics, morality, and decency.[58] He was backed up by Ulbricht, who openly threatened that the Central Committee would restore "order" if necessary.[59]

One person to raise her voice in protest during the meeting against what was going on was Christa Wolf, who for her pains found herself removed from her position as a candidate for membership of the SED Central Committee. She also had difficulties with the publication of her next novel, *Nachdenken über Christa T.* (Reflections on Christa T.), which appeared in 1968 in a limited edition of 15000 copies, received few reviews, and was only reprinted four years later — all measures that were quite frequent in the GDR and that amounted to censorship. Another casualty of the party's crackdown at this time was the singer Wolf Biermann. After he was thrown out of the SED in 1963, he was only allowed to perform in public to a limited extent in 1964, and the publication of his songs in the West in 1965, after protracted negotiations with Eastern publishers, led him to be singled out for criticism by Honecker. Thereafter, until he was forced to leave the GDR in 1976, he was no longer allowed to sing officially in public at all. The main literary casualty of the 1965 clampdown was undoubtedly Werner Bräunig's novel *Rummelplatz* (Fairground), which was only published in 2007, along with background documentation about how it fell foul of the censors, when the manuscript was rediscovered.[60] Most of the work is set around the Wismut uranium mine, the production from which helped the Soviet Union to become a nuclear power. It and the surrounding area are presented as a kind of wild frontier rather than a socialist model, although there are positive socialist characters. This was clearly too much for the authorities to stomach. In the area of film, too, the 1965 meeting had major negative consequences. Films that had already been made disappeared from circulation until 1989/90 — for example, the film version of Manfred Bieler's novel *Maria Morzeck oder Das Kaninchen bin ich* (M. M. or I Am the Rabbit), in which the eponymous heroine has an affair with the married prosecutor who has helped put her brother in prison.

Another event that soured the atmosphere with some writers at least was the participation, however minimal, of GDR troops in the Soviet-led invasion of Czechoslovakia in 1968. The poet Reiner Kunze left the SED in protest and came under increasing surveillance by the Stasi secret police until he left the GDR in 1977. His literary response to the 1968 invasion had appeared in the book *Die wunderbaren Jahre* (The Wonderful Years), published in the Federal Republic in 1976.[61] Other younger intellectuals protested, too, including Thomas Brasch, the son of the deputy minister of culture, who produced leaflets condemning the invasion. His 1977 volume, which appeared when he too had moved to the West, has the telling title *Vor den Vätern sterben die Söhne* (The Sons Die from the Fathers).[62] It encapsulates the situation of GDR society as a whole until the collapse of 1989: a gerontocracy, in which those expressing unorthodox ideas were frequently subjected to harassment and exclusion.

Conclusion

In a book largely critical of intellectuals, *Der Wahnsinn des Jahrhunderts* (The Madness of the Century), Hans Dieter Zimmermann singles out at least one major exception — Hans Werner Richter, to whom he dedicates the volume — and the writers associated with the Gruppe 47. Zimmermann claims that intellectuals made a significant contribution to the change of government in 1969, which in turn was a vital step in the democratic development of the Federal Republic.[63] This is certainly an argument that deserves to be taken seriously.

What this chapter has sought to show is how intellectuals attempted to facilitate this process of change that, it is fair to say, helped make the Federal Republic a more normal European democracy. In the area of intellectual life, postwar skepticism had given way to a more specific West German intellectual identity, marked by a greater identification with the state and a desire to show commitment to democratic values. At the same time, the western part of Germany still faced turbulent times, as the next chapter will show, with writers and intellectuals again in the vanguard of the movement for change, but for changes that this time were far more radical than a change of government within the existing political framework. As for the GDR in the 1960s, it was still largely a case of the state imposing its will on, in its view, potentially destabilizing intellectuals. Hopes for change were crushed in the middle of the decade and had to wait for the end of the Ulbricht era to surface again.

Notes

[1] Wolfgang Weyrauch, "Bemerkungen des Herausgebers," in *Ich lebe in der Bundesrepublik,* ed. Wolfgang Weyrauch (Munich: List, [1961]), 7–9, here 7. Further citations given in parentheses.

[2] Martin Walser, "Skizze zu einem Vorwurf," in *Bundesrepublik,* ed. Weyrauch, 110–14, esp. 114.

[3] Hans Magnus Enzensberger, "Schimpfend unter Palmen," in *Bundesrepublik,* ed. Weyrauch, 24–31, here 25. Further citations given in parentheses.

[4] Wolfgang Koeppen, "Wahn," in *Bundesrepublik,* ed. Weyrauch, 32–36, here 34. Further citations given in parentheses.

[5] Kasimir Edschmid, "Aus meinem Notizbuch," in *Bundesrepublik,* ed. Weyrauch, 50–59, here 59.

[6] Johannes Gaitanides, "Von der Ohnmacht unserer Literatur," in *Bundesrepublik,* ed. Weyrauch, 10–23, here 22.

[7] Koopmann, Helmut, "Die Bundesrepublik Deutschland in der Literatur," *Zeitschrift für Politik* 26:2 (1979): 161–78.

[8] The statement against the proposed channel is reproduced in *Die Gruppe 47: Bericht, Kritik, Polemik. Ein Handbuch,* ed. Reinhard Lettau (Berlin: Luchterhand, 1967), 454–55.

[9] See Lettau, ed., *Die Gruppe 47,* 458–59.

[10] Wolf Jobst Siedler, "Die Linke stirbt, doch sie ergibt sich nicht," in *Die Mauer, oder Der 13. August,* ed. Hans Werner Richter (Reinbek: Rowohlt, 1961),111–15, here 111.

[11] See *Die Mauer,* ed. Richter, 132. Where, as in this case, references are to short untitled pieces, no more detailed references will be given.

[12] Wolfdietrich Schnurre, "Von der Verantwortlichkeit des Schriftstellers," in *Die Mauer,* ed. Richter, 116–19.

[13] Enzensberger, Hans Magnus, "Bürgerkrieg im Briefkasten," in *Die Mauer,* ed. Richter, 175–77, here 175.

[14] Hans Magnus Enzensberger, "Über die Schwierigkeit, Inländer zu sein," in *Deutschland, Deutschland, unter anderem* (Frankfurt am Main: Suhrkamp, 1967), 7–13, here 9. The original essay appeared in *Encounter,* vol.XXII: 4 (1964): 16–19.

[15] Hans Magnus Enzensberger, "Versuch von der deutschen Frage Abschied zu nehmen," in *Deutschland,* Enzensberger, 37–48, here 47.

[16] Paul Schallück, "Vorurteile und Tabus," in *Bestandsaufnahme,* ed. Hans Werner Richter (Munich, Vienna, Basel: Kurt Desch), 1962, 432–43.

[17] Martin Walser, "Das Fremdwort der Saison," in *Die Alternative oder Brauchen wir eine neue Regierung?,* ed. Martin Walser (Reinbek: Rowohlt), 124–30, esp. 129.

[18] Peter Rühmkorf, "Passionseinheit," in *Die Alternative,* ed. Walser, 44–50, here 45.

[19] Heinz von Kramer, "Es ist so spat, wie es schon einmal war," in *Die Alternative,* ed. Walser, 85–96, here 87.

[20] Hans Magnus Enzensberger, "Ich wünsche nicht gefährlich zu leben," in *Die Alternative,* ed. Walser, 61–66, here 66.

[21] Erich Kuby, "Und ob wir eine neue Regierung brauchen," in *Die Alternative,* ed. Walser, 146–54.

[22] Gerhard Schoenberner, "Zerstörung der Demokratie," in *Die Alternative,* ed. Walser, 137–45.

[23] Siegfried Lenz, "Die Politik der Entmutigung," in *Die Alternative,* ed. Walser, 131–36.

[24] Hans Werner Richter, "Von links in der Mitte," in *Die Alternative,* ed. Walser, 115–24, here 123.

[25] Franz Schonauer, "Das schmutzige Nest," in *Die Alternative,* ed. Walser, 73–75, here 74.

[26] Martin Walser, "Das Fremdwort," in *Die Alternative,* ed. Walser, 126.

[27] Carl Amery, "Eine kleine Utopie," in *Die Alternative,* ed. Walser, 7–13.

[28] Heinz von Cramer, "Es ist so spät," in *Die Alternative,* ed. Walser, 87.

[29] Axel Eggebrecht, "Soll die Ära der Heuchelei andauern?" in *Die Alternative,* ed. Walser, 25–35, esp. 30.

[30] Gerhard Szczesny, "Humanistische Union," in *Die Alternative*, ed. Walser, 36–43, here 38.

[31] Inge Aicher-Scholl, "Wohlstand ohne Konzept?," in *Die Alternative*, ed. Walser, 104–14.

[32] Hans Werner Richter, "Die Alternative im Wechsel der Personen," in *Plädoyer für eine neue Regierung oder Keine Alternative*, ed. Hans Werner Richter (Reinbek: Rowohlt, 1965), 9–16, esp. 10.

[33] Jürgen Becker, "Modell eines möglichen Politikers," in *Plädoyer*, ed. Richter, 121–25.

[34] Peter Härtling, "Eine natürliche Opposition," in *Plädoyer*, ed. Richter, 177–81, here 181.

[35] Rudolf Augstein, "Der geschundene Siegfried," in *Plädoyer*, ed. Richter, 63–65.

[36] Reinhard Lettau, "It's time for a change," in *Plädoyer*, ed. Richter, 129–31.

[37] Erich Fried, "Englische Randglossen," in *Plädoyer*, ed. Richter, 140–46.

[38] Robert Havemann, "Nach zwanzig Jahren," in *Plädoyer*, ed. Richter, 132–39.

[39] Peter Weiss, "Unter dem Hirseberg," in *Plädoyer*, ed. Richter, 147–49, here 148.

[40] Ulrich Sonnemann, "Vom Preis des Unrechts und der Rentabilität des Rechts," in *Plädoyer*, ed. Richter, 153–69, here 166. Further citations given in parentheses.

[41] Rolf Hochhuth, "Klassenkampf," in *Plädoyer*, ed. Richter, 65–87, here 83.

[42] See *VLMS*, 229.

[43] Günter Grass, *Über das Selbstverständliche* (Munich: DTV), 1969. (Many of the texts are contained in Grass, Günter *Speak Out!* [London: Secker and Warburg, 1969]).

[44] Grass, "Es steht zur Wahl," in *Selbstverständliche*, Grass, 10–20, here 15.

[45] Grass, "Des Kaisers neue Kleider," in *Selbstverständliche*, Grass, 42–57, here 47.

[46] Grass, "Loblied auf Willy," in *Selbstverständliche*, Grass, 21–31, here 31.

[47] Grass, "Des Kaisers neue Kleider," 51. Further citations given in parentheses.

[48] See Heinz Ludwig Arnold, ed., *Günter Grass — Dokumente zur politischen Wirkung* (Munich: Richard Boorberg Verlag, 1971), 51.

[49] Günter Grass, "Rede über das Selbstverständliche," in *Selbstverständliche*, Grass, 68–83.

[50] Grass, "Offener Briefwechsel mit Willy Brandt," in *Selbstverständliche*, Grass, 95–99, here 95.

[51] Grass, "Rede über das Selbstverständliche," 73. Further citations given in parentheses.

[52] Grass, "Des Kaisers neue Kleider," 45.

[53] Grass "Vom mangelnden Selbstvertrauen der schreibenden Hofnarren unter Berücksichtigung nicht vorhandener Höfe," in *Selbstverständliche*, Grass, 84–89, here 89.

[54] See *Dafür*, no. 1 (1969), 56.

[55] Heidrun Abromeit and Klaus Burkhard, eds., "Die Wählerinitiativen im Wahlkampf 1972," supplement to *Das Parlament*, 15 September 1973.

[56] Werner Mittenzwei, *Die Intellektuellen. Literatur und Politik in Ostdeutschland 1945–2000* (Leipzig: Faber & Faber, 2001), 182.

[57] Klaus Schlesinger, "Am Ende der Jugend," in *Heute — und die 30 Jahre davor,* ed. Rosemarie Wildemuth (Munich: Ellermann, 3rd ed., 1979), 98–101, here 101.

[58] See Hermann Weber, ed., *DDR; Dokumente zur Geschichte der Deutschen Demokratischen Republik 1945–1985* (Munich: DTV, 1986), 282.

[59] See Günter Agde, ed., *Kahlschlag. Das 11. Plenum des ZK der SED 1965* (Berlin: Aufbau, 2001), 332.

[60] Werner Bräunig, *Rummelplatz* (Berlin: Aufbau, 2007).

[61] Rainer Kunze, *Die wunderbaren Jahre* (Frankfurt am Main: Fischer, 1976).

[62] Thomas Brasch, *Vor den Vätern sterben die Söhne* (Berlin: Rotbuch, 1976).

[63] Hans Dieter Zimmermann, *Der Wahnsinn des Jahrhunderts* (Stuttgart, Berlin, Cologne: Kohlhammer, 1992), 103.

4: A West German Interlude: Writers and Politics at the Time of the Student Movement

Introduction

THE MAIN OUTLINES OF POLITICAL AND LITERARY developments in the Federal Republic in the 1960s were sketched at the beginning of the previous chapter. This chapter will deal with events (and writers' reactions to them) that can be linked to the student movement, a phenomenon that ran parallel to mainstream political developments, although of course the two worlds did influence one another. Specifically, large parts of the student movement sought to change the nature of the Federal Republic and set up a different kind of society that would be based on socialism, albeit not that of the GDR. In this they appeared to have the support of a number of writers and intellectuals, not least those who at the beginning of the 1960s had supported the SPD but had become increasingly disillusioned by the party's apparent drift to the right. Hans Magnus Enzensberger, for example, claimed in 1967 that it was no longer possible to repair the political system of the Federal Republic. The choice was either the status quo or a new system (*VLMS,* 257). It is the ideas and events that can be linked to this view that will form the subject of this chapter.

The Return of Ideology

The first two postwar decades in the western part of Germany can be seen as characterized by suspicion of political ideologies. The experience of Nazism had put right-wing ideology, or at least that of the extreme kind, beyond the pale, while the negative example of the GDR acted as a deterrent to the adoption of ideologies based on Marxism. Enzensberger's advice to sixth-formers in his frequently anthologized poem "ins lesebuch für die oberstufe" appeared to sum up the mood of the time perfectly, not least in the lines: "nützlich / sind die enzykliken zum feueranzünden, / die manifeste: butter einzuwickeln und salz" (Encyclicals are useful for lighting fires, manifestos for wrapping up butter and salt).[1] At the same time, critical intellectuals, as one would expect, did seek to put their views and activities into some kind of theoretical perspective.

One example of this was the 1963 volume edited by Horst Krüger *Was ist heute links?* (What Does Left-wing Mean Today?). In his introduction, Krüger rejects orthodox Marxism, as well as pointing out that the terms "left" and "right" have reduced significance for the majority in a society where production and consumption are the main concerns. Ultimately, he appears to reduce being left-wing to an attitude of mind, which he defines as individualism complemented by a willingness to swim against the tide and to maintain the courage of one's convictions.[2] Incidentally, one wonders how many of these virtues might be claimed by rightists in certain circumstances. Hans Werner Richter is even more minimalist in his contribution, more or less admitting that currently the term "left-wing" cannot be defined. After embracing the ideas of convergence theory, which was popular in the 1960s and which claimed that both East and West were faced with the same problems, he expresses the hope that a new generation, faced with technological challenges on a global scale, will find a new definition on the basis of new knowledge.[3] If one looks for approval of any kind of socialist thinking in Krüger's volume, then it can be found in the publisher Klaus Wagenbach's endorsement of the ideas of the British politician Richard Crossman, as expressed in his Fabian essays of 1952. What he likes about Crossman, though, is the lack of any rigid ideological framework, his skepticism, and his self-imposed limits. Specifically, he praises Crossman for his gradualist rather than revolutionary approach.[4]

When, toward the end of the 1960s, students adopted Marxism or their own version of it and demanded revolutionary change, it was something that could hardly have been expected a few years earlier, given the kind of ideas expressed by Krüger and his fellow contributors and the perceived state of affairs at German universities. In his essay for the 1962 volume *Bestandsaufnahme,* the longtime cultural editor of *Die Zeit* Rudolf Walter Leonhardt laments the state of German universities, noting that they have not fulfilled the hopes placed in them immediately after the war.[5] He speaks of the need for students to be able to express themselves more freely and for the role of the professor to be challenged. Despite all the problems, however, he expresses the hope (it would seem rather the expectation) that perhaps one day the universities might be the starting point for a process of renewal in Germany (359).

How then could things change so quickly? It can be pointed out that Marxist thought, in the shape of the Frankfurt School, was never entirely dead in the Federal Republic. As has been seen, Adorno, Horkheimer, and their colleagues can be regarded as having laid the intellectual foundations of the Federal Republic. Equally significantly, by the late 1960s, a new generation of students and writers was more receptive to their and other left-wing ideas. This can be explained in part by the apparently natural process whereby a particular intellectual climate provokes an opposite reaction — in this case, an anti-ideological period being followed by one that became much more ideological. Equally significant in this case, though, were a series of political events involving not just the Federal Republic, reactions to which will be discussed later in this chapter.

It is now time to turn to some of the ideas that became current at the time of the student movement, although it would go beyond the scope of this book to attempt to summarize all of these. What is significant here is the role of writers in the formulation and dissemination of these ideas. Of particular significance here is the magazine *Kursbuch* (Timetable), founded by Enzensberger in 1965 and published initially by Suhrkamp. Increasingly associated from the 1960s onwards with the latest cultural developments, the Suhrkamp publishing house gave rise to the shorthand term *Suhrkamp-Kultur* to describe fashionably progressive writing. The initial edition spoke of a literary magazine that would also include areas beyond the traditional spheres of literature. Nevertheless, contributions by established writers — for example Walser, Jürgen Becker, and Samuel Beckett in the first edition — enjoyed a leading place. There was also a good deal of poetry in the early numbers. Gradually, though, the magazine began to develop into what some saw as the mouthpiece of the *Außerparlamentarische Opposition* (Extra-Parliamentary Opposition), the increasingly used umbrella term for those who, in association with the student movement, sought radical change in the Federal Republic. A significant caesura came with edition 20 in 1970. This was the last to be published by Suhrkamp and the last for some time to have a significant literary content. Thereafter, the magazine appeared for many years under its own imprint, beginning with an edition entitled *Kapitalismus in der Bundesrepublik* that sought to show, partly with the aid of tables and diagrams, that the Federal Republic was in thrall to monopoly capitalism. Ironically, the magazine came to an end in 2008, exactly forty years after it can be said to have had its major impact.

Well before that, the magazine had been a vehicle for the expression of left-wing ideas. One example was a "Gespräch über die Zukunft" (Conversation About the Future) between Enzensberger and various student leaders, including Rudi Dutschke, that appeared in 1968, almost a year after the actual deliberations. In this discussion, plans for creating a socialist society in West Berlin are discussed. It should, according to is proponents, be based on decentralized communes and *Rätedemokratie* (council democracy), the original ideal of the Russian Revolution expressed in the cry "All power to the Soviets." No judges would be needed, nor would the agricultural land that remained in West Berlin. According to Dutschke, it should be replaced by "Lebenszentren für die freie Zeit" (life centers for leisure time),[6] an idea that is not defined. Dutschke also demands the establishment of large-scale kitchens that would still be able to provide quality to satisfy sophisticated tastes (172). At this point, Enzensberger suggests that the art of cooking is not revolutionary, thus wittingly or unwittingly helping to undermine ideas that, almost four decades later, can only be seen as highly bizarre.

In general, though, Enzensberger contributed fully to the increasingly radical discourse of *Kursbuch*. A good example was his long piece "Berliner Gemeinplätze" (Berlin Commonplaces) that appeared in early 1968. In this essay, unlike in the discussion about the future, he does not seem to have his feet on the ground, arguing, for instance, that debates about whether opponents of the system should use violent or nonviolent methods are pointless — it is the protesters who should set the agenda rather than accepting concepts used by their opponents.[7] What is more, Enzensberger appeared to be putting his revolutionary beliefs into action when in early 1968 he resigned from a fellowship at the Center for Advanced Studies at the Wesleyan University of Middletown, Connecticut — clearly a place with an inappropriate name for him at that particular time! In a well-publicized open letter to the university's president, following criticism of the Vietnam War and imperialist exploitation of the Third World, he announces his intention of spending a long period in Cuba, where he feels he can be of use and also learn a lot.[8] This move underlines how far he had moved since his decision to return to the Federal Republic at the beginning of the decade, as seen in the volume *Ich lebe in der Bundesrepublik* and referred to in the previous chapter.

Political Developments in the Federal Republic

To obtain a fuller insight into attitudes of writers, including Enzensberger, associated with the student movement, it is necessary to look in more detail at how they reacted to political events. It will be recalled from the previous chapter that a number of writers who had previously supported the SPD were no longer willing to do so in 1965. Others, including the novelist Christian Geissler, went so far as to support the Deutsche Friedens-Union (German Peace Union), which, although not a successor party as such, occupied the place of the Communist Party in the party spectrum since the latter's prohibition in 1956.[9] All these writers and other intellectual groups, including the increasingly restless students, had their worst fears confirmed with the formation of the Grand Coalition with the former member of the Nazi party Kurt Georg Kiesinger as chancellor. This appointment came at a time when, thanks to the increasing number of war trials, especially that of the Auschwitz guards, awareness of the past was growing among younger people. Whereas, as seen in the last chapter, Günter Grass gritted his teeth and continued to support the SPD despite everything, others broke with the party, apparently forever. Nowhere did this stance find clearer expression than in a bitter poem by Friedrich Christian Delius, who, as seen in the previous chapter, had been part of the team of young writers employed by the

SPD in 1965. This began: "Brandt: es ist aus. Wir machen nicht mehr mit." (Brandt, it's all over. We'll go along no more).[10]

There followed a series of events that appeared to confirm some of the worst fears of those writers who had lost faith in the institutions of the Federal Republic, and that triggered off the most intense phase of the student movement. On the 2 June 1967 the student Benno Ohnesorg was shot dead by a policeman in West Berlin during a student demonstration against the visiting Shah of Iran. This tragic event was followed by a letter of protest signed by many writers, including not only Enzensberger, but also Günter Grass. Blame for the event was attributed in part to the press tycoon Axel Springer, who was accused of "Beihilfe zu Körperverletzung bis Totschlag" (aiding and abetting anything from wounding to manslaughter; VLMS, 247). Three months later, at the final regular Gruppe 47 meeting, a protest against the Springer Press — the publications of which, especially the tabloid Bild-Zeitung, were characterized at this time by a strong condemnation of the student movement — was signed by most, if not all the writers present, who also decided to boycott Springer publications. Springer himself was also singled out for blame when in April 1968 Rudi Dutschke was shot and badly injured by a mentally unstable individual. In his song, the East Berlin writer Wolf Biermann used the fact that three bullets were fired to blame directly three individuals: alongside Springer, the West Berlin mayor Klaus Schütz, and Chancellor Kiesinger, who, as a former member of the National Socialist party, was not an acceptable figure to many intellectuals (VLMS, 265–66). It has to be pointed out that Biermann is guilty of gross simplification in seeing a direct cause-and-effect relationship between views expressed by individuals and attempted murder. His stance in fact largely prefigures that of those who in the following decade, accused writers of being directly responsible for terrorism.

However sensational these two shootings in West Berlin may have been, there was another longstanding issue that provoked arguably more concern: namely, the question of emergency laws. At the time of its creation and even after it achieved sovereignty in 1955, the Federal Republic had no legislative powers to deal with political emergencies; any crisis of that nature would have had to be resolved by the Allies. By the early 1960s the CDU was clamoring for legislation, while the prospect of such legislation filled with horror all those haunted by the memory that Hitler had achieved absolute political power by using the emergency powers available under the Weimar constitution following the Reichstag fire. The advent of the Grand Coalition made the passing of the required laws more likely, as the two-thirds majority required for a change to the Basic Law was now arithmetically available to the governing parties. In due course the laws, which made possible the suspension of democracy in extreme situations, were introduced. The hostile reaction of writers and intellectuals, whose fears had been expressed as early as 1961 in *Die Alternative,* was only to be expected. Along with students, they took part in a sustained campaign that included a number of congresses and a march in Bonn to try to prevent the passing of the legislation. Nearly all leading writers were involved, although Grass was somewhat reluctant to criticize the role of the SPD very much. In 1966, with the Grand Coalition imminent and the issue already under discussion, a campaign entitled *Notstand der Demokratie* (Emergency for Democracy) was launched with Böll, Enzensberger, Walser and Erich Kästner as members of the organizing committee.

Predictably, it was Enzensberger, who expressed some of the most trenchant criticisms of the planned laws. He began a somewhat demagogic speech at a 1966 Frankfurt meeting of *Notstand der Demokratie* with a series of rhetorical questions: "Leben wir in einer Bananenrepublik? Werden wir von Gorillas regiert? Liegt Bonn in Haiti oder in Portugal? (Do we live in a banana republic? Are we governed by gorillas? Is Bonn to be found in Haiti or Portugal?; *VLMS,* 238). At the same time, he still identified with the Federal Republic, saying that the Federal Republic, as it existed at the time, was still needed (*VLMS,* 239). Two years later things had changed, with Enzensberger now using a public platform to demand more radical action in protest at the planned legislation. After saying that misgivings, distrust and protest were insufficient, he demanded "französische Zustände" (French conditions) in Germany.[11] That this plea became almost a part of folk memory in accounts of the era of student protest does not alter its essential inappropriateness in terms of the political situation of the day. Moreover, the Emergency Laws were duly passed, coming into force on 24 June 1968. That they have never been close to being used does suggest that the protests were exaggerated, although they did lead to a concession in the form of a change to the Basic Law. Article 20 was amended to include the right of resistance if the constitutional order were under threat, something that gave a legitimacy to protest, at least in certain limited circumstances.

The late 1960s were certainly a time when many writers adopted radical stances in a number of areas. Martin Walser, one of the few writers to have consistently taken an interest in economic questions, as many of his novels show, made the following comment in 1967:

> Kant hat gesagt, die beste Verfassung sei die, die noch eine Gesellschaft von Teufeln dazu zwänge, einander Gutes zu tun. Von den marktwirtschaftlichen Spielregeln, nach denen unser Leben sich richten muß, könnte man sagen, daß sie auch noch eine Gesellschaft von Engeln zwänge, einander Ungutes zu tun.[12]

> [Kant said that the best constitution is one that would force even a society of devils to do good to one another. It would be possible to say

of the rules of the market economy, by which our lives must be guided, that they would even force a society of angels to do ill to each other.]

Yet, it is important not to exaggerate. When *Der Spiegel,* in the worst traditions of sensationalist journalism, asked fellow writers to react to Enzensberger's apparent plea for revolution quoted at the beginning of this chapter, few either believed that a revolution was either possible or desirable. Jürgen Becker, for example, said he preferred the current political system, however deficient, to any that might emerge from a revolution, while Walser, in a perfect example of dialectical thinking, claimed revolutionary activity would promote evolution (see *VLMS,* 257–60). One writer to react to the emergency-laws controversy within the framework of the existing political institutions was Rolf Hochhuth. After supporting the SPD in 1965, as seen in the previous chapter, he now began to look toward the Free Democrats, the only opposition party inside parliament during the Grand Coalition and the only grouping to reject the emergency laws, although individuals in the other parties, including one Christian Democrat, did so. In a speech in 1968 during a protest meeting against the legislation, Hochhuth castigated the Social Democrats for preventing even the discussion of FDP amendments. He goes on to criticize several individual Social Democrats, justifying this in terms of his overall view of politics that, as his plays also show, is based on a belief in the moral responsibility of the individual. According to Hochhuth, individuals determine the cause of history, being anything other than *beliebig austauschbar* (interchangeable at will), as is frequently claimed.[13] Such a viewpoint clearly showed how much closer Hochhhuth's views were to liberalism than the ideology of much of the student movement, even if he did make common cause with them on the issue of emergency legislation.

It would also certainly be wrong to see all the political writing at this time as dour and disapproving. Delius and his colleague Nicolas Born wrote in verse form a series of "Berliner Para-Phrasen," in which the clichés of those opposed to the students were reversed in an amusing manner — for example, "Wir haben es satt, uns von gewaschenen Schlägern schlagen zu lassen" (We are sick of letting ourselves be beaten by washed thugs; *VLMS,* 264). On the specific issue of the emergency laws, the much-older Günter Eich, who was not usually prominent in political debates, produced a satirical piece entitled "Episode" that describes an imaginary emergency by using literary techniques reminiscent of Kafka to make his point:

> Ich wache auf und bin gleich im Notstand. Die Gründe weiß ich nicht genau, verhafte aber vorsorglich meine Kinder, Verhaftungen müssen sein. Im Rundfunk stelle ich Tanzmusik ein, drehe die Antenne in Richtung Luxemburg. Mit den Handschellen klirrend patrouilliere ich durch die Etagen.[14]

[I wake up and am immediately in an emergency situation. I don't know the exact reasons, but as a precautionary measure I immediately arrest my children. Arrests are necessary. I turn on dance music on the radio and turn the aerial in the direction of Luxembourg. Rattling handcuffs, I patrol throughout the floors.]

Subsequently the police surround the house, and even the narrator is arrested. The purpose of this text is to point to a danger that goes beyond that of an externally declared "emergency" — that such laws might encourage a submissive mentality alien to the ideals of democracy. In other words, emergency laws could create emergency citizens, who take on the state's dirty work themselves. Moreover, by tuning to dance music of the type offered at the time by Radio Luxembourg, they eschew the world of politics.

The Vietnam War

Alongside the domestic issues that provoked the kinds of reactions discussed in this chapter, there were numerous international questions that were of interest to students and their supporters from the world of literature. These can be subsumed under the general heading of revolutionary activity in the Third World, with the conflict in Vietnam overshadowing everything else. At their 1965 meeting, the writers of the Gruppe 47 published a declaration on the war, recalling what had happened since independence in 1954, highlighting the number of civilian casualties, and warning of the danger of genocide.[15] At about the same time, students too began public demonstrations against American policy. It should be recalled in this context that such protests against the United States represented a major break with prevailing attitudes in the Federal Republic. The mass of the population had been and remained, despite Vietnam, solidly pro-American because of the Berlin blockade and the role of the United States in facilitating the economic success of the country. Despite its misgivings over Vietnam, the Gruppe 47 had held its 1966 meeting at Princeton, while the title and descriptions of youth culture in Delius's story *Amerikahaus und der Tanz um die Frauen* (House America and the Dance Around Women, 1997), set in 1966 with anti-Vietnam War demonstrations playing a role, implied the significance of American culture for young Germans at this time.

Although most politically committed writers were opposed to the Vietnam War, there were differences of tone. In 1965 Enzensberger published in *Kursbuch* an essay entitled "Europäische Peripherie" (European periphery). His argument is that the real divide in world politics was between north and south, rich and poor — at the time, a bold proposition in divided Germany.[16] It certainly did not meet with the approval of Peter Weiss, who during the course of the 1960s moved much closer to Marxist positions. In a reply that appeared the following year, Weiss took exception to what he saw as Enzensberger's noncommittal approach and expressed his solidarity with all opponents of capitalism. His essay sees the divide in the world much more in the traditional East-West terms of the Cold War era, rejecting any idea that the Soviet Union is part of a rich world indifferent to the struggles of the oppressed. His essay concludes with a rhetorical question asking whether "we" are capable of solidarity with the oppressed and of supporting them in their struggle "der auch der unsere ist" (which is also ours).[17] It is this kind of stance that inspired at least two of Weiss's plays of that era, *Vietnam-Diskurs* (1968) and the attack on Portugese colonialism *Gesang vom lusitanischen Popanz* (Song of the Lusitanian Bogeyman, 1967), both of which espoused the cause of those fighting an imperial power.

Enzensberger's response to Weiss's essay, published alongside it as part of what was labeled a controversy, was that it is impossible to speak of authors endangering themselves by supporting revolutions: Whatever they do, "es ist immer noch was zum Trinken im Kühlschrank" (there is still always something left to drink in the refrigerator).[18] He advises people like Weiss to go to Vietnam or Peru and fight a revolutionary war if they want to experience a real struggle. His conclusion is particularly scathing:

> Die Moralische Aufrüstung von links kann mir gestohlen bleiben. Ich bin kein Idealist. Bekenntnissen ziehe ich Argumente vor. Zweifel sind mir lieber als Sentiments. Revolutionäres Geschwätz ist mir verhasst. Widerspruchsfreie Weltbilder brauche ich nicht. Im Zweifelsfall entscheidet die Wirklichkeit. (176)

> [I can do without left-wing Moral Rearmament. I am not an idealist. I prefer arguments to feelings. I prefer doubts to convictions. Revolutionary prattle is anathema to me. I do not need one-dimensional world views. In cases of doubt, reality decides.]

It must be concluded that Enzensberger's precise verbal blows gave him much the better of the argument. At the same time, his credo of skepticism did not fit in too well with his own political activity a little later, as described above.

Martin Walser also used the pages of *Kursbuch* to try to mediate between the extreme stances adopted by his colleagues. His essay "Praktiker, Weltfremde und Vietnam" (Realists, the Unworldly, and Vietnam) concentrated much more exclusively on protests against the Vietnam War. He points out that Enzensberger had inadvertently come up with a new version of the right-wing cry of the time that protesting individuals should go to live in the East. He also suggests Enzensberger's unwillingness to identify with any group is based on psychological factors. As for the issue of Vietnam itself, he proposes both a practical and nonpractical approach. He is unwilling to concede that moral protest is worthless: "Ein Verbrechen ein Verbrechen zu nennen, kann nicht sinnlos sein" (It cannot be senseless to call a crime a crime),[19] adding that writers' attempts to inform other members of society have not proved worthless over the course of history. On the practical level, he suggests the creation of a Vietnam office to disseminate information, and the preparation of a petition urging the Federal Parliament to debate the issue, something that did eventually occur during the Grand Coalition. This demand is also present in other statements on Vietnam by Walser, who arguably took the leading role among authors on this issue. It also, on the evidence of his short piece "Auskunft über den Protest" (Information on Protesting), led him to abandon previous doubts about the value of such activities. He concludes his remarks by a rather strange comparison, saying that protest is as necessary for him as war is to those making war.[20]

The Death of Literature

This idea became current at the height of the student movement when many writers were increasingly concerned with political issues, and a body of theoretical writing emerged that appeared to be claiming that traditional literature no longer had any relevance. As early as 1965, Peter Schneider had suggested that it was possible to conceive of occasions when writers should turn their efforts to writing manifestos rather than aesthetically pleasing literature.[21] Such an attitude certainly seemed, at least partially, to lie behind a comment by the writer and critic Reinhard Baumgart about an incident when the antifascist campaigner Beate Klarsfeld slapped Chancellor Kiesinger. He said that such an action might be better politics than the (political) poetry of Yaak Karsunke.[22] At the very least, Baumgart's admittedly noncommittal statement did not claim that Klarsfeld's deed might be poetic.

Not surprisingly, it was in the pages of *Kursbuch* that much of the debate over the "death of literature" took place. In the eleventh edition, dated January 1968, Enzensberger took his fellow writers to task for failure in the area of politics. Undoubtedly thinking of those associated with the Gruppe 47, he describes them as decent and modest, but only interested in reform or avoiding the worst. What is more, they lack vision and failed to produce "eine politische Theorie, die diesen Namen verdient" (a political theory worthy of the name).[23]

This kind of comment can be seen as a precursor to the real debate that took place in *Kursbuch 15*, in which three significant essays appeared. The first (taking them by their order in the magazine), by Yaak Karsunke, was principally an attack on literary critics, who are seen as the heirs of National Socialism.[24] That Warsaw ghetto–survivor Marcel Reich-Ranicki is mentioned in the following paragraph in the same critical way as no different from his colleagues is, to say the least, regrettable. The offense of which the critics are said to be guilty was expressed by Karsunke very much in conventional Marxist terms: They contribute to false consciousness, which, in turn, prevents the development of a literature that might be "funktional und gesellschaftsabhängig" (functional and dependent on society; 167). The second essay, by the co-editor of *Kursbuch,* Klaus Markus Michel, entitled "Ein Kranz für die Literatur. Fünf Variationen über eine These" (A Wreath for Literature. Five Variations on a Thesis), took contemporary literature to task. Not only does he see it as irrelevant to the political struggle, as the student demonstration against the Gruppe 47 demonstrated, but he also accuses it of diverting attention away from social questions even where it seeks to be socially aware and committed. In this way, it only gained Pyrrhic victories and allowed those in power to continue as usual.[25] These assertions, which are as unproven as those that claim a direct influence for literature, amount to a denial of any social function for traditional literature.

Not surprisingly, given his prominence, it was Enzensberger's essay "Gemeinplätze, die Neueste Literatur betreffend" (Commonplaces in Relation to the Most Recent Literature) — the title of which recalled Lessing's "Briefe (Letters), die Neueste Literatur betreffend" of two centuries earlier — that attracted the most attention in the debates about the death of literature. A careful reading of the text, however, shows that he is not crudely dismissing all literature as irrelevant or dead. He begins by pointing out that to talk of the death of literature is itself to use a metaphor that has been current for 150 years. His main point, nonetheless, is that it cannot be shown that literature can contribute to major changes in society, at least not at the time he is writing: "Für literarische Kunstwerke läßt sich eine wesentliche gesellschaftliche Funktion in unserer Lage nicht angeben" (An essential social function for literary works of art cannot be stated in our situation.)[26] Writers can only undertake their work without certainty, that is to say, unsure of whether they will achieve anything. Despite these doubts, Enzensberger does suggest types of writing that could be valuable, giving as examples books providing information about the Third World and Ulrike Meinhof's columns in the magazine *Konkret.* Moreover, he castigates those whose political activism exhausts itself in attacking literature; he adds that such people should turn their attention to those parts of cultural life that, unlike literature, can be seen as positively dangerous, doubtlessly meaning the mass media.

In many respects, it seems that what can be perceived as obituaries for literature were in fact pleas for different kinds of writing to be accepted as literature. Indeed, the time of the student movement did spawn new types of writing. In what can be regarded as an extension of documentary drama, there developed what might be called documentary literature, that is to say, the attempt to capture the authentic voice or situation of those members of society who were usually excluded from literary discourse. One example was a volume entitled *Bottroper Protokolle* (Bottrop Transcripts, 1968) — which includeed an introduction by Martin Walser — where Erika Runge claimed to present residents' views of life in the Ruhr town during the recession of

1967.[27] In that it is the people of Bottrop who are supposedly speaking, the role of the author (in this case Runge) is at least in theory reduced to that of recorder. The same search for "authenticity" also inspired Walser to arrange the publication of two autobiographies of social outsiders.[28] A somewhat different route was taken by the investigative writer Günter Wallraff, who began to publish his firsthand accounts of life as an ordinary worker in the Federal Republic, something he continued in the following decades.[29]

The main issue that arose in connection with many of these works was that of authenticity. Were those who facilitated their publication not merely faithful recorders but rather manipulators of the material they had gathered? Certainly, there were many who were not enamored by this particular development. These included not just traditionalist critics such as Benno von Wiese and Marcel Reich-Ranicki, but also younger authors. Writing in 1970, Hans Christoph Buch, for example, expressed the fear that such methods as Runge's transcripts and Wallraff's reports did not truly give workers the chance to express their needs. At the same time, he champions the role of the subjective in literature. Remaining within the parameters of Marxist discourse, Buch even goes so far as to challenge those writers who scoff at literature that seeks to induce social change. They are seen as falling into a trap set by the ruling classes to prevent any politically effective links between workers and intellectuals.[30]

Dieter Wellershoff, too, in an essay "Fiktion und Praxis" (Fiction and Praxis) saw literature as a challenge to the established world, since it offered the reader the chance to extend his or her experiences. He criticizes Enzensberger for judging literature in terms of its visible achievements and in this way indulging in a crude cult of success.[31] Wellershoff is closer to Adorno's view that the influence of literature is achieved more subtly than by direct political statements.

With hindsight, the whole "death of literature" debate can be seen as merely a brief episode. In the 1970s, as will be seen, the subjective came back to the fore. If anything more lasting was achieved, it was arguably in the publications of the Werkkreis Literatur der Arbeitswelt (Workshop for the Literature of the World of Work), officially founded in 1970. This went beyond the Gruppe 61, which had been created primarily to promote literature about the working class, in that nonprofessional writers presented their experiences without intermediaries, and frequently with the subjective dimension demanded by Buch.

Writers Organize Themselves

It seems no coincidence, during a period in which politics became such a major, if not the exclusive, concern of so many writers, that they began to consider their own position in society and to seek further ways of improving their status, at least materially. One phrase that became current was *Ende der*

Bescheidenheit (end of modesty), stemming from a speech by Heinrich Böll in 1969. He complains that writers let themselves be exploited by publishers when it comes to royalties and also receive harsh treatment from the tax authorities, which regard them as entrepreneurs.[32] The speech goes beyond material questions, however, by claiming a significant role for writers in the Federal Republic, stating: "Wir verdanken diesem Staat nichts, er verdankt uns eine Menge" (We owe this state nothing, it owes us a great deal; 356), Böll is here no doubt referring to the prestige he and his fellow writers had undoubtedly given his country after Nazism, while seeing the freedom of speech allowed to him and his colleagues as a right rather than a privilege.

This speech was made at the first gathering organized to create a writers union at the federal level. The first congress of this newly formed Verband deutscher Schriftsteller (Association of German Writers), usually referred to by the initials VS, took place in 1970 in Stuttgart under the slogan *Einigkeit der Einzelgänger* (Unity of the Individualists). At this meeting, the hope that the newly founded organization would develop close links with the wider trade union movement was expressed by Böll, Enzensberger, Hochhuth, and Walser, among others. Walser went as far as proposing an "IG Kultur" (Culture Trade Union), that is to say, a force comparable to such industry-wide trade unions as the engineering union, IG Metall.[33]

Subsequent events have seen this part of Walser and the other writers' ambitions realized to a degree. First, the VS associated itself with the printing trade union IG Druck und Papier in 1973, and is currently linked with ver.di (or *Vereinigte Dienstleistungsgewerkschaft*), the larger trade union that covers a number of service industries. Where there have been problems, particularly since the 1980s, has been in retaining the unity that was spoken about in the early days of the association. At this time, the VS embodied the general leftist consensus among most writers. While expressing their hopes for its future, the four writers mentioned above talked about the need for them and their colleagues to contribute to the struggle against capitalism and imperialism.[34]

Similar sentiments, although stated in less rigid terms and with an admission of failure, were expressed at the second congress in 1973 by Siegfried Lenz, who complained that writers had done little to curb those in power, to prevent hunger, or to further the cause of social justice.[35] Cracks began to show at the third congress in 1974, when Günter Wallraff demanded that writers incite their fellow citizens to opposition against hard-hearted technocrats like Helmut Schmidt.[36] Not surprisingly, such a viewpoint did not meet with the approval of those writers who still supported the SPD, in particular, Günter Grass.

This kind of spat was of nothing in comparison with what happened in the early 1980s. By this time, the chair of the VS was the left-wing historian and novelist Bernt Engelmann, who was particularly keen on establishing contacts with GDR writers. This policy roused suspicions among authors who had left the GDR, in some cases after periods of imprisonment. Things came to a head at the 1983 congress in Mainz and a year later in Saarbrücken. A major issue at this time were events in Poland, where, in the face of the challenge presented by the Solidarity trade union, the communist system was only sustained by the introduction of martial law. The wave of popular protest in Poland did not impress the journalist Erasmus Schäfer from the magazine *Kürbiskern*, which from its beginnings was closely associated with the reborn West German communist party (DKP). At the Mainz conference, he plumbed the depths of bad taste by comparing the ten million supporters of Solidarity with the millions who had supported Hitler.[37] A year later, the dissolution by the authorities of the Polish Writers Union was the bone of contention. The first motion at Saarbrücken only spoke of the need for a new union in Poland, not the reinstatement of the old one. Eventually, a resolution calling for a lifting of the original ban and an end to the persecution of intellectuals in Eastern Europe was passed by one vote.

Following these events, there was a wave of resignations, including those of Uwe Johnson, Rainer Kunze, and Gerhard Zwerenz, and the creation of a rival Freier Deutscher Autorenverband (Free German Writers Association). Clearly, there was not much left of the unity vaunted a decade earlier. That such hopes were misconceived had been pointed out in 1983 by Hans Christoph Buch, who strongly supported the writers who had left the East. He stated that it was an illusion to believe that writers, trade unionists, and intellectuals all shared the same interests. Moreover, terms such as *Literaturproduzent* (producer of literature) reflected a false view of the position of writers, who cannot be organized like other workers since they work individually and prosper in accordance with the quality of their work.[38] Although the substance of Buch's arguments cannot be denied, the survival of the VS within the wider trade union movement does show that its foundation at the time of the student movement was more than a mere flash in the pan inspired by the atmosphere of the time.

Conclusion

By the mid-1970s, it was impossible to speak of the student movement as a single phenomenon, and probably impossible to speak of such a movement at all. Insofar as they retained an interest in left-wing politics at all, the class of 1968 went their separate ways. Some, taking the advice of Rudi Dutschke who had spoken of a "long march through the institutions," joined the mainstream, while others split into various Marxist subgroups. In the case of a very few, protest gave way to terrorism, an issue that, as will be seen in the next chapter, became a major concern for intellectuals in the 1970s. Similar processes were at work among writers and intellectuals. A decade after 1968,

Enzensberger published his long poem *Der Untergang der Titanic* (The Sinking of the Titanic, 1978), which can be read in part as a farewell to the kind of socialism he was previously advocating.

One organization that did attract support from a number of writers was the DKP, which, following its creation in 1968, pursued an orthodox Marxist-Leninist line of the kind associated with the Soviet Union and specifically the GDR. Writers associating with it included Uwe Timm and Franz Xaver Kroetz, who was a candidate for the party in the 1972 federal election and remained a member until 1980. At the time of the 1972 election, Martin Walser, although not a member, also spoke up for the DKP. He pointed out that, although the party was theoretically legal, it was excluded from a full part in the political process.[39] While there was some justification in this claim — Walser having some difficulty in finding an outlet for his comments — in the longer term, it is Walser's criticisms of the DKP that are of interest. Specifically, he accused the party of a lack of West German identity, of being too closely linked with the GDR. To this extent, the essay can be seen as pointing to what some see as the nationalist phase in Walser's political development, something that will feature strongly in the latter part of this volume.

Given the dubious credentials of the GDR as a role model at any time, not to mention its subsequent collapse, writers' involvement with the DKP has to be seen as an aberration. The question also arises of whether the same can be said of the whole era discussed in this chapter. Certainly, Günter Grass never had much time for the 1968 generation, describing in *Aus dem Tagebuch einer Schnecke* the student revolutionaries in a somewhat sweeping generalization as "Vergrämte Streichelkinder, die ihre Schwierigkeiten zur Litanei knüpfen: die Eltern, die Schule, die Verhältnisse, alles" (Embittered coddled children, who turn their troubles into a litany: parents, school, conditions, everything; *TS,* 16). In recent years, too, there has been no shortage of criticism of those associated with the student movement. The role of the then–foreign minister Joschka Fischer became an issue at one point, with the daughter of the journalist-turned-terrorist Ulrike Meinhof taking on the role of accuser. Subsequently, the attitude of Rudi Dutschke toward violence and, in particular, the question of whether the student movement was anti-Semitic came to the fore, the latter issue following the publication of a book about a failed plan to bomb a West Berlin Jewish center in 1969 on the anniversary of *Kristallnacht* (The Night of Broken Glass), the anti-Jewish pogrom of 1938.[40]

It is such events that, even if they involved only a small minority, raised questions about claims that the student movement was marked by shame about the Nazi past that had its origins in, for example, the trial of Auschwitz guards in the early 1960s that had brought to light the full horror of Nazi crimes. Undoubtedly, they were an underlying factor, as Peter Schneider stresses in his memoir of 1968 *Rebellion und Wahn* (Rebellion and Delusion, 2008), one of the many books to appear forty years after the events. After a childhood and adolescence in which he learned little about the Nazi past, he was suddenly confronted with the events referred to above. For him, antifascism remains "das bestimmende emotionale Motiv" (the determining emotional motif) behind the rebellion.[41] While not denying this, in another book with the provocative title *Unser Kampf 1968* (Our Struggle, 1968) that appeared in the same year, the historian Götz Aly, himself a member of the relevant generation and an actor in 1968, suggested that the student movement suppressed any sense of shame and avoided personal confrontation with the Nazi crimes of their parents, taking, for instance, no interest in the many war crimes trials going on at the time. Instead, they looked instead for perpetrators of genocide in Washington and chanted, as part of the Vietnam campaign, "USA-SA-SS." According to Aly, this *Zauberspruch* (magic phrase) amounts to an acquittal verdict for young Germans.[42] Aly's claims may have something of what might be called the zeal of the reconverted; nevertheless, he does raise difficult issues. In his book he also quotes Enzensberger's claim that he was a "teilnehmender Beobachter" (participating observer) in the events of the time, an oxymoron that seeks to suggest a desire to dissociate himself from them (114).

If some writers did undoubtedly involve themselves with a movement that had its negative sides, it would be wrong to condemn everything that can be associated with the year 1968. There was undoubtedly merit in two comments made about the student movement by writers, one in the early 1970s by Horst Krüger and the other much later by Enzensberger. Writing in *Die Zeit* in 1971, Krüger pointed to the dismantling of taboos, the greater tolerance toward minorities and the expression of utopian ideas, considering the last point to be the most important.[43] Enzensberger's comments made in 1995 were not entirely dissimilar. He sees the student movement as helping to break down Germany's authoritarian traditions, thus helping to make relations — for example, between doctor and patient, pupil and teacher — much more human.[44] That the late 1960s brought the kind of positive changes in society noted by Krüger and Enzensberger cannot be denied, although the question of the value of utopian ideas is much more difficult. It is relevant to much that will be considered later, the environmental and peace movements, and the GDR at the time of its collapse.

Notes

[1] Hans Magnus Enzensberger, *Gedichte* (Frankfurt am Main: Suhrkamp, 1962), 28.

[2] Horst Krüger, "Das Thema wird gestellt," in *Was ist heute links?*, ed. Horst Krüger (Munich: List, 1963) 11–29, here 27.

[3] Hans Werner Richter, "In einem zweigeteilten Land," in *Was ist heute links?*, ed. Krüger, 94–100, esp. 100.

[4] Klaus Wagenbach, "Ernüchtert oder heimatlos," in *Was ist heute links?*, ed. Krüger, 84–89, here 89.

[5] Rudolf Walter Leonhardt, "Die deutschen Universitäten," in *Bestandsaufnahme*, ed. Hans Werner Richter, 351–59, esp. 352. Further citations given in parentheses.

[6] "Ein Gespräch über die Zukunft mit Rudi Dutschke, Bernd Rabehl und Christian Semler," *Kursbuch 14* (1968): 146–74, here 169. Further citations given in parentheses.

[7] Hans Magnus Enzensberger, "Berliner Gemeinplätze," *Kursbuch 11* (1968): 151–69, here 166.

[8] See Hans Magnus Enzensberger, "Warum ich nicht in den USA bleibe," *Tagebuch* März/April 1968, 12–13.

[9] For the declaration of Geissler and others see *VLMS*, 229.

[10] F. C. Delius, "Abschied von Willy," in *Heute — und die 30 Jahre davor*, ed. Rosemarie Wildermuth (Munich: Ellermann Verlag, 3rd ed., 1979) 135.

[11] Hans Magnus Enzensberger, "Notstand," in *Tintenfisch 2* (Berlin: Klaus Wagenbach Verlag, 1969), 19–20, here 20.

[12] Martin Walser, "Die Parolen und die Wirklichkeit," in *Heimatkunde* (Frankfurt am Main: Suhrkamp, 1968), 58–70, here 65.

[13] Rolf Hochhuth, "Die Sprache der Sozialdemokraten," in *VLMS*, 267–69, here 268.

[14] Günter Eich, "Episode," in *Heute — und die 30 Jahre davor*, ed. Rosemarie Wildemuth (Munich: Ellermann, 3rd ed., 1979), 163.

[15] See Lettau, *Die Gruppe 47*, 459–62.

[16] Hans Magnus Enzensberger, "Europäische Peripherie," *Kursbuch 2* (1965), 154–73.

[17] Peter Weiss and Hans Magnus Enzensberger, "Eine Kontroverse," *Kursbuch 6* (1966): 165–76, here 170.

[18] Weiss, Enzensberger, "Eine Kontroverse," 175. Further citations given in parentheses.

[19] Martin Walser, "Praktiker, Weltfremde und Vietnam," *Kursbuch 9* (1967): 168–76, here 173.

[20] Martin Walser, "Auskunft über den Protest," in *Heimatkunde*, 36–39.

[21] Peter Schneider, "Politische Dichtung. Ihre Grenzen und Möglichkeiten," in *Theorie der politischen Dichtung*, ed. Peter Stein (Munich: Nymphenburger Verlagshandlung, 1973), 141–55, here 154.

[22] Reinhard Baumgart, "Die verdrängte Phantasie oder Sechs Thesen über Literatur und Politik," in *Poesie und Politik*, ed. Wolfgang Kuttenkeuler (Stuttgart: Kohlhammer, 1973), 358–66, here 362.

[23] Enzensberger, "Berliner Gemeinplätze," 158.

[24] Yaak Karsunke, "Anachronistische Polemik," *Kursbuch 15* (1968): 165–68, here 166. Further citations given in parentheses.

[25] Klaus Markus Michel, "Ein Kranz für die Literatur," *Kursbuch 15* (1968): 169–86, here 178.

[26] Hans Magnus Enzensberger, "Gemeinplätze, die Neueste Literatur betreffend," *Kursbuch 15* (1968): 187–97, here 195.

[27] Erika Runge, *Bottroper Protokolle* (Frankfurt am Main: Suhrkamp, 1968).

[28] The two volumes in question are Ursula Trauberg, *Vorleben* (Frankfurt am Main: Suhrkamp, 1968) and Wolfgang Werner, *Vom Waisenhaus ins Zuchthaus* (Frankfurt am Main: Suhrkamp, 1969).

[29] Some of Wallraff's reports on poor working conditions in the Federal Republic are collected in Günter Wallraff, *13 unerwünschte Reportagen* (Cologne: Kiepenheuer und Witsch, 1969).

[30] Hans Christoph Buch, "Von der möglichen Funktion der Literatur," *Kursbuch 20* (1970): 42–52, here 50.

[31] Dieter Wellershoff, "Fiktion und Praxis" in *Poesie und Politik,* ed. Kuttenkeuler, 329–40.

[32] Heinrich Böll, "Ende der Bescheidenheit," in *Poesie und Politik,* ed. Kuttenkeuler, 347–57, here 356.

[33] Martin Walser, "Für eine IG-Kultur," in *Wie und wovon handelt Literatur,* Walser (Frankfurt am Main: Suhrkamp, 1973), 67–75.

[34] See Dieter Lattmann, ed., *Einigkeit der Einzelgänger* (Munich: Kindler, 1971), 82.

[35] Siegfried Lenz, "Das Dilemma der Außenseiter," in *Entwicklungsland Kultur,* ed. Dieter Lattmann (Munich: Kindler, 1973), 64–68, here 67.

[36] Günter Wallraff, "Autoren Radikale im offentlichen Dienst," in *Phantasie und Verantwortung,* ed. Horst Bingel (Frankfurt am Main: Fischer, 1975), 24–38.

[37] Schäfer's comments are quoted in *Frankfurter Rundschau,* 26 March 1983, 15.

[38] Hans Christoph Buch, "'Herdentiere oder Einzelganger' Uber die Krise der VS und Moglichkeiten zu deren Überwindung," *Vorwärts,* 24 March 1983, 13.

[39] Martin Walser, "Wahlgedanken," in *Wie und wovon,* Walser, 100–118.

[40] See Wolfgang Kraushaar, *Die Bombe im jüdischen Gemeindehaus* (Hamburg: Hamburger Edition, 2005).

[41] Peter Schneider, *Rebellion und Wahn* (Kiepenheuer & Witsch, 2008), 124.

[42] Götz Aly, *Unser Kampf* (Frankfurt a.M: Fischer, 2008), 148. Further citations given in parentheses.

[43] Horst Krüger, "Was bleiben sollte," *Die Zeit,* 13 August 1971, 13.

[44] Hans Magnus Enzensberger, "Ich will nicht der Lappen sein, mit dem man die Welt putzt," *Die Zeit,* 20 January 1995, 47–48.

5: The 1970s: Writers on the Defensive

Political Developments

A LTHOUGH IT ENDED WITH THE same SPD/FDP coalition with which it
began, and the two parties had their positions confirmed in the 1980
federal election, the decade of the 1970s was a time of massive changes in
political mood in the Federal Republic. While the Christian Democrats licked
their wounds following the events of 1969, the new government under
Chancellor Willy Brandt proposed changes on both the domestic and foreign
political fronts. At home, Brandt spoke of reforms and of daring to be more
democratic. In foreign affairs, he turned his attention to negotiations with
the Federal Republic's eastern neighbors, to what became universally known
as *Ostpolitik*. Treaties were signed in 1970 with the Soviet Union and Poland,
1971 saw a four-power agreement on Berlin, and the following year the two
German states signed a "Basic Treaty." All that was then left was the less
controversial treaty with Czechoslovakia, by which the infamous Munich
Agreement of 1938 was accepted as null and void. In essence, all the treaties
signed by the Federal Republic amounted to an acceptance of postwar realities, specifically, the loss of Germany's former eastern territories to Poland
and the Soviet Union and the division of Germany itself, although the
possibility of reunification was left open. To their detractors, the treaties were
the abandonment of long-held positions — in particular, the notion of a
single Germany in its 1937 frontiers — in return for very little. Their supporters pointed to the humanitarian improvements that had been negotiated, like the increased contacts across the intra-German frontier. What was
also important to them was the element of reconciliation with countries that
had suffered dreadfully at German hands in the Second World War. The
1972 federal election, which came a year before the end of a normal four-
year legislative period because the Brandt government's slim 1969 majority
had been eroded by defections, was in many respects a plebiscite on *Ostpolitik,* with the SPD for the first time ever overtaking the CDU/CSU in the
popular vote.

At home, the new government achieved certain changes — for example,
to the previously very restrictive abortion law — but soon after the 1972
triumph was overtaken by events like the oil price shock of 1973. Brandt
himself seemed to have lost his drive even before the discovery of the GDR

spy Günter Guillaume in his immediate entourage led to his resignation in 1974. His successor Helmut Schmidt was a very different kind of politician. He was much more a pragmatist than Brandt, whose foreign policy at least had an idealistic dimension, seeing himself as a crisis manager; indeed, he liked to use the term "crisis management" (in English) himself. His opponents preferred the derogatory term *der Macher* — literally, "the doer," but which might be rendered as "Mr. Fix-it." Given the economic problems of the middle of the decade, Schmidt, along with his FDP partner Hans-Dietrich Genscher who had replaced Brandt's charismatic foreign minister Walter Scheel, only just scraped through the 1976 election. Their triumph in 1980 had much to do with the CDU/CSU choice of candidate for chancellor: Franz Josef Strauß was, as seen in previous chapters, the bête noire of intellectuals, and his popularity among the general public waned the further away they lived from Strauß's native Bavaria. The post-1976 legislative period was dominated by the issue of terrorism, to which much of this chapter will be devoted. In short, the latter part of the 1970s was not a happy time for the Federal Republic.

The 1970s also saw change in the GDR. When confronted with the figure of Willy Brandt, whose antifascist credentials as an émigré from Hitler's Germany prevented his being denigrated in the same way as his predecessors, the GDR leadership seemed unsure how to react: whether to welcome the new *Ostpolitik* or to see it as a cunning strategy to undermine their own position. In reality, what counted was the Soviet Unions's willingness to negotiate with Brandt. When the ageing Ulbricht was increasingly unwilling to go along with his major ally, he was replaced by Erich Honecker in 1971. Honecker was more willing to deal with the Federal Republic, although he also set great store on the policy of *Abgrenzung* (delimitation), which stated that the two German states no longer had anything in common and that reunification was to be postponed to sometime after the Second Coming. The new constitution of 1968 was amended to stress the separateness of the GDR, with, for example, all reference to a single German nation being excised. Except for the title of the SED newspaper *Neues Deutschland,* the word "Deutschland" more or less disappeared from the official vocabulary, which meant ironically that the words of the GDR national anthem with its imprecation of a united Germany in the words "Deutschland, einig Vaterland" (Germany, one fatherland) were no longer sung.

At home, Honecker promised more economic prosperity and better living conditions. He embarked on a massive building program, the results of which are still visible in most towns in the east of Germany. Even if these new flats were decried by some as *Arbeiterschließfächer* (lockers for workers) because of their small dimensions, they did bring improved sanitary conditions to many and were much sought after. As it turned out, however, Honecker could not deliver the goods, literally, as the long waiting periods for new cars showed. By the end of the 1970s, the GDR was in decline, also intellectually, as this chapter will show.

Literary Developments

Undoubtedly, the main event of the 1970s in the world of West German literature, at least in public perception at the time, was the rapid end to all talk of the death of literature. This idea had always been dubious, as not many authors, and not even Enzensberger himself, had abandoned tradi-tional literary forms. What now took center stage was writing that was sub-sumed under the term New Subjectivity — that is to say, works in which writers presented (or at least appeared to present) their own experiences and feelings directly to the reader. One work that can be connected to this development is Peter Schneider's 1973 story *Lenz*. The main character is an intellectual who becomes increasingly disenchanted with the German left-wing circles he frequents, and takes himself off to Italy where politics can be combined with a zest for life. The following passage gives a flavor of his growing alienation:

> Es kam Lenz im Moment so komisch vor, daß all diese Genossen mit ihren heimlichen Wünschen, mit ihren schwierigen und aufregenden Lebensgeschichten, mit ihren energischen Ärschen nichts weiter vonein-ander wissen wollten als diese sauberen Sätzen von Mao Tse-tung, das kann doch nicht wahr sein, dachte Lenz.[1]

> [It appeared so funny to Lenz at this moment that all these comrades with their secret desires, their difficult and exciting biographies, with their energetic arses did not want to know anything more about each other than these clear-cut sentences from Mao-Tse-tung, that cannot surely be true, thought Lenz.]

By contrast, in Italy, Lenz notes, political meetings are frequently followed by musical sessions. It was not only younger writers who turned to the sub-jective. Max Frisch's *Montauk* of 1975 narrates what are presented as the author's own experiences in the first person, thus giving the impression of total authenticity.

The development of *Frauenliteratur* (women's literature) can also be linked with New Subjectivity, given that the first works inspired by the fe-minist thinking of the 1970s appeared autobiographical. Indeed, the first one to make substantial impact, *Häutungen* (Shedding, 1975) by the Swiss writer Verena Stefan, spoke in its subtitle of autobiographical notes.[2] In this work, the first-person narrator, following unsuccessful relationships with men, gradually discovers her true identity as a woman. Thirty years on, the importance of works like that of Stefan should not be underestimated. Since the 1970s, writing by women has progressed from mainly portraying personal themes to become a major element in German literature.

The 1970s were also a decade that promised major changes in GDR literature. On his accession to power, Honecker famously promised that there would be no taboos in the area of literature, although he did hedge his bets by saying that writers should remain committed to socialism. One work that seemed to capture the new mood was Ulrich Plenzdorf's *Die neuen Leiden des jungen W.* (The New Sorrows of Young W., 1973).[3] This work, too, has a subjective element, as it recounts the personal and professional problems of a young GDR citizen who finally kills himself by accident thanks to experimenting recklessly with electricity. It was not only the descriptions of life in the GDR that caused a stir, but the obvious use made by Plenzdorf of Goethe's *Die Leiden des jungen Werthers* (The Sorrows of Young Werther), a much-thumbed copy of which his hero carries round. The Honecker era saw increasing attempts to place GDR culture in the tradition of all that was best in German cultural history, what was called the *humanistisches Erbe* (humanist inheritance). This concern led to all kinds of what might seem unlikely developments, not least the restoration of the statue of Frederick II of Prussia to pride of place in East Berlin. What it did not see was a true liberation of GDR culture. This chapter will show how "no taboos" quickly degenerated into repression of certain forms of artistic activity and of artists themselves.

Writers and Politics

A Brief Honeymoon

The change of government as a result of the 1969 election led initially to a changed relationship between the worlds of politics and literature, at least as far as those writers who had maintained support for the SPD were concerned. Instead of hurling insults at each other under Erhard's chancellorship, writers and politicians sought each other's company, as when Willy Brandt attended the founding congress of the Verband Deutscher Schriftsteller. The chancellor's speech could hardly have been more conciliatory. The former journalist stressed his desire that the dichotomy between the two spheres be reduced; at the end of his speech, he went further by asking for help from writers so that "nicht abermals die Vernunft an der Ignoranz scheitert" (reason does not again flounder on the rock of ignorance).[4]

Brandt was an attractive figure to many writers because of his anti-Nazi past. He enhanced his reputation further with his *Ostpolitik*, which for many intellectuals was a break from the anticommunist shibboleths of the early years of the Federal Republic. Specifically, Brandt's gesture during his 1970 visit to Poland of kneeling in front of the memorial to the Warsaw ghetto created a major impression. Writing in 1972, Horst Krüger spoke of a gesture he would never forget. What is more, he is equally happy with Brandt's domestic policy, seeing the Federal Republic as the most liberal state in Europe with the possible exception of the Scandinavian countries. Significantly, he contrasts this feeling with his previous attitudes to the Federal Republic, saying that he could not identify with it during the years of CDU rule, although he admits that it was not an unpleasant place to live.[5]

The year 1972 probably represented the zenith of writers' identification with the SPD-led government, not least because of the CDU's attempts to remove Brandt. The election of that year saw the first president of the VS, Dieter Lattmann, enter parliament as an SPD member, a position he held for eight years. It is small wonder that a year earlier, the writer and journalist Klaus Harpprecht, who was close to Brandt, saw a new relationship between the SPD and intellectuals, claiming that the party had achieved the integration of the Federal Republic's intellectuals.[6] At the same time, he did temper this claim by admitting that there were tensions between the party and younger intellectuals, meaning no doubt those he associated with the student movement.

These tensions were, in fact, never far below the surface. As early as 1972, the Brandt government sullied its reputation for many with what became known as the *Radikalenerlass* (radicals decree), the letter it sent out to the federal states reminding them that only those who were loyal to the constitution were acceptable as civil servants. This group in the Federal Republic includes teachers and lawyers in the public service, but at that time encompassed also different kinds of professions, such as many railway personnel. The word *Berufsverbot* (professional disbarment), which recalled the Nazis' banning of Jews from numerous professions, became current again, also beyond the frontiers of the Federal Republic. The West German PEN center expressed its disapproval of the measure, as did the signatories of an open letter to the Federal Parliament, who included Alfred Andersch, Uwe Johnson, and Günter Wallraff (*VLMS*, 287–88). Peter Schneider recounted his own difficulties in being accepted as suitable for the teaching profession in a text entitled . . . *schon bist du ein Verfassungsfeind* (. . . and That's all it Takes to Make you an Enemy of the Constitution, 1975).[7]

It was, however, Brandt's resignation in 1974 that marked the true end of the honeymoon. Writing at the time in *Die Zeit*, the journalist Dieter E. Zimmer spoke correctly about the end of an era, claiming that Brandt, along with Federal President Heinemann, the first Social Democrat to hold the office and whose 1969 election preceded that of Brandt by a few months, had done more to reduce the seemingly unbridgeable gap between the worlds of politicians and writers than any of their predecessors.[8] Zimmer also pointed out that even Martin Walser, at the time no friend of the SPD, had had good things to say about Brandt. In fact, at the time of Brandt's resignation, Walser wrote an open letter to the GDR leader, Honecker, telling him that his regime's role in the downfall of Brandt was reason enough for him to quit the political stage (*VLMS,* 289–90). Not surprisingly, this suggestion was not followed. It did, however, show that Walser was moving away from positions that could be associated with the second German state. At the same time, with the resignation of Brandt, other writers were less willing to engage in political activity at all. This was noticeable at the time of the 1976 federal election when the journalist Hermann Schreiber noted that it was no longer fashionable for writers and intellectuals to be involved with the campaign.[9]

Tendenzwende

This term, the sense of which can possibly best be rendered in English by "change of mood," became current in the 1970s. It referred to the increasing unwillingness of large sections of the middle class in the Federal Republic to support the domestic reforms of SPD-led governments at either the federal or state level. One major issue was education, with controversies in Hessen over a planned new syllabus for German and in North Rhine-Westphalia over the organization of secondary education. This latter issue still dogs educational debate thirty years later: many politicians and parents still regard the tripartite system of secondary education, with the *Gymnasium* (grammar school), as a perceived pinnacle of excellence, as sacrosanct.

Generally, *Tendenzwende* did not refer, initially at least, to large numbers of writers abandoning their left-of-center positions, although it must be remembered that there were well-known authors such as Rudolf Krämer-Badoni and Hans Habe who had always generally supported conservative positions. Habe, for instance, was a strident opponent of *Ostpolitik,* claiming that it would open the door to communist influence.[10] (From today's standpoint, it seems more reasonable to claim that it was Western influence that spread eastwards to undermine communism.) Rather than authors changing their views, however, it was rather that intellectuals as a social group came under fire. When Helmut Schmidt became chancellor, he was reported as saying that he had fired the intellectuals who had been members of the previous cabinet.[11] These included Brandt's minister for overseas development Erhard Eppler, a favorite among writers. Intellectuals also came under fire from within their own ranks with two well-known academics launching scathing attacks. The sociologist Helmut Schelsky — best known for having dubbed the postwar generation "the skeptical generation" because of its distrust of all political ideology after Nazi indoctrination — published a 1975 book with a title that, given the importance attached to work at that time by most Germans, did not lack a touch of demagogy: *Die Arbeit tun die anderen* (The Work Is Done by Others). The subtitle made Schelsky's thesis clearer: "Klassenkrieg und Priesterherrschaft der Intellektuellen" (Class Warfare and Priest-like Rule of Intellectuals). What Schelsky is claiming is that intellectuals have come to occupy a dominant role in society, which they use to undermine the existing order. It is true that Schelsky speaks of people of all political persuasions having the same power through the media to achieve a monopoly position for their points of view — what he calls "Gesinnungs-herrschaft"[12] — but his main wrath is undoubtedly reserved for the political Left. This can be seen by his comments on the new class of intellectuals who stand opposed to those whose productive work assures the functioning of society (14) and his scathing attack on Heinrich Böll, who is scornfully described as a cardinal and martyr (342–63).

A year after Schelsky, the political scientist Kurt Sontheimer published his book *Das Elend unserer Intellektuellen* (Our Sorry Intellectuals), which was a clear attack on the political thinking of the intellectual Left. Its appearance was more surprising in that the author had been involved in the Sozialdemo-kratische Wählerinitiative during the 1969 election campaign. His argument is that the democratic consensus of the Federal Republic is under threat from the leftist theory associated with the student movement. Specifically, he claims that core values and ideas of the Federal republic are being undermined.[13] Although he concedes that left-wing radicals have no success at the electoral or governmental level, he nevertheless maintains that they can have an unsettling effect on the world of politics. One wonders, however, how a set of ideas can be both ineffective and dangerous at the same time.

The widening gap between writers and intellectuals and the world of politics in the 1970s can also be illustrated by two publications by Dieter Lattmann that reflected his experiences as a practicing politician. The first, with the telling title *Die Einsamkeit des Politikers* (The Loneliness of the Politician, 1978), appeared when he was still a member of parliament. The hint of resigned self-pity in the title is immediately confirmed in the opening pages:

> Kaum jemand ist verlassener als ein Abgeordneter, der nach einer Abend-versammlung im Wahlkreis spät in der Nacht hinter Scheinwerfern hundert oder mehr Kilometer nach Hause fährt. Auf die Rolle im Mittel-punkt der Diskussion, die er eben noch ausgeübt hat, folgt jäh die Isolation.[14]

> [Hardly anyone is more abandoned than a member of parliament, who, after an evening meeting in his constituency, drives home at night behind his headlights for a hundred or more kilometres. After his role at the center of discussion, which he has just performed, isolation follows abruptly.]

He goes on to criticize the tone of parliamentary debates and to list his various disappointments, for example, at the low priority given to cultural policy.

If this first volume was a collection of brief impressions, then the second, *Die lieblose Republik* (The Cold Loveless Republic, 1981), which appeared shortly after the end of his parliamentary career, provided a wider sense of the frustrations he experienced. One element of political life Lattmann criticizes is the way parliamentarians are obliged to follow the party whip, a process he describes under the chapter heading "Erpressung" (Blackmail).[15] He himself fell foul of the whips when he refused to support the Schmidt government's antiterrorist legislation. It seems, however, to have been more than concerns over individual issues that turned him against staying on as a politician; he shows a much-wider unhappiness about the whole ethos of the Federal Republic, as in his comments on the economic system that recall the title of his book. He speaks of the all-pervading power of money and the way most people buy goods of which they have no need, summing his remarks up with the metaphor "Immer häufiger friert uns in geheizten Räumen" (More and more often, we freeze in heated rooms; 146). The tone here recalls the 1950s when the dichotomy between the worlds of politics and literature was particularly wide. Certainly, Lattmann is expressing himself in a literary rather than a political register. Moreover, he speaks of the relationship between writers and politicians as being fundamentally damaged (45).

It is small wonder that Lattmann came in for major criticism from Kurt Sontheimer in another book *Zeitenwende?* (A Change of Era?), which again was highly critical of German intellectuals. Lattmann is taken to task for not confronting and trying to bridge the gap between literature and politics, but for instead retreating into the idealistic moral isolationism of the critical intellectual.[16] Despite the passages referred to above, this does appear a harsh judgment. Lattmann remains aware of the realities of politics — for instance, the need for a government to retain a majority in order to pursue its program — while he does show human sympathy for the arch-pragmatist Helmut Schmidt.[17] Especially in *Die Einsamkeit des Politikers* there is an awareness of the difficulties of politics, expressed by Max Weber in his distinction between the ethic of the politician and that of the intellectual and in his celebrated image of politics as being "ein starkes und langsames Bohren von harten Brettern mit Leidenschaft und Augenmaß zugleich" (drilling down strongly and slowly through thick boards with passion and a sense of perspective at the same time).[18]

It is ironic that Lattmann left politics in the year that Helmut Schmidt indulged in a major public political debate with the two leading writers Günter Grass and Siegfried Lenz at the time of the 1980 elections, although he had met privately with them and some of their colleagues on occasions before. As it turned out, there was not a great meeting of minds. Where Grass expressed his disappointment over the gulf between writers and politics in Germany, Schmidt saw it as more or less part of the natural order of things. Moreover, the federal chancellor did not see it as part of his duty to educate

his fellow citizens by taking part in debates on cultural matters.[19] Any rapprochement between writers and the SPD at the end of the 1970s has, in
fact, to be seen not so much as a great meeting of minds but as a result of a
single shared purpose: preventing Strauß becoming Federal Chancellor. The
fear of this brought several writers, even Martin Walser, back to the SPD, at
least to the extent of supporting the Sozialdemokratische Wählerinitiative.

Terrorism I: The Case of Heinrich Böll

Undoubtedly the major issue that had alienated writers from the political
world and other sections of society was terrorism. As the student movement
disintegrated at the end of the 1960s and early 1970s, a few of those associated with it began to indulge in acts of terrorist violence. These included the
journalist Ulrike Meinhof whose columns in the magazine *Konkret*, which in
the late 1960s combined left-wing politics with something approaching soft
porn, carried a certain weight in student circles. Meinhof's participation in
the violent freeing of Andreas Baader, who had been involved in an arson
attack on a Frankfurt department store, from detention in May 1970 marked
the beginning of the Baader-Meinhof Group or Red Army Faction. There
followed a series of bank raids and clashes with the police that led to deaths
on both sides. When a bank raid, during which a policeman was killed, took
place in Kaiserslautern in late 1971, the mass-selling Springer daily *Bild-
Zeitung* immediately assumed that the Baader-Meinhof Group was to blame.
This provoked an angry response from Heinrich Böll, the aftermath of which
showed up the extent of hostility now felt in certain sections of society toward those they associated with the intellectual Left.

Böll's essay "Will Ulrike Gnade oder freies Geleit?" (Does Ulrike Want
Mercy or Safe Conduct?) first appeared in *Der Spiegel* in early 1972. Firstly,
it is a general attack on the Springer Press for its treatment of the subject of
terrorism, denouncing its reporting as "nackter Faschismus, Verhetzung,
Lüge, Dreck" (naked fascism, incitement, lies, filth).[20] Specifically, Böll expresses his anger over how the issue of who might be responsible for the events
in Kaiserslautern has been prejudged. Secondly, the essay represents an attempt to consider the position of the terrorists and offer a way out. He combines the two issues in his proposed solution: that Meinhof be offered safe
passage prior to trial and that Springer should be tried for incitement (228).

Insofar as it appeared to equate Meinhof and Springer, such a statement
was bound to create controversy. What is more, even some of those who
were in sympathy with the attack on the Springer Press could be unhappy
that Böll was not taking the phenomenon of terrorism seriously enough. In
the essay, he concedes that the terrorists have declared war on society, but
regards it as an unequal struggle of six against sixty million, also claiming
somewhat dubiously that the terrorists are more violent in theory than in
practice. Equally, he sees them to a degree as victims, as they are constantly

persecuted and denounced (223). Toward the end of this essay, he goes even further in this direction when he turns to the question of the possible arrest and trial of the terrorists. He seeks to remind his readers, particularly any who were once persecuted by the Nazis, of what it is like to be an outcast, posing the rhetorical question: "Waren auch nicht sie, die ehemals Verfolgten, einmal erklärte Gegner eines Systems, und haben sie vergessen, was sich hinter dem reizenden Terminus 'Auf der Flucht erschossen' verbarg?" (Were they, those formerly persecuted, not once declared opponents of a system, and have they not forgotten what lay behind the charming expression 'shot while trying to escape'?"; 228). Compassion for those he sees as victims is a frequent element in Böll's fiction. Hence, it is not surprising that, during the subsequent controversy about the essay, Böll states that those being persecuted or sought for whatever reason were ultimately in the same position.[21] It is interesting to note that he includes Nazis fleeing justice in this category, while suggesting that they might find it easier than others to find a refuge.

The attacks on Böll, following the publication of his essay, were numerous and violent. Not surprisingly, the Springer Press was in the vanguard. In addition to its own journalists, it was able to field the rightist duo Rudolf Krämer-Badoni and Hans Habe. The first shots by Krämer-Badoni were fired the day after the appearance of Böll's essay. They take the form of frequent rhetorical questions aimed at undermining Böll's logic, along with scathing references to Böll's position at that time as president of the International PEN club. Taking into account the club's role in the struggle to preserve authors' rights to free expression, Krämer-Badoni coins the unlikely compound noun *Meinungsfreiheitspräsident* (freedom-of-opinion president) in a way that, at the very least, smacks of demagogy (*FG*, 36) In his comments, Habe compares Böll's position on the Baader-Meinhof question with his stance on another controversy of the day, the Soviet dissident Bukovsky, who had just been sentenced to two years imprisonment, five years forced labor, and five years internal exile. In a television interview, Böll had said that he was not permitted by the statutes of the PEN club to protest in his role as president and that, before making private protests, he would have to consider whether he might do more harm than good. Such a cautious tactic, which was in no way an acceptance of Soviet actions, does not meet with Habe's understanding. His polemics reach their height (or rather plumb their depths) when he insinuates that someone like Böll would not have stood up against the Nazis:

> Es sei dringlich geworden, sagte Böll in London, daß der PEN zur Umweltverschmutzung Stellung nehme. *Aber von der intellektuellen Umweltverschmutzung der Sowjets will Moskaus westlicher Liebling, der sich, wie die Amerikaner sagen würden, als "Goodie-Goodie" ausgibt, als ein Hans*

*Wohltäter-in allen-Gassen, nichts wissen. Er hat keine arroganten Freiheits-
begriffe, der Präsident. Er hätte wohl, ware er zur Zeit Ossietzkys PEN-
Präsident gewesen, die Hitlerschen Freiheitsbegriffe respektiert.* (*FG,* 56)

[It had become urgent, Böll said in London, for PEN to take up a position on environmental pollution. *But Moscow's Western darling, who presents himself, as the Americans would say, as a 'goodie-goodie,' as a Lord
Bountiful, does not want to know about Soviet intellectual pollution. He, the
president, has no proud concepts of freedom. He would presumably, if he had
been PEN-President at the time of Ossietzky, have respected the Hitlerian
concepts of freedom.*]

Habe's attack, too, has to be condemned as demagogic. It seems unlikely,
for instance, that Alexander Solzhenitsyn would have stayed with Böll following his enforced emigration from the Soviet Union if he had perceived
Böll's attitude to that state in the same way or, alternatively, that a pro-
Soviet Böll would have given him hospitality.

Attacks on Böll were not limited to the Springer Press. Other areas of
the media, which might have felt more inhibitions, also did not mince their
words. The daily newspaper published in his birthplace of Cologne, the
Kölnische Rundschau, did not seek to defend the city's famous son, but
spoke of understanding words for terrorism as part of a critical climate
breeding violence (*FG,* 70). The public service broadcasting system, despite
the legal requirement of balance, also transmitted highly critical material. On
24 January 1972, a television commentary by Ulrich Frank-Planitz spoke of
drawing-room anarchists in general and of Böll specifically as the advocate of
anarchist gangsters (*FG,* 85). Böll's response was to describe the commentary as denunciatory and fascist and to state that he would no longer
contribute to that particular station, the Südwestfunk (*FG,* 86). He was then
accused of not being willing to accept freedom of expression for others, an
accusation he turned on its head with the tongue-in-cheek reply that he was
in fact limiting his own freedom of expression by closing down this avenue
of communication with the public (*FG,* 101). Given the clamor, publications
such as *Die Zeit* and *Der Spiegel* that defended Böll found it difficult to calm
the overall charged atmosphere.

A more measured criticism of Böll came from the SPD politician Diether
Posser, at that time the minister of justice in North Rhine-Westphalia. While
condemning the reporting of the *Bild-Zeitung,* as indeed the German Press
Council did, Posser also criticizes Böll on four counts. Firstly, although he
accepts that Böll does not sympathize with terrorism, he points out that the
terrorists' claim — quoted by Böll — that they do not shoot first is not
borne out by the facts, of which examples are given. His second point is that
Böll, by stating that the terrorists were more violent in theory than in practice, is in fact playing down the offenses committed by them, which range

from murder to arson and armed robbery. Hence, it is totally inappropriate to compare them with the victims of National Socialism. Posser's third point concerns the prosecution of captured terrorists. Quoting examples, he maintains that terrorist trials are conducted in a proper manner and that acquittals are not unknown. Fourthly, he takes exception to Böll's terminology, particularly the two terms "mercy" and "safe conduct." He points to a disparity between their usage by Böll and the requirements of the law. He concludes that, although Böll has raised his voice on important issues, he has let his emotions run away with him. Specifically, in Posser's view, Böll wanted *Besinnung* (reflection), but had failed to follow his own advice (*FG*, 84).

Replying, Böll shows some acceptance of the criticisms made, conceding that Posser was right both in general terms and on some points of detail (*FG*, 142). He also admits in an interview that his reaction to Planitz had been wrong, blaming it on his sense of isolation at the time (*FG*, 182), although he never concedes that he underestimated terrorism in his essay, quite simply because it had not reached its height in 1972.[22] What is particularly interesting in his reply to Posser, however, is his emphasis on his position as a writer. This, he claims, means that he uses language differently from other professions In other words, terms such as "mercy," "persecuted," and "crime" have a different meaning for him than for lawyers, civil servants, ministers, and police officers (*FG*, 142). The implied refusal in this statement to differentiate between fictional work and political essays contrasts sharply with the standpoint of Grass, as described in chapter 3 of this volume, and leaves him arguably open to the charge of impractical dilettantism.

In the light of this possibility, it was as well that Böll's most powerful and successful response to his critics, particularly to those in the Springer Press, came in literary form. The story *Die verlorene Ehre der Katharina Blum oder: Wie Gewalt entstehen und wohin sie führen kann* (The Lost Honor of Katharina Blum, or: How Violence Develops and Where It Can Lead, 1974), is principally a critique of the workings of the tabloid press and specifically the *Bild-Zeitung*.[23] The story shows how the eponymous heroine, who had spent one night with a young man suspected of being a terrorist, is hounded by a tabloid reporter until she is finally driven to procure a gun and shoot him. That Böll gives his fictional newspaper the generic title *die ZEITUNG* (the PAPER) shows how he is also interested, beyond one particular publication, in the whole issue of journalistic responsibility. There is also a major contrast between the methods of sensationalist journalism and those used by the book's narrator, who seeks objectivity and avoids emotion by reporting the murder at the beginning of the text. (This example is not followed in Volker Schlöndorff's film version, where the narrative is linear and thus can be accused of seeking to rouse emotions.) It is equally significant that Katharina is in most senses a very ordinary and conventional young woman, as is shown by her using much of the money she earns to pay off the mortgage on her flat, her most prized possession. The point is that even such a person is not safe from prurient intrusion and is capable of being driven to an act of despair. That Böll's attack hit home was not only confirmed by the sales figures (half a million copies of the paperback edition within just over a year), but also by the suspension by the Springer Press of the publication of bestseller lists as long as this particular text formed part of them. Those who criticized Böll at this time often made fools of themselves — for example, the CDU politician and subsequent federal president Karl Carstens, who in a speech in Duisburg in December 1974 showed his inability to understand this particular work and, one suspects, any work of fiction by totally identifying Böll with his fictional character and seeing the story as a justification of violence.[24]

Another of Böll's fiercest critics found himself in judicial hot water. In November 1974, in a broadcast for Radio Free Berlin, the journalist Matthias Walden accused Böll of having fertilized the soil of violence. In a case that went as far as the Federal Constitutional Court, the station was forced to pay 40,000DM in compensation. This is not to say that the attacks on Böll did not have a lasting effect. In September 1977, at the height of the crisis to be discussed in the next section, Die Zeit reported that spectators present at the scene of the kidnapping of the industrialist Hanns Martin Schleyer suggested that the terrorists responsible would be drinking coffee with the famous author.[25]

Terrorism 2: The German Autumn

As terrorism grew more serious in the Federal Republic during the 1970s, culminating in 1977 with the murder of three prominent citizens from the worlds of industry and the law, writers in general, but particularly those who could be linked with the student movement, came under increased pressure. Their longstanding adversary, Franz Josef Strauß, made the claim that there was a causal link between New Left ideology in the 1960s and the terrorism of the 1970 that was seeking to destroy the state through violence, blackmail, and murder.[26] In a parliamentary debate in the autumn of 1977, the right-wing CDU politician Alfred Dregger at least insinuated that the intellectual Left was guilty of destroying the values of the Federal Republic in the same way as Hitler had been of destroying the basic values and historical consciousness of most Germans.[27]

It was not just writers who were put under pressure by the CDU/CSU over terrorism. The SPD-led government, too, was urged to respond — not only by its political adversaries but also by large sections of the media who were undoubtedly reflecting parts of public opinion. The result was tighter antiterror legislation, which in turn mobilized writers to protest out of the fear that democracy itself was being undermined. The bleakest picture of what was happening was undoubtedly presented by Alfred Andersch in a highly controversial poem of 1976 entitled "Artikel 3 (3)," a reference to the section of the Basic Law that forbade discrimination on all kinds of grounds including political opinions. Andersch speaks of the new Gestapo, the new concentration camp, torture, and the "geruch einer maschine, die gas erzeugt" (stench of a machine producing gas) (*VLMS,* 297–98). When asked how he could speak of torture, Andersch refused to differentiate between mental torture inflicted on those falling foul of the Radicals Decree and the physical brutality of the Gestapo (*VLMS,* 298–99). How far such a view was correct remains a matter of opinion. What is undoubtedly true is that Andersch's choice of words, even in the context of a poem, cannot have helped to overcome entrenched positions held at this time.

Other writers preferred a different kind of stance, seeing themselves not as undermining the state, as Strauß claimed, but rather as defenders of the Federal Republic's democracy. The chairman of the VS, Bernd Engelmann, in a declaration during a press conference in October 1977, made a point of saying "Noch ist dies auch unsere Republik" (This is still our republic too), an intertext with what Tucholsky had said in the Weimar years (see the introduction, above), but expressing an entirely opposite sentiment (*VLMS,* 310). In this way, he was seeking to combat in advance any claim that intellectuals were turning their back on the state, as it was often claimed their predecessors had done during the Weimar period, thereby contributing to democratic society's failure to combat the menace of Hitler. In similar vein, a volume that appeared in the autumn of 1977 (the time when terrorism dominated the political agenda, and which opponents of the prevailing climate dubbed the "German autumn," and this not just because of the season of year) was entitled *Briefe zur Verteidigung der Republik* (Letters in Defense of the Republic). In this collection, which achieved an edition of 110,000 by the end of the year, writers and others expressed their concerns in the form of letters about what was happening to the country in the name of combating terrorism. Of the roughly 25 letters, some were addressed to named individuals, some to institutions, and some to a nonidentified group or individual — for instance, a neighbor or an educated liberal. Among the contributors were the writers Heinrich Böll, Siegfried Lenz, and Nicolas Born, the artist Klaus Staeck, and the theologian Dorothee Sölle. Various generations were also represented. Two older writers, Axel Eggebrecht and Hans Erich Nossack, speak somewhat resignedly about their fellow countrymen. Eggebrecht points out that democracy has always been implanted into Germany rather than being an achievement of the German people itself,[28] while Nossack perceives an abiding petit bourgeois trait in Germans that comes to the surface at certain times, creeping up the walls "wie Hauschwamm" (like dry rot) and destroying the whole superstructure.[29] If Nossack resorts to this mixture of Marx and literary metaphor to express his pessimism, others adopt a different and more incisive stance, and none more so than the academic and critic Walter

Jens. Not only does he reject any idea that writers are to blame for terrorism, but he also states that the correct response is more, not less, democracy, as his title "Isoliert die Desperados durch mehr Demokratie" (Isolate the Desperados Through More Democracy) shows.[30] This kind of more positive thinking is also found elsewhere. Nicolas Born rejects any idea that the Federal Republic has become a police state,[31] while, despite everything, Martin Walser finds words of praise for the SPD government.[32]

After this first volume, a companion appeared the following year with the title *Briefe zur Verteidigung der bürgerlichen Freiheit* (Letters in Defense of Civil Liberty). Here the impression given is of a more structured work, with the letters appearing under five different headings. The first deals with the plight of seven individuals regarded, or in one case regarding herself, as suffering because of the climate of intolerance, while the second turns more generally to the defense of liberality in the Federal Republic. Of the remaining three sections, the most substantial deals with the Filbinger affair, which will be discussed separately below. In general, the impression is that the issues of late 1977 are no longer so pressing. Although the book concludes with two warnings, one of the issues raised cannot be described as dealing with a potentially apocalyptic issue: the radical Catholic writer Carl Amery's open letter to Franz Josef Strauß is an unsuccessful request to the Bavarian first minister not to include Otto von Habsburg, the son of the last Austrian emperor, in the list of CSU candidates for the European Parliament.[33]

As was the case with the events surrounding Böll discussed in the previous section, the terrorism crisis of 1977 also afforded opportunities for writers to respond with more literary means. One such occasion was offered by comments made by the Lower Saxon minister for higher education, Eduard Pestel. On the murder of one of the prominent victims of terrorist violence in 1977, the federal prosecutor Siegfried Buback, a Göttingen student published an obituary that, while criticizing the murder itself, spoke of a feeling of "klammheimliche Freude" (superclandestine joy) on hearing of the murder. This was enough to provoke outrage, which intensified when forty-three academics re-published the obituary and their reactions to it. This in turn prompted Pestel to demand that the academics in the service of the state who were involved in this publication sign a loyalty declaration rejecting violence and declare their willingness to support the state actively. This demand, which certainly smacked of totalitarianism, prompted a volume of reactions that appeared under the title *Nicht heimlich und nicht kühl* (Not Secret and Not Cool). Peter Schneider ironically suggests that a mere signature under a document was not sufficient as a proof of loyalty and declares his love for Herr Pestel personally.[34] Peter O. Chotjewitz, in his "Beichte des Staatsbürgers" (Confession of the Citizen) uses religious language to profess his loyalty: "Herr, im Lichte Deiner Wahrheit erkenne ich, daß ich gesündigt habe in Gedanken, Worten und Werken. Ich soll Dich meinen Staat und

Herrn über alles lieben, aber ich habe mich selbst mehr geliebt als Dich" (Lord, in the light of Your Truth, I admit that I have sinned in thought, word and deed. I shall love You my state and lord above all else but I did love myself more than You.)[35]

Chotjewitz also reacted to the issues raised by terrorism and the response to it in the traditional literary form of the novel, publishing *Die Herren des Morgengrauens* (Gentlemen of the Dawn) in 1978. The main character — like Chotjewitz himself, a writer and a lawyer (Chotjewitz was one of Baader's defense team) — runs afoul of the eponymous gentlemen of the dawn (namely, the security services) because of his political activities. The similarities between author and character link this work with the subjective dimension found in much 1970s literature; the other link is with Kafka and specifically *Der Prozeß* (The Trial). Not only does Chotjewitz call his work a fragment, he also begins it with a clear reference to the opening words of Kafka's novel: "Jemand musste in Fritz Buchonia ein schlechtes Gewissen erzeugt haben, denn ohne daß er sich einer Schuld bewußt gewesen wäre, hatte er eines Morgens einen Traum" (Somebody must have produced a bad conscience in Fritz Buchonia, because without his being aware of any guilt, one morning he had a dream).[36] In this case, the literary intertext seems to work better than the rather heavy satire quoted above.

The literary canon also played a central part in Heinrich Böll's contribution to another important response to the events of 1977, the film *Deutschland im Herbst* (Germany in Autumn). Böll contributed a script that presented a discussion in a committee about whether it was still possible to perform Sophocles's *Antigone*. Sad to relate, Böll was not only indulging his talent for satire. There was a link with reality, as performances of the play had indeed been canceled in Stuttgart because of the sensitivity of the theme of resistance to the state.

However ludicrously some of those in positions of authority had reacted to the events of 1977, there remained the question of whether writers did share some responsibility for the phenomenon of terrorism in the 1970s. One certainly was directly involved. Peter Paul Zahl shot at a policeman while trying to escape arrest in 1972. He received a sentence of fifteen years, of which ten (an unusually high proportion) were served. Looking back in 1984, Peter Schneider admitted that he had been attracted to terrorism and added that he was far from alone, with the concepts of armed struggle and the urban guerrilla being frequently discussed during teach-ins attended by thousands.[37] A volume that appeared a decade after the events with the telling title *Der blinde Fleck* (The Blind Spot, 1987) was based on the idea that the Left had been unwilling in the past decade to reflect on the phenomenon of terrorism. Like Schneider, the journalist Klaus Hartung specifically claims that sympathy for terrorism was not a figment of the state's imagination.[38] It does not of course follow from this that leftist writers and intellectuals were somehow responsible for the phenomenon of terrorism; what motivates individuals to specific actions cannot be determined by such simplistic explanations. At the time, Max Frisch suggested that it was potentially the whole of society that was to blame. Speaking to the SPD party conference in 1977, he put forward the idea of a shared guilt because of a lack of understanding for the concerns of a whole generation (*VLMS*, 312–13). Given the difficult relationships between generations in Germany because of the Nazi past, these were reasonable issues to raise. Nevertheless, it remained true that many terrorists came from the same middle-class backgrounds and had similar educational backgrounds to the writers of the same generation. This perhaps explains why, in the years after Hartung and other contributors to the aforementioned volume spoke of a reluctance to consider the phenomenon of terrorism, numerous literary works have sought to portray both it and those responsible for it.[39] As for the issue of terrorism itself, it remained — although not on the same scale — along with the Nazi period and the years of division, an uncomfortable part of German history, as the dispute before the opening of an exhibition in 2005 in Berlin about the Rote Armee Fraktion showed.

Moments of Triumph

Even if the 1970s were such a difficult time for writers, there were moments of triumph. One such was the part played by Rolf Hochhuth in unseating Hans Filbinger from his post as first minister of Baden-Württemberg (incidentally, one of the few occasions when it is possible to assert that political intervention by a writer had direct consequences). In 1978, Hochhuth published the fruits of his research, which showed that Filbinger as a military judge during the Second World War had played a part in at least one extremely unjust death sentence and, even after the defeat of Germany, had continued to apply Nazi legal criteria in Norway in the spring of 1945, when German troops had surrendered to the British but internal disciplinary matters remained officially in German hands. Presenting his findings in *Die Zeit*, Hochhuth coined the term "ein furchtbarer Jurist" (a fearsome lawyer) to describe Filbinger, which went into the language as a description of Nazi lawyers.[40] Hochhuth's discoveries created an almighty stir. He was attacked both in the press and by CDU/CSU politicians. The affair prompted Franz Josef Strauß to refer to him and his ilk as "Ratten und Schmeißfliegen" (rats and blue bottle flies), an insult with Nazi undertones that helps to explain why so many writers flocked to the anti-Strauß cause during the 1980 election campaign. Other CDU politicians like Helmut Kohl flocked to Filbinger's defense, prompting a reply by Hochhuth in the volume *Briefe zur Verteidigung der bürgerlichen Freiheit*.[41] As for Filbinger himself, he ignored the famous political adage of not digging when in a hole by refusing to recognize anything amiss in his previous conduct and by his apparent inability to distinguish between statute and the ideal of justice. He was duly forced into resignation.

Another success was achieved in 1977 when the investigative writer Günter Wallraff, suitably disguised, managed to obtain a job at the *Bild-Zeitung* and reported on his experiences in the volume *Der Aufmacher* (The Lead Story), which immediately became a bestseller.[42] Wallraff tells, for example, of invented stories, such as one about Majorca holidays spoiled by bad weather when in fact the sun had shone continuously, and more seriously, of the power of the Springer Press to destroy individuals' lives. Following publication, *Der Aufmacher* faced several challenges in court; in the end, however, Wallraff was not forced to omit any part of his original text. In that the *Bild-Zeitung* did not substantially change its ways and become a minority taste, Wallraff's book did not have the same direct effect as Hochhuth's researches. On the other hand, he did set up a support fund for those who wished to fight against what they considered to be inaccurate reporting by the paper.

One of the measures taken by the Schmidt government with the aim of combating terrorism was to make it illegal to advocate in written texts violence that might endanger the constitutional order of the Federal Republic. Since this was potentially a form of censorship, many writers were exceedingly unhappy. One book to fall victim to the thinking behind this law was the autobiographical *Wie alles anfing* (How Everything Began) by the former terrorist Michael "Bommi" Baumann, even though it partially repudiated the path of violence and advised terrorists to throw their guns away. In fact, the book was confiscated by police in the autumn of 1975 before the new legislation had gone through parliament. In that it anticipated the new legislation, this action was *de facto* the first time it was invoked, as the introduction to the new edition of 1977 suggests.[43] This was prefaced by the names of so many celebrated editors, including Delius, Handke, Enzensberger, and a number of publishing houses, that prosecution of them all would no doubt have kept the courts busy for decades. As it turned out, the act was repealed in 1980, something that might be regarded as a victory over the return to the kind of censorship practiced in the Adenauer era. It had become clear that administrative methods were highly unlikely to be an effective way of defeating terrorism.

The 1970s in the GDR

Although the GDR continued to exist until 1990 and its traditional structures remained intact until the events of the autumn of 1989, it could be argued that its fate was sealed in the 1970s. How far this might be true politically and economically is a topic beyond the scope of this book but certainly such a claim is not inappropriate with reference to the field of culture. By the end of the decade, it was clear that the Honecker era, despite all talk of "no taboos," did not mean the creation of a climate in which the aspirations of those writers and intellectuals who were loyal to the GDR but wanted change and reform could be met. In fact, by this time, official policy was as rigid as ever and many of those who had once identified with the ideals of the state had left or been obliged to leave for the Federal Republic or West Berlin.

The double-edged nature of Honecker's "no taboos" promise was referred to at the beginning of the chapter. What this might mean in practice became clear in the debate surrounding Plenzdorf's work *Die neuen Leiden des jungen W.* The GDR's leading lawyer, Friedrich Karl Kaul, for example, who had represented the state's interests in the Auschwitz trial of the 1960s, expressed his disgust at such a dubious character as Plenzdorf's Wibeau being the hero of a socialist work of literature. However, when the leading journal *Sinn und Form,* in which the text of the story first appeared, included in its first edition of 1973 a documentation of a debate that had taken place at the GDR Academy of Arts in the autumn of 1972, other leading figures — for instance, the established writer Stephan Hermlin, who apparently enjoyed a good personal relationship with Honecker — were willing to defend Plenzdorf, saying that his work provided a convincing picture of young working-class youths in the GDR.[44] This view was not apparently shared by Honecker himself, who spoke of society being blamed for personal sufferings (see *GDL,* 188).

Nevertheless, Plenzdorf's work, not least its stage adaptation, remained popular, while others were emboldened to speak out. Christa Wolf, for instance, was critical of censorship that in turn could lead to the even-more-problematical self-censorship in a 1974 journal article (*KP,* 157), while at the Seventh Artists Conference in 1973, the newly elected chairman Willi Sitte spoke of the need for an atmosphere of trust and understanding in the field of culture (*KP,* 156). Trust and understanding were also core themes in Volker Braun's story *Unvollendete Geschichte* (Unfinished Story, 1977), which can be seen, with the benefit of hindsight, as almost prophetic of the dangers that engulfed the GDR in 1989. The two main characters are Karin, the daughter of a party functionary, and her boyfriend Frank, an ordinary worker who runs afoul of the state because of suspicions that he wishes to leave the GDR. When Karin becomes aware of these unfounded suspicions, which she believes could be cleared up without difficulty, she asks a series of rhetorical questions including "Warum habt ihr uns nicht gefragt?" (Why didn't you ask us?) and, addressed to those in official positions, "Warum bemißtraut ihr einander, statt zu sagen, was euch Sorge macht?" (Why do you distrust one another instead of saying what is worrying you?).[45] The message of the book, where the word *Geschichte* in the title also appears to include its other meaning of "history," is that unless those in power change their ways, the GDR will fail. Now that the history of the GDR is finished, it is clear which path was taken. As for Braun's work itself, it was not reprinted in the GDR until the end of the 1980s, in itself a sign of the increasingly frosty intellectual climate.

That the GDR was beginning to dig its own grave is a conclusion that can also be drawn from the events of 1976. When the writer and singer Wolf Biermann, who, as noted above, had not been allowed since the mid-1960s to perform in the GDR, except for occasional concerts in churches, the one area of GDR society where the government's writ did not run completely, was away on a concert tour in the Federal Republic, he was stripped of his citizenship. Here was the GDR turning its back on a critical socialist, a native of Hamburg who had elected to live in the eastern part of Germany. The result was a letter of protest signed by other critical writers and intellectuals (*VLMS*, 303–4). They pointed out that, notwithstanding the criticisms of the GDR made by Biermann in his first Western concert in Cologne — criticisms that had provided the pretext for that state to rid itself of its long unwanted citizen — he had clearly shown his preference for the East over the Federal Republic. The signatories, too, in the most part wanted reform in the GDR rather than the Western model; nevertheless, a number of them, for example Jurek Becker and Rolf Schneider, were soon to move to the West, although these two and others retained their GDR citizenship, at least for a time.[46] The mass exodus of writers and others involved in the area of culture was the lasting result of the Biermann affair. Rather than seeking to maintain the loyalty of its critical intellectuals, in many cases the GDR seemed just to want to be rid of them, even if, in some cases, they did not really want to go. Some did stay — for example, Volker Braun and Christa Wolf — while some of those who left turned into fierce critics of the GDR and their former colleagues — for example, Hans Joachim Schädlich.

The end of the decade saw another event that cast the cultural policy of the GDR in the worst possible light. The main target was Stefan Heym, who had published his critical novel *Collin* in the Federal Republic without official permission and was fined 9,000 Marks for his pains. Heym had returned to live in Germany after the war following his exile in the United States, where he had also had citizenship. This was not a particularly appealing pedigree to the GDR authorities, even if Heym was a socialist who, like Biermann, had chosen to live in the GDR. Following an orchestrated campaign, Heym was excluded from the Berlin branch of the Writers Association along with other critical colleagues like Klaus Schlesinger and Rolf Schneider. Based on the evidence of the transcripts published in 1991 under the title *Protokoll eines Tribunals,* the process itself can only be described as a witch-hunt. An opening salvo was fired by the loyalist novelist Dieter Noll who spoke of *kaputte Typen* (an equivalent of which might be "deadbeats") who cooperated with the GDR's Western enemies.[47] The meeting at which the miscreants were expelled did at least offer Heym the chance to defend himself.

He pointed out that he had always been a socialist, having been persecuted by the Nazis not solely on account of his *Hakennase* (hooked nose; 48), whereas the person he undoubtedly saw as his chief tormentor, the chairman of the GDR Writers Union Hermann Kant, had once worn the Nazi uniform (47). Given Kant's youth at the time, this was undoubtedly a blow below the belt, but arguably justified against someone who, despite his talent and status, generally retained an unswerving loyalty to the GDR authorities.[48]

Conclusion

If the 1960s were marked by many writers' increased identification with their respective states — West German writers involving themselves in the democratic process and East Germans like Christa Wolf creating a GDR literature with its own specific themes relating to the development of the country — then the 1970s became a time of increased alienation. The hopes of the earlier part of the decade in both countries for a better relationship between the worlds of politics and literature were not fulfilled. At the same time, it is important to differentiate. Western writers were not forced to leave the country, nor did they have the wish to do so, as they continued to recognize the merits of the Federal Republic and strove to defend its democratic values. In the GDR, writers were afforded no such chance, unless they supported official policies more or less completely. What happened in the GDR at this time, specifically the departure of critical writers to the Federal Republic and West Berlin, did play a part in reawakening an interest in the issue of Germany as a whole, an important question throughout the 1980s, which was of course to be resolved at the end of the decade.

Notes

[1] Peter Schneider, *Lenz* (Berlin: Rotbuch, 1973), 28.

[2] Verena Steffen, *Häutungen* (Munich: Verlag Frauenoffensive,1975).

[3] Ulrich Plenzdorf, *Die neuen Leiden des jungen W.* (Rostock: Hinstorff, 1973).

[4] Willy Brandt, "Braucht die Politik den Schriftsteller?," in Lattmann, *Einigkeit der Einzelgänger*, 9–18, here 18.

[5] Horst Krüger, "Der Staat und die Intellektuellen," *Frankfurter Hefte* 27:7 (1972): 488–95, esp. 491–92.

[6] Klaus Harpprecht, "Die SPD und ihre Intellektuellen," *Die neue Gesellschaft*, 18:11 (1971): 824–27, here 824.

[7] Peter Schneider, *. . . schon bist du ein Verfassungsfeind* (Berlin: Rotbuch, 1975).

[8] Dieter E. Zimmer, "Ein Kapitel Geist und Macht," *Die Zeit*, 17 May 1974, 13–14.

[9] Hermann Schreiber, "Dabei sein ist out," *Der Spiegel*, 6 September 1976, 46–52.

[10] See Hans Habe, *Leben für den Journalismus,* vol.3 (Munich, Zurich: Knaur, 1976), 146.

[11] See Dietz Bering, *Die Intellektuellen: Geschichte eines Schimpfwortes* (Stuttgart: Klett/Cotta, 1978), 1–6.

[12] Helmut Schelsky, *Die Arbeit tun die anderen* (Opladen: Westdeutscher Verlag, 1975), 333. Further citations given in parentheses.

[13] Kurt Sontheimer, *Das Elend unserer Intellektuellen* (Hamburg: Hoffmann und Campe, 1976), 63.

[14] Dieter Lattmann, *Die Einsamkeit des Politikers* (Frankfurt am Main: Fischer, 1982), 7.

[15] Dieter Lattmann, *Die lieblose Republik* (Frankfurt am Main: Fischer, 1984), 134–40. Further citations given in parentheses.

[16] See Kurt Sontheimer, *Zeitenwende?* (Hamburg: Hoffmann und Campe, 1983), 155–59.

[17] See Lattmann, *Die lieblose Republik,* 60.

[18] Max Weber, *Politik als Beruf,* 82.

[19] For more information, see "'Der Kanzler ist kein Volkserzieher.' Gespräch zwischen Helmut Schmidt und Siegfied Lenz, Günter Grass, Fritz J. Raddatz," *Die Zeit,* 22 August 1980, 29–31.

[20] Heinrich Böll, "Will Ulrike Gnade oder freies Geleit," in *Ende der Bescheidenheit: Schriften und Reden 1969–72* (Munich: DTV, 1985), 222–29, here 225. Further citations given in parentheses.

[21] Frank Grützbach, ed. *Freies Geleit für Ulrike Meinhof. Ein Artikel und seine Folgen,* 143. As this volume consists of short pieces, individual references will not be made.

[22] See "Rufschädigung ist eine ansteckende Krankreit," in Heinrich Boll, *Werke. Interviews I,* ed. Bernd Balzer (Cologne: Kiepenheuer und Witsch, no year), 696–701, esp. 698.

[23] Heinrich Böll, *Die verlorene Ehre der Katharina Blum* (Cologne: Kiepenheuer und Witsch, 1974).

[24] For the context of these remarks, see the volume published by the City of Cologne in 1992, *Heinrich Böll und sein Verlag Kiepenheuer und Witsch,* 69.

[25] See *Heinrich Böll und sein Verlag,* 69. The original comments were published in the 9 September 1977 edition of *Die Zeit.*

[26] Franz Josef Strauß, "Die Zeit der Entscheidung ist da," in *Gegen den Terror,* ed. Walter Althammer (Stuttgart: Verlag Bonn Aktuell, 1978), 22–30, esp. 23.

[27] See *Verhandlungen des Deutschen Bundestags 8. Wahlperiode. Stenographische Berichte,* Band 103 (Bonn 1977), 4103.

[28] Axel Eggebrecht, "Die Enkel der Hitlergeneration," in *Briefe zur Verteidigung der Republik,* ed. Freimut Duve, Heinrich Böll, and Klaus Staeck (Reinbek: Rowohlt, 1977), 39–42, esp. 39.

[29] Hans Erich Nossack, "Unser Feind ist immer das Kleinbürgertum. An meinen in Brasilien lebenden Bruder," in Duve, Böll, and Staeck, *Briefe zur Verteidigung der Republik*, 124–25, here 125.

[30] Walter Jens, "Isoliert die Desperados durch mehr Demokratie," in Duve, Böll, and Staeck, *Briefe zur Verteidigung der Republik*, 86–90.

[31] Nicolas Born, "Eines ist dieser Staat sicher nicht: ein Polizeistaat," in Duve, Böll, and Staeck, *Briefe zur Verteidigung der Republik*, 20–24.

[32] Martin Walser, "An die Sozialdemokratische Partei Deutschlands," in Duve, Böll, and Staeck, *Briefe zur Verteidigung der Republik*, 156–59.

[33] Carl Amery, "Brief zur Verteidigung des Freistaates," in Duve, Böll, and Staeck, *Briefe zur Verteidigung der bürgerlichen Freiheit* (Reinbek: Rowohlt, 1978), 224–29.

[34] Peter Schneider, "PS zur Unterschrift der Professoren unter die Erklärung des Ministers Pestel," in *Nicht heimlich und nicht kühl*, ed. Heiner Boehncke and Dieter Richter . (Berlin: Ästhetik und Kommunikation Verlag, 1977), 28–29.

[35] Peter O. Chotjewitz, "Beichte eines Staatsbürgers," in Boehncke, *Nicht heimlich*, 38–39, here 38.

[36] Peter O. Chotjewitz, *Die Herren des Morgengrauens* (Berlin: Rotbuch, 1978), 5.

[37] Peter Schneider, "Plädoyer für einen Verräter," *Der Spiegel*, 13 February 1984, 66–69, here 66.

[38] Klaus Hartung, "Die Linke und die RAF," in *Der blinde Fleck* (Frankfurt am Main: Verlag Neue Kritik, 1987), 148–59, esp. 158.

[39] For a review of recent fiction dealing with the subject of terrorism, see Julian Preece, "Death and the Terrorist in Recent German Fiction," in *Politics in Literature: Studies on a German Preoccupation from Kleist to Améry*, ed. Rüdiger Görner (Munich: iudicium, 2004), 171–86.

[40] Rolf Hochhuth, "Schwierigkeit, die wahre Geschichte zu erzählen," *Die Zeit*, 17 February 1978, 41.

[41] Rolf Hochhuth, "Parteien und Autoren," in *Briefe zur Verteidigung der bürgerlichen Freiheit*, ed. Duve, 180–96. Strauß's comments are to be found on 180.

[42] Günter Wallraff, *Der Aufmacher* (Cologne: Kiepenheuer und Witsch, 1977).

[43] Michael Baumann, *Wie alles anfing* (Frankfurt am Main: Anabas Verlag et al., 1977).

[44] For a concise overview of the debate surrounding Plenzdorf, see *KP*, 153–54.

[45] Volker Braun, *Unvollendete Geschichte* (Frankfurt am Main: Suhrkamp, 1989), 76.

[46] For the names of some of the writers leaving the GDR, see *KP* 187.

[47] Reprinted in Joachim Walther et al., eds., *Protokoll eines Tribunals* (Reinbek: Rowohlt, 1991), 97–98, here 97. Further citations given in parentheses.

[48] For a review of Kant's career as Chairman of the Writers Union, see *KP*, 167–69.

6: The 1980s: On the Threshold

Political Developments

THE RESULT OF THE 1980 ELECTION, which saw the governing parties increase their share of the vote, can, as noted earlier, be regarded less as an endorsement of Helmut's Schmidt's government than as a rejection by the electorate of Franz Josef Strauß as a potential chancellor. Given that he was particularly unpopular in the north German states, the election emphasized the traditional German divide between Protestant north and Catholic south, which had been overshadowed by the postwar East-West division. Nor was the continuation of the SPD-FDP coalition the cause of any widespread enthusiasm. Without Strauß it might have come to an end earlier, as one reason for its existence, Willy Brandt's *Ostpolitik*, was no longer at the top of the political agenda and divergent attitudes within the coalition on economic policies were becoming more apparent. It was these divergences, together with the desire of the FDP to show it was not tied to one coalition partner forevermore, that led to the end of the coalition in 1982, with Schmidt being ousted and replaced by the CDU leader Helmut Kohl as a result of the FDP switching its allegiance. Specifically, the change of government was made possible by the mechanism of the constructive vote of no confidence, which means that, unlike in the Weimar Republic, a government can only be toppled if there is a majority for a successor administration. The new government was confirmed in office in early 1983 when the federal election was brought forward. This election also brought a change in the number of parties represented in the parliament, for the first time in two decades. The Greens emerged as a serious political force and were able to enter parliament by virtue of achieving more than five per cent of the popular vote.

On becoming chancellor, Helmut Kohl spoke of a *Wende* (change of direction), the first use of that term (the second being at the time of unification). As it turned out, there was at least as much continuity as change. Despite the tensions of the Reagan years, relations with the Soviet Union and its allies never broke down completely, with Honecker even making an official visit to the Federal Republic in 1987. It is true that, faced with the challenge of the increasingly popular Gorbachev, Kohl did compare the Soviet leader to Goebbels, but in the longer term that remark did not prove too damaging. In the area of domestic policy, Kohl was helped by the recovery of the world economy from the oil-price shocks of the 1970s and early 1980s. The German model, proclaimed by the SPD a decade earlier, seemed to be continuing to prove its worth. It appeared to matter little that Kohl, because of his perceived provinciality and culinary tastes — in particular, his predilection for *Saumagen* (pig's stomach) — was the butt of jokes in academic and intellectual circles. He led his coalition to another victory in 1987 and was set to achieve to further triumphs after unity in 1990 and 1994.

If the 1980s were a time of improvement in economic terms for the Federal Republic, for the GDR they were a time of a decline that in the end turned out to be terminal. Faced with increasing economic problems at the beginning of the decade, the GDR negotiated a major loan in the Federal Republic, with the role of intermediary being played by none other than the ideological enemy, Franz Josef Strauß. In another reversal of the previous situation, relationships with the Soviet Union became strained on Gorbachev's assumption of power, as the increasingly geriatric leadership rejected any notion of reform or liberalization. Even the Soviet youth publication *Sputnik* was banned in 1988, while chief ideologue Kurt Hager responded to Gorbachev's reforms by saying that just because one's neighbor was repapering his house, there was no need to follow suit. This kind of comment was enough to drain away any remaining hopes among increasingly large sections of the population that the GDR would become an attractive alternative to its Western neighbor. When in 1989 on the fortieth and last anniversary of the state's founding Gorbachev famously commented that those who come too late are punished by life, the die was already cast. The Soviet Union was no longer willing to maintain the existence of the GDR through the ultimate threat of military intervention — and the country's citizens had lost all belief in its future.

Literary Developments

In the 1980s, literary life in the Federal Republic was more diffuse than in earlier decades. The major figures of earlier times, who had been associated with the Gruppe 47, no longer held such a dominant position, and the death of Heinrich Böll in 1985 underlined that an era was coming to an end. It was not that the older generation stopped writing or lost popularity — Martin Walser, following the success of his novella *Ein fliehendes Pferd* (Runaway Horse, 1978), enjoyed more popularity than with some earlier works. Nor did the themes of earlier decades — for example, the Nazi past — disappear from literature. This was shown by what were called *Vater-Bücher*. The year 1980 saw the publication of Christoph Meckel's *Suchbild. Über meinen Vater* (Puzzle Picture. About My father) and Peter Härtling's *Nachgetragene Liebe* (Love Carried Forward), in which the authors tried to come to terms with their fathers' conduct during the Third Reich. Later,

Peter Schneider used the magazine articles of the son of the infamous Auschwitz doctor Josef Mengele as the basis for his work *Vati* (Daddy, 1987), in which the son of a Nazi war criminal recounts his relationship with his father. The difference between such works and, for instance, the early works of Günter Grass was that their authors' direct experience of National Socialism did not go beyond childhood, and so they had much more the perspective of outsiders. The narrator in Grass's *Katz und Maus,* roughly of the author's own generation, was racked by guilt about his wartime role in corrupting his friend Mahlke and thus leading him to perdition. The questions were different for those born just a little later, as was the case with Härtling and Meckel, born in 1933 and 1935 respectively. They can already be said to belong to a different generation, whose perspective brought change to one of the enduring themes of postwar literature.

In his history of preunification German-language literature, Ralf Schnell entitled his chapter on the period 1978–89 "Zwischen 'Post-Histoire' und 'Widerstandsästhetik'" (Between "post-histoire" and the "aesthetic of resistance"; *GDL,* 441–512). If the second term suggested the continued importance of the sociopolitical themes of previous decades, the first implied a break from the social realist and/or modernist writing associated with those decades, and the dawn of the era of postmodernism. One work of the 1980s that can be associated with this elusive concept and that — sadly, a rare occurrence for texts written in German in recent decades — became an international bestseller, was Patrick Süskind's 1985 novel *Das Parfüm.* In recounting the story of a bestial murderer, a relevance to the German past can be seen. Nevertheless, the novel is most remarkable for its use of language and for its literary and historical allusions that, regardless of the eighteenth-century setting, make it anything but a conventional historical novel.

The generational change taking place in the 1980s can also be underlined by the full emergence of Botho Strauß and the Austrian Peter Handke. It was in connection with the latter that the present author, together with colleagues, entitled a volume of essays on 1980s literature *Literature on the Threshold.*[1] The metaphor of the threshold implies a time of transition, as did Schnell's chapter heading. One crosses a threshold to move to a new location or situation, which was what German literature did with German unity. In their political statements and activities, as will be seen later in the chapter, some writers were, either consciously or unconsciously laying the groundwork for this change.

It is as difficult to categorize the literature of the GDR of the 1980s as that of the Federal Republic. If in previous decades they had seen their role as being critical socialists, hoping to contribute to necessary change, such a stance was no longer desired or tolerated by the state. Many emerging authors, such as Monika Maron and Wolfgang Hilbig, were only published in the Federal Republic. Maron's *Flugasche* (Flight of Ashes, 1981) dealt with the problem of industrial pollution, which was topical enough, given the growing importance of the environmental issue in the Federal Republic and elsewhere, but which was largely a taboo subject in the GDR. Other younger authors appeared to turn away from the direct treatment of political questions altogether, preferring to concentrate on the aesthetic and the production of texts that owed a great deal to contemporary French literary theory. Insofar as this literature — primarily associated with the then-rundown East Berlin suburb Prenzlauer Berg — sought new forms of expression, it was critical of wooden official discourse. It was, however, as an underground counter-culture, with many works produced outside the official publishing industry in very small runs or small magazines, that Prenzlauer Berg attracted attention, not least in the Federal Republic and other Western countries.

More established GDR writers showed a distinct lack of enthusiasm for their society. A good example was provided by Christoph Hein's novel *Der Tangospieler* (The Tango Player, 1989), which was set in the Ulbricht era. The eponymous hero Dallow has provided the musical accompaniment to satirical sketches that were unacceptable to the authorities, and finds himself dismissed from his university job and sent to prison. He then leads a cynical and somewhat dissolute life working at a holiday resort, until the year 1968 offers him the chance to return to academia — an idealistic colleague dismisses reports of the Soviet-led invasion of Czechoslovakia as Western propaganda and is suspended from his job, thus providing an opening for Dallow. The implication is that hard-bitten cynicism is the quality needed to survive in the GDR. It is of course also significant that the events of 1968 in Czechoslovakia play an important role; they too contributed to the loss of credibility for the GDR as an alternative to the Federal Republic.

Writers and Politics

The End of Commitment?

In 1988, Hans Magnus Enzensberger — as ever in the vanguard of contemporary thinking, or even arguably an influential force in creating such thinking — published an essay suggesting that the German dichotomy between the worlds of politics and the intellect was no longer a serious subject. Rather, this dichotomy manifests itself at the level of playground games; hence the essay's title: "Macht und Geist: Ein deutsches Indianerspiel?" (Power and Intellect: A German Game of Red Indians?). For example, he compares the sniping between the two realms with the bickering of old married couples.[2] The questions Enzensberger raises about the political role of the writer will be considered in more detail in the conclusion of this work; in this context it is only important to note his major thesis that society has changed, with the state, as he provocatively puts it, withering away in the face of an increasing plurality of social forces. Accordingly, neither politicians nor writers enjoyed the same status or played the same role as before (216).

This essay was written half a decade after the CDU's return to power, which, as noted above, was accompanied by proclamations of a change of direction. Whatever was intended, this did not involve the kind of open warfare against writers and intellectuals that had been a feature of the Adenauer and Erhard years. It is true that the relatively hardline CSU minister of the interior Friedrich Zimmermann prevented the film *Das Gespenst* (The Ghost) — by the avant-garde Bavarian writer Herbert Achternbusch — from receiving public financial support; in general, however, the world of the arts went its way without interference from the Kohl government, while writers, in keeping with Enzensberger's diagnosis of changed times, did not involve themselves in party politics as in the previous two decades. The 1980s saw the demise of the Sozialdemokratische Wählerinitiative, although a successor organization, the August-Bebel-Kreis, initially chaired by Walter Jens, was intended to be a place where intellectuals could scrutinize new SPD policies. This body was complemented by the party's Kulturforum, the brainchild of the then–general secretary, the donnish Peter Glotz, which sought to influence the general intellectual climate of the Federal Republic.

Events around the 1987 federal election offered the opportunity to capture the atmosphere of the early Kohl years. Initially, it should be noted that for the first time in over two decades Günter Grass, who incidentally had finally become a member the SPD out of a sense of solidarity at its loss of power in 1982, was not present on the campaign trail, having taken off to Calcutta, a place he continued to visit as part of his growing interest in Third World topics. To an extent, his role was taken over by the artist Klaus Staeck, who organized mass meetings in support of the SPD and gained support from, for example, Jürgen Habermas and the dramatist Tankred Dorst. There was also, as in the 1960s, the publication of a paperback volume in time for the election, but this time the title did not proclaim an alternative to a despised government but asked a question: *Wählen — aber wen?* (Vote — but For Whom?). It is true that the answers provided to the question do not contain ringing endorsements of the CDU. Equally, there is a sense of *déjà vu* to some of the reluctant endorsements of the SPD — for example, that given by the novelist and journalist Ralph Giordano: the party will gain his vote "trotz ihrer bekannten historischen Fehler, ihres Zaudertums, ihres blanken Opportunismus, ihrer gräßlichen Unentschuldbarkeiten" (despite its known historical failings, its dithering, its naked opportunism, its hideous unforgivable mistakes).[3] The younger Berlin writer Bodo Morshäuser does not even go as far as this. In a piece that can hardly be described as subtle, he damns more or less all contemporary politicians and their works, noting of those in his own generation intent on a political career that they are *Streber und Schleimer* (strivers and greasers), distinguished by their spots and stuttering.[4] It seems small wonder that an essay by that close observer of social developments Michael Rutschky, which appeared shortly before the election, should proclaim a lack of interest in it among "us," meaning no doubt younger intellectuals. His argument is, in fact, similar to that of Enzensberger's. The Federal Republic has progressed far enough for there to be no danger of a relapse into authoritarian structures.[5]

Despite much of the above, it would be wrong to say that writers' traditional concerns about the world of politics had disappeared entirely. A year after the 1987 election, the publisher and scholar Heinz Ludwig Arnold edited a volume titled *Vom Verlust der Scham und dem allmählichen Verschwinden der Demokratie* (Concerning the Loss of Shame and the Gradual Disappearance of Democracy), the contributors to which expressed their concern about, the political direction the Federal Republic was taking. It contains a typical barnstorming piece by Günter Grass attacking the CDU campaign, which did indeed use highly dubious methods against the SPD leader in Schleswig-Holstein, Björn Engholm.[6] The same affair, specifically its treatment by the *Frankfurter Allgemeine Zeitung,* is the subject of the contribution by Friedrich Christian Delius.[7] Dieter Lattmann sees a more general danger in keeping with the book's title. Recalling in time-honored and arguably exaggerated way the negative course of German history, he sees a danger that a renewed threat to democracy might not even be recognized.[8]

If many of the contributors to Arnold's volume, who also include Peter Rühmkorf and Klaus Staeck, can generally be associated with the SPD, then other authors turned toward the Greens. Indeed, this new party is the answer given by some respondents in the 1987 election publication to the question of which party they will vote for. However, it can be claimed that support for the Greens, or at least concern about the issues they raise, represents a break with the old type of political involvement. Although participating in political life, the Green party did, in its early years, see itself as an "anti-party party," seeking to break with the political establishment of the Federal Republic.

Going Green?

Interest among German writers and intellectuals in the environment and related issues associated with the Green movement was not something that suddenly developed in the late 1970s and 1980s, as the example of Hans Henny Jahnn quoted in chapter 2 above shows. Nevertheless, such interest did come much more to the fore at the same time as ecological concerns began to play a major part in German political life with the emergence of the Greens. Among those who openly supported the party were, at the end of his life, Heinrich Böll and, at the time of the 1987 election, two prominent women writers: Luise Rinser and Karin Struck. Rinser was even the candidate for the Greens in the 1984 election for federal president, albeit with no prospects of success given the balance of power in the Bundesversammlung (electoral college), which has the responsibility for choosing the incumbents for that office. In her supportive essay for the 1987 election, while not being entirely uncritical of the Greens, she expressed strong support for one of their major ideas of that time — an increase in direct democracy.[9] By contrast, one of Karin Struck's major reasons for supporting the Greens appears to have been the need to teach the SPD a lesson. The feminist metaphor that titles her piece in the 1987 election volume is taken from within her text: "SPD wählen hieße, dem Chefarzt die Blumen zu bringen, nachdem Mutter und Hebamme ein Kind zur Welt gebracht haben" (To vote SPD would mean giving the senior doctor the flowers after mother and midwife have brought a child into the world).[10] The child is of course the environmental movement, to whose coat tails Struck now sees the SPD somewhat hypocritically attaching itself. Another writer, who, while not necessarily a Green supporter, showed a strong environmental awareness at this time, was Siegfried Lenz, who writes plaintively in a 1980 essay of lakes and rivers being allowed to die, water being poisoned and wasted so that there is a real danger of shortage in the foreseeable future.[11] Lenz's solution is greater public investment and putting environmental protection on the school curriculum, arguably both as much Social Democratic as Green ideas.

Lenz makes his comments in a volume entitled *Kämpfen für eine sanfte Republik* (Fighting for a Gentle Republic, 1980), which, given the continuity of editorship, can be seen as a sequel to the two earlier ones in defense of democracy and civil liberty in the Federal Republic referred to extensively in the previous chapter. At the same time, the adjective *sanft* indicates the hope for a change of political paradigm of the kind aspired to by the Greens. In fact, it became a very fashionable word in the early 1980s among those who sought to change societal values. That values did change, at least in intellectual life, is suggested by a 1984 article by the literary critic Fritz J. Raddatz, who discerned the end of an era that had been dominated by the rationalism of enlightenment-based ideas.[12] The committed Social Democrat Günter Grass, it will be recalled, had always seen himself as a child of the Enlightement, while Jürgen Habermas continued to consider the achievement of modernity an unfinished project in the Federal Republic.[13]

The movement in many quarters away from enlightenment values in the 1980s manifested itself in a variety of ways. A group of young Tübingen-based intellectuals established a new periodical, *Konkursbuch* (literally, bankruptcy book), as a counter to *Kursbuch,* which retained the reputation of being in the vanguard of leftist rationalism, an opposition underlined by the subtitle *Zeitschrift für Vernunftkritik* (Magazine for the Critique of Reason). A best-selling author in the 1980s who expressed ideas that can be associated with the changed mood was Michael Ende. His novel *Die unendliche Geschichte* (The Neverending Story, 1979) is ostensibly a children's book that

juxtaposes the real world with the imaginary kingdom of Fantastica, a place
that ultimately only exists through human imagination. In the novel, it has
to be rescued by a boy, Bastian Balthasar Bux — in the real world an unhappy isolated individual, but one capable of making the necessary leap of
the imagination to rescue the other kingdom. He is in fact transported to
Fantastica, where he not only has wonderful adventures but also learns important lessons — in particular, the value of love. The novel is manifestly
didactic and carries clear political implications. In one passage, the world of
Fantastica is contrasted with the real world of lies and power. Before Balthasar
rescues it, Fantastica is in danger of being sucked into the void along with its
inhabitants. One of these, Atreju, who subsequently befriends Balthasar, is
told by a werewolf of the dangers this would entail, many of which sound
like a litany of many intellectuals' worries. The first problem is that he will be
"ein willenloser und unkenntlicher Diener der Macht" (a mindless servant of
power, with no will).[14] Then he is told that, with his aid, people might be
made to buy superfluous goods, hate those they do not know, and fall prey
to beliefs that make them easy to manipulate. From this, Artreju is able to
draw the conclusion that the more of Fantastica that is destroyed, the more
lies will flood the human world. It is small wonder that Ende became a kind
of guru to environmentally conscious young people opposed to the consumer society, with some of them even making pilgrimages to his home in Italy.

Ende's specifically political views can be gleaned more directly from a
volume that appeared in 1982 under the title *Phantasie, Kultur, Politik* (Imagination, Culture, Politics). It is a record of conversations held at his home
between himself, the actor and head of a Stuttgart theater project Hanne
Tächl, and the former Social Democrat minister Erhard Eppler. The discussions between the three reveal a remarkable degree of unanimity about
the need for a new kind of politics, with Ende, however, being most radical
in his rejection of a society driven by technology. He goes as far as to question the whole tradition of logical Socratean thought, saying that it is necessary to question urgently where the world is being led by what he calls "die
ganze wissenschaftliche Aufklärung" (the whole scientific enlightenment).[15]
His ideal is that of a new human consciousness that could change political
life completely. What is more, imagination, culture, and politics should not
be separate domains but be integrated to create a new kind of politics. He
gives as an example of this the possibility that in some cases a decision about
a new law might depend on a theatrical performance (52).

It is not easy to place Ende's views on a traditional left-right scale. He
speaks of capitalism as "der eigentliche Krankheitsherd" (the real source of
the sickness; 53), but equally rejects state intervention whenever there is a
problem. In his ideal world, the state would be banished from such spheres
as higher education, where institutions would have to rely on the drawing
power of professors to attract students. In a rare disagreement, Eppler takes

up a traditional Social Democratic stance against what seems an extreme form of liberalism, saying that it is only the state that at present protects the weakest in society and promotes more equality. Ende's ideal, however, remains the creation of a new form of democracy based on totally different institutions.

It has to be concluded that Ende's ideas are largely unpolitical and impractical. The same can be said of much of the thinking associated with the early years of the Greens, who, in the light of experience, did change a great deal over the next two decades. It is small wonder either that there were challenges at the time. Kurt Sontheimer's book *Zeitenwende?* — referred to in the previous chapter — not only takes Dieter Lattmann to task, but also denies that the real nature of politics has changed. In a 1983 essay, Peter Schneider, too — who was by this time abandoning many of his previous leftist standpoints — showed his skepticism about the ideals of the Green movement. He accuses the Greens of having an unrealistic vision of a harmonious world from which conflict can be eradicated. Because of this, they come to regard all that is evil as extraneous to the true nature of man, something that makes them more akin to a revivalist movement than a political grouping. Hence, they come to make absolute demands that are ultimately unpolitical or alternatively potentially dangerous. Instead of accepting that politics is an area where experiments are necessary in the search for solutions, they adopt "einen rechthaberischen, im Prinzip totalitären Gestus" (a self-opinionated, basically totalitarian pose).[16] With hindsight, this does seem exaggerated, given the direction the Greens eventually took, with the so-called "Realos" (realists) triumphing over the "Fundis" (fundamentalists). It should also not be forgotten that they raised serious ecological issues of continuing relevance today.

War and Peace

If the adjective *sanft*, as referred to above, expressed the hope for a future where the aggressive use of technology might give way to a more ecologically aware society, then the noun *Angst*, which was also much used in intellectual circles in the 1980s, reflected a related sentiment: worry that a continuation of current confrontational foreign policies would lead to atomic destruction. In the late 1970s Chancellor Schmidt detected what he saw as an imbalance in the nuclear arsenals of the major powers — namely, that the Soviet Union was developing medium-range missiles that had no equivalent on the Western side. The result of this was what became known as the NATO dual-track policy; if negotiations (the first track) with the Soviet Union over the new missiles failed, then the West would respond (the second track) by arming itself with its own weapons (Cruise and Pershing missiles) to counter the perceived threat. The German word of the time, *Nachrüstung*, made clear how the official policy was being presented: This was new weaponry to "catch up," this idea being expressed by the preposition *nach* in the sense of "after."

To many writers it was no such thing; rather, it was a dangerous escalation that made nuclear war all the more likely and with it, if not universal destruction, at least the destruction of Germany, which was likely to be turned into a nuclear battleground in the event of war. This is, in fact, the title of a 1983 article by the novelist Gerhard Zwerenz — "Deutschland automatisiertes Schlachtfeld" (Germany, Automated Battlefield) — in which he wonders how he can still sit comfortably in his chair.[17] It was worry about this kind of scenario that gave rise to such a sense of fear among numerous writers and intellectuals in the early 1980s. One example is the volume entitled *Mut zur Angst* (The Courage to Have Fear, 1982), in which many famous authors express their anxieties over the threat of war. It includes, for example, an open letter to Chancellor Schmidt written in 1980 and signed by Günter Grass, Peter Schneider, Sarah Kirsch, and Thomas Brasch, the last two being authors who left the GDR at the time of the Biermann affair. The letter makes peace the ultimate priority, in the interests of which not just compromises, but also utopian fantasies have to be accepted.[18] In his contribution to the collection, Heinrich Böll presents, on his own admission, such a fantasy — that the word *Frieden* (peace) should be given a special place in official vocabulary. Thus, soldiers would greet each with the cry "Frieden."[19]

The columns of *Die Zeit* from the early 1980s provide a picture of what might be called the anxiety debate, brought about by reactions to the perceived military and ecological threats. The thesis of a 1981 piece by the cultural editor Dieter E. Zimmer is that it is remarkable how little anxiety there is in society.[20] In the same year, the psychologist Horst Eberhard Richter speaks of fear and unrest being the appropriate responses to the current political situation.[21] By contrast, in the same edition as Zimmer's article, the sociologist Erwin K. Scheuch speaks of fearfulness becoming arrogance,[22] while the newspaper's one-time proprietor Gerd Bucerius tells his readers not to wallow in fear.[23] A little later, the former chancellor Schmidt adopted a sovereign pose in telling the readers in Biblical terms, "Fürchtet Euch nicht" (Fear not). He admits, it is true, to having felt fear himself, but sees it as a purely private emotion with no place in politics, where it is likely to have a number of disastrous effects. Some politicians might exploit citizens' fears, idealistic visions might replace practical politics, and power might fall into the hands of inexperienced dilettantes.[24] It is not difficult to conclude who does not fall into the dilettante category. More surprising is the conclusion to the article: the existence of God as the ultimate determining force in history makes anxiety inappropriate. Such a view contrasts strongly with the reactions of many Christians, especially in the Protestant churches, at that time.

The all-German nature of the concern over the growth of nuclear weaponry has already been illustrated by reference to the open letter signed by writers from both Western and Eastern backgrounds. This aspect was further underlined by the discussions that took place in the early 1980s on the issue between writers from both German states. That such gatherings took place at all, albeit within the framework of other discussions between European writers from both East and West, was a major new development. Even if it has to be accepted that the participation of East German writers in discussions with their Western counterparts could not have taken place without official approval and might therefore be regarded as part of the general propaganda exercise of the GDR and its allies against new American missiles, such approval did imply the existence of a specific and significant German dimension to the debate. Moreover, what was said, not least by some GDR writers, frequently did not fit in with the state's official standpoints.

The first, largely intra-German discussion took place in East Berlin in December 1981, with no further aim in mind than a general exchange of views. The suggestion by Grass that there should be some final resolution or communiqué was not acceptable to the majority. As the transcript shows, a variety of topics were raised, including the role of the superpowers, the German dimension, and the influence writers might be able to exercise over events. Whereas nobody present was willing to defend the policies of the United States, attitudes to the Soviet Union showed considerable variation. Grass saw both superpowers in an equally negative light, but many of the East German writers — for example, Erik Neutsch and Helmut Baierl — identified totally with the official stance of their government and hence with the Soviet Union. Nevertheless, other GDR writers made critical comments: Günter de Bruyn spoke about the negative attitude toward unofficial peace movements in the GDR. Forcing them underground would, in de Bruyn's view, hamper the cause for peace and undermine the state's credibility in this area.[25]

As for the German dimension, this, too, was expressed powerfully by a GDR writer, Jury Brežan, who claimed that action by Germans could move the world toward peace and that as a people they carried a particular responsibility for peace (43). The question of the role of writers in the peace movement also gave rise to a number of interesting comments. The Westerner Günter Herburger stressed the connection between writing and the whole issue of survival: as a writer, it was his task to preserve things from destruction, and books, even if they remained comparatively unknown for a century or more, might survive to emerge at some future date (146). For many writers, it was important to stress the difference between their world and that of the politicians. Peter Rühmkorf pointed to the significance of language in this respect. Writers should preserve their own kind of language to resist that of bureaucrats involved with the technology of war (92). Ingeborg Drewitz made a similar point but reached a more concrete conclusion. It was the very weakness of writers as peripheral members of society that gave them the strength as part of the peace movement to find alternatives to the present militarized world (25–27).

Notwithstanding the variety of views expressed, the general feeling gained from reading the transcript of this first Berlin meeting is that of a common purpose among the writers from the two German states in the search for peace. This is much less the case with the second meeting that took place in West Berlin in April 1983, when controversy was much more the order of the day. It was pointed out, for instance, that the records of the first debate had never been published for the general public in the GDR. Additionally, there was the question of the harsh treatment meted out shortly before the meeting to unofficial peace activists in the university town of Jena. The major controversy, however, centered round the nature of peace itself. Was peace merely the absence of armed conflict — in other words, the situation that had existed in Europe since 1945 — or did it imply something more? The first view was taken by the GDR writers largely in sympathy with their government's policies, with Hermann Kant rejecting any equation of the superpowers and laying particular emphasis on the Soviet Union's policy of no first use of nuclear weapons.[26] By contrast, other writers wished to connect the issue of peace with that of human rights, specifically the imposition of martial law in Poland and more generally the whole question of the postwar division of Europe following the 1945 Yalta conference. It was a Hungarian guest, György Konrád, who first raised the issue of Yalta. He was strongly backed up by Peter Schneider, who, in comments on Poland, maintained that Yalta had spoken of free elections in that country and not the establishment of a single-party dictatorship (113). Hans Christoph Buch adopted a similar position on human rights, saying that peace and human rights were inextricably linked (95). A contrasting position from the West German side came from Bernt Engelmann, the chair of the VS at the time. While acknowledging the right to criticize the status quo in Eastern Europe, he maintained that the desire to make the other side change could not be the basis of peace and disarmament (134). In the case of diplomats this may well be true, but is arguably less so for writers with a different vision from that of negotiators.

How any joint efforts should continue was an issue at the West Berlin meeting. Grass wanted a meeting near a Pershing base, while the mercurial Stefan Heym, referring to the new Soviet weaponry, suggested an SS20 launching pad. As it turned out, the next mass gathering of writers in the cause of peace took place in Heilbronn, close to an American base but without the presence of GDR writers, something that, given the location, would have been somewhat problematic. At this meeting, Grass was very much to the fore. Along with Hans Christoph Buch, Peter Härtling, and others, he launched the Heilbronn Appeal of December 1983. The appeal called on those concerned to reject military service in the Federal Army since the new weapons — regarded by the writers as offensive — gave the army as part of NATO an unconstitutional role: the Basic Law mandated a purely defensive role for the armed services. This appeal caused considerable controversy, particularly because, in his speech at Heilbronn, Grass had used the term *Wehrkraftzersetzung* (subversion of military strength) to describe his future attitude to the military.[27] Earlier in the year he had called upon parliamentarians to reject the deployment of missiles, comparing a vote for them as equivalent to the sanctioning of the Enabling Act that gave Hitler absolute power in 1933.[28]

A good twenty years later, what is one to make of these debates? There is no doubt that there was a major concern about peace, as is shown by the phenomenal success of the book *Frieden ist möglich* (Peace is Possible, 1983) by the television journalist Franz Alt, with nine editions in the year of its appearance.[29] Nevertheless, it is important to note that there was criticism at the time. The head of an institute for peace and conflict research in Bonn, Hans-Adolf Jacobsen, took Grass to task both for his arguments — specifically, the invalid comparison between 1933 and fifty years later, since there was now no party wanting war — and for the way he advanced them, using the word "infantile" to describe those in favor of the new missiles and at the same time castigating those who called the Soviet Union the enemy for their excessive language.[30] The meetings between writers from the two German states did not find favor with some who had left the GDR following persecution. One such writer was Jürgen Fuchs, who refused to attend the West Berlin meeting and drew particular attention to the role of the GDR Writers Union, some of the leading members of which, including the chair, Hermann Kant, were present. Fuchs listed the following as being among the methods used by the GDR and the Writers Union against dissident authors: slander, blackmail, fines, expulsion from the Union, and bans on public readings.[31] While this was undoubtedly true and, with hindsight, the danger to peace was undoubtedly less than thought at the time, the peace campaign did have the effect of bringing writers from both parts of Germany together to seek common ground. Moreover, the wider pressure exerted by the peace movement certainly kept politicians on their toes in both German states. Chancellor Kohl, for instance, responded to the peace movement's call to create peace without weapons by speaking of achieving the same goal with fewer weapons.

The Theme of Germany

The all-German dimension of the issue of peace coincided with a growing, and arguably related, reawakening of interest in the question of Germany as a whole, since any nuclear threat concerned both parts of the country. Clearly, the issue of German unity had never gone away for the political Right, while the move to the Federal Republic or West Berlin by so many

GDR writers inevitably raised questions about the nature of the relationship between the two German states. After all, in some cases, the GDR writers did not choose to go, nor were they sent to Austria or any other German-speaking area.

The name that became most associated with a more intense interest in matters German was that of Martin Walser. Some of his earlier work — for example, some of the short pieces collected in "Ein deutsches Mosaik" (A German Mosaic) — showed, if not an endorsement of division, at least an exasperation with how the issue of German unity was exploited by certain political forces. By the late 1970s, however, he was directly expressing his strong dislike of the division of Germany. In a 1977 speech, for example, he speaks of his "Bedürfnis nach Deutschland" (need for Germany).[32] Two years later, in a collection edited by Jürgen Habermas to mark the thirtieth anniversary of the Federal Republic, Walser asks why division was accepted as natural when it arose out of a temporary constellation of events.[33]

In the same volume, Dieter Wellershoff, while conceding that re-unification is an "unträumbarer Traum" (undreamable dream),[34] admits that he cannot forget the idea of Germany as a whole. He also admits that he approves of the internal order of the Federal Republic but, because of this idea of Germany as a whole, he is unable to develop much of an emotional attachment to it. His love of Germany as a whole prevents him from seeing the Federal Republic as anything other than a merely acceptable place to live (78–79). If these kinds of sentiments are not surprising for a generation that retained memories of a united Germany — Walser was born in 1927 and Wellershoff in 1925 — this was hardly the case with Peter Schneider, who also turned his attention to German questions in the 1980s, influenced no doubt by the fact that he lived in West Berlin and was thus geographically close to the country's division. His story *Der Mauerspringer* (The Wall Leaper, 1982) contains many documentary elements — specifically, references to events in which and to people for whom the division of Germany had been a central element in their lives. There is also a central plea for the German language as a uniting element, expressed, however, in such a way that there seems to be a political inference. The basis for a common German language must begin, in Schneider's view, by a refusal "das Kirchenlatein aus Ost und West nachzuplappern" (to parrot the Church Latin from East and West);[35] the implication of this is that citizens of both German states need to emancipate themselves from their respective great powers. In another essay from the same period, he puts forward, as admittedly a utopian dream, the idea of equal competition between the two German states within a confederation: "BDDR."[36]

Given the admission, by Wellershoff and Schneider, for example, that any idea of a change to the political status quo was unrealistic (which was soon of course to be proved wrong), it is not surprising that much of the interest in the question of Germany in the 1980s was not concerned with the issue of political unity. This is the case with Günter Grass's story *Kopfge-burten oder Die Deutschen sterben aus* (Headbirths or The Germans Are Dying Out, 1980), which has at least three major themes. The first, encapsulated in the title, has to do with questions of demography, both in Germany and the world. The second, influenced by the approaching federal election, is the perceived continuing threat posed by Strauß. The third is the need to maintain German cultural unity. Not surprisingly, given his opposition to the events of 1989/90, this seems the only kind of unity Grass seems able to countenance. Specifically, he puts forward the idea of a German National Foundation, suggesting that it could be housed in a building spanning the Berlin Wall at Potsdamer Platz. Like his aforementioned colleagues, he has to admit, though, that this idea is a "hellwacher Tagtraum" (wide-awake day dream).[37]

How far interest in the question of Germany had spread in the 1980s is further illustrated by the devotion of the fifteenth edition of *Tintenfisch,* an annual collection of texts by writers and others published by the left-leaning Wagenbach publishing house, to the theme of Germany. Many of the texts are hostile to all things German, a tradition among German writers, as some of the incorporated quotations from Goethe and Hölderlin show. This is especially the case with the text of Peter Paul Zahl, who lists all kinds of reprehensible phenomena and people, including "Speichellecker, Arsch-kriecher, Radfahrer, Denunzianten, Schleimer" (lickspittles, brown-nosers, creeps, informers, slimebags),[38] saying that they are found in other countries but in the greatest number in Germany. If there is nationalism in this volume, it is not expressed in conventional political terms. Hermann Peter Piwitt, for instance, combines his regrets over the lack of interest in language, culture, and tradition with an attack on those who have turned their homeland into a "riesige schmutzige Produktionsanlage" (massive filthy production plant).[39]

How, then, from today's perspective, is this growing interest in Germany among writers in the 1980s to be regarded? It is tempting to see some link with the events that began to unfurl at the end of the decade, to attribute to writers an early sense of forthcoming developments of the kind claimed by Heinrich Mann.[40] Clearly, no such assertion can be proved; equally, it is now hard to dismiss the interest in the theme of Germany in the way it was by some at the time. The political scientist Eckhard Jesse, for instance, wrote of a phenomenon with no political relevance,[41] while Andreas Roßmann, in the title of a short piece reporting a discussion between writers and politicians on the subject of Germany, asked whether Germany was a (literary) fiction.[42] That the worlds of literature and politics could come together is shown by a volume that was conceived before the events of 1989/90 but published during them in April 1990. The title *Mein Deutschland findet sich in keinem Atlas* (My Germany Is Not to Be Found in Any Atlas) smacks at first sight of nonpolitical interest in the idea of Germany. Many of the earlier pieces, dating from before the political upheaval, reflect this, responding directly to the editors' five questions to potential contributors about what they associate with the word Germany. A typical reply is that of Peter Härtling, who associates the term with language and history.[43] Later contributions, however, respond to the events of the weeks and months before the book's publication, with Bernd Wagner, an oppositional GDR writer, seeing a chance for the future in the breaking down of frontiers in Germany and Europe.[44]

Political questions inevitably came to the fore with the changes at the end of the decade. At the same time, it is important to remember that earlier debates had a political dimension, especially in the case of Martin Walser. In 1988, he delivered what proved to be a very controversial speech published under the title "Über Deutschland reden" (Speaking About Germany). In it he argues that division had been a suitable punishment for Germany, given the horrors of the Nazi past, but he goes on to say that the period of probation should now be regarded as over. He also argues at a personal level, speaking about his "elementares Bedürfnis" (elemental need) to be allowed to visit Saxony and Thuringia in quite different circumstances than the current ones.[45] Among those to react angrily to this kind of argument was one of the prominent GDR writers who had moved to the West: Jurek Becker. The title of his response, "Gedächtnis verloren — Verstand verloren" (Memory Lost — Sense Lost), sums up his argument.[46] For someone who, as he states, lost around twenty family members in the gas chambers, it is impossible to forget the past. He also dislikes the emotional level of Walser's arguments, that he advances no concrete reasons for change. Clearly, the stage was already set for the arguments between writers and others that, as will be seen in the next chapter, accompanied the process of unification.

Developments in the GDR

Despite the example of Monika Maron's treatment of the subject of industrial pollution, as mentioned at the beginning of this chapter, in general the political concerns of GDR writers in the 1980s tended to move away from purely internal issues. The all-German dimension of the concern for peace has already been dealt with in the discussion of the meetings between writers from both German states. This theme also found its way into a major novel of the decade: Christa Wolf's *Kassandra* (1983), set at the time of the Trojan War but undoubtedly written with the current situation in mind. The main character is intent on trying to prevent war, but is ultimately defeated by the bellicose forces on both the Roman and Trojan sides.[47] Another work by Wolf from later in the decade, *Störfall* (Accident: A Day's News 1986), takes up the other major theme of the Western Green movement: environmental pollution. In this case, it is not caused by the GDR's own industry but by the Chernobyl disaster of 1985, which, it will be remembered, had an effect as far away from the Soviet Union as Britain.[48]

As mentioned above, GDR writers also took part in the debate on Germany in the volume *Mein Deutschland findet sich in keinem Atlas*. Some did follow the official line, not least the dramatist Peter Hacks, who had moved to the GDR from the Federal Republic in the 1950s. He sees the Federal Republic as simply a neighboring Western foreign country.[49] While he admits it is easy to talk with the inhabitants because of the common language, he also states that it is not a problem to talk with cultivated French or British people either. Günter de Bruyn's contribution, at least by implication, contains a rejoinder to this kind of stance. For him, even those in the GDR who stress the differences with the Federal Republic are influenced by the other German state because they are "fixated" on it.[50] Elsewhere in the text, he stresses, as its title shows, the existence of a single German culture, as does Helga Schubert, who speaks of being part of it.[51] De Bruyn also speaks of the political dimension, asking whether the Germans in the two states had shown a lack of character or been clever in accepting what the rival great powers had imposed in the two parts of the country.[52] Like Walser and Wellershoff in the West, de Bruyn, born in 1926, had memories of a single Germany, as had Stefan Heym, who, despite his identification with the GDR, in 1983 spoke of the division of Germany as an open wound that would continue to fester.[53] Clearly, the theme of Germany had retained its relevance in the GDR despite official attempts in the Honecker era to deny the existence of a single nation.

One reason why specific GDR themes were less prominent in the 1980s may have been the diminution of official pressure. Manfred Jäger speaks, in the title of his chapter on the 1980s, of a chaotic cultural policy lacking a strategic concept (*KP,* 187–263). In fact, writers and others were able to go more on the offensive against official policies, especially over the issue of censorship. Christoph Hein, for example, spoke out strongly against it at the tenth congress of the GDR Writers Union, finding some original arguments that, however tongue-in-cheek, contain a lot of truth. One of these is based on a literal interpretation of the GDR's criminal code and the offense, used as a blunt instrument to stifle criticism, of *Öffentliche Herabwürdigung* (public disparagement of the state) — he suggests that because censorship damages the GDR's reputation, it should itself be classed as coming within the parameters of public disparagement.[54] In fact, publishing and re-publishing policy became more liberal in the late 1980s, while some critical plays were also given first performances (*KP,* 257–60). Occasionally, it was possible to fool the censor, as Uwe Kolbe did with a text entitled "Kern meines Romans" (Core of My Novel), which was published by the Mittel-deutscher Verlag in 1981. It consists of a rhythmically linked list of words, the first letters of which add up to highly critical statements, culminating in "Eurem Heldentum widme ich einen Orgasmus. Euch mächtige Greise zerfetze die tägliche Revolution" (To your heroism I dedicate an orgasm, may the daily revolution rip apart you powerful geriatrics).[55] Less than a decade later, this wish was history's command.

Conclusion

The 1980s clearly marked the end of an era, if only for the reason that the political entities with which writers had had to grapple since 1949 would cease to exist in the same way following the events of 1989/90. The pre-1990 Federal Republic had been marked by initial distance and even enmity between the worlds of literature and politics. There followed a brief period of coming together before concerns over state reactions to extremism and terrorism soured the relationship once again. By the mid-1980s, many writers and politicians were still at loggerheads on certain issues, but the hostilities of earlier decades were no longer present insofar as the two sides often chose to ignore each other — certainly over aesthetic issues on the one side and everyday politics on the other. In a sense, this can be seen as part of the overall normalization process that characterized the development of the Federal Republic.

In the GDR, such normalization was not possible, not least because the state had its own conception of the role of the writer as someone contributing to the development of socialism as it understood the term. As has been shown, many writers were certainly favorable to the idea of socialism, as indeed were swathes of the general population. The dilemma of the state was how to let the population, including intellectuals, participate; if in doubt, the decision was almost invariably to repress anything that challenged its absolute power. The situation is summed up in a story by one of those authors who left the GDR in the wake of the Biermann affair: In "Versuchte Nähe" (Attempted Proximity), Hans Joachim Schädlich portrays the mentality of a leading party functionary. He is to take the stand at a celebratory march past by the people. He would like to be close to them, but retains a feeling of insecurity in the face of the "Unübersehbarem, das vorbeugender Kontrolle vielköpfig sich zu entziehen scheint" (immensity, which seems in its mass to be beyond preventative control).[56] If such was the sentiment toward the majority of citizens, it was felt particularly strongly toward writers, even at the times when it appeared they were being given greater latitude to express themselves. It has to be concluded that the GDR was no place for critical writers any more than for critical citizens of any kind. Since the majority consisted of such citizens, even if their discontent was based primarily on material considerations, it is scant wonder that the state collapsed once the external constraint posed by the threat of Soviet intervention disappeared.

Notes

[1] Arthur Williams, Stuart Parkes, and Roland Smith, eds., *Literature on the Threshold* (Oxford: Berg, 1990).

[2] Hans Magnus Enzensberger, "Macht und Geist: ein deutsches Indianerspiel?," in *Mittelmaß und Wahn* (Frankfurt am Main: Suhrkamp, 1991), 207–21, here 212. Further citations given in parentheses.

[3] Ralph Giordano, "Über meine Unfäigkeit, konservativ zu wählen oder von Zwangs-demokraten und Gegenradikalen," in *Wählen — aber wen?*, ed. Dieter Gütt (Hamburg: Grüner & Jahr, 1987), 25–40, here 38–39.

[4] Bodo Morshäuser, "Über das Risiko, von der Leiter zu fallen oder auf die Strahlung kommt es an," in *Wählen*, ed. Gütt, 83–92, here 83.

[5] Michael Rutschky, "Warum uns die Bundestagswahl nicht interessiert," *Die Zeit*, 2 January 1987, 29..

[6] Günter Grass, "Geißlers Schüler," in *Vom Verlust der Scham und dem allmählichen Verschwinden der Demokratie*, ed. Heinz Ludwig Arnold (Göttingen: Steidl, 1988), 159–61.

[7] Friedrich Christian Delius, "Strickmuster einer Verstrickung," in *Vom Verlust der Scham*, ed. Arnold, 186–98. A decade later, Delius wrote a whole volume criticizing the journalism of the *Frankfurter Allgemeine Zeitung*: *Konservativ in 30 Tagen* (Reinbek: Rowohlt, 1998).

[8] Dieter Lattmann, "Unsere real existierende Demokratie," in *Vom Verlust der Scham*, ed. Arnold, 37–46, here 46.

[9] Luise Rinser, "Für eine grüne Politik, oder Über den Mut zu denken," in *Wählen*, ed. Gütt, 111–18.

[10] Karin Struck, "SPD wählen hieße, dem Chefarzt die Blumen zu bringen, nachdem Mutter und Hebamme ein Kind zur Welt gebracht haben," in *Wählen*, ed. Gütt, 143–52.

[11] Siegfried Lenz, "Das Wasser der Republik," in *Kämpfen für die sanfte Republik*, ed. Freimut Duve, Heinrich Böll, and Klaus Staeck (Reinbek: Rowohlt, 1980), 88–93, here 89–90.

[12] Fritz J. Raddatz, "Die Aufklärung entlässt ihre Kinder," *Die Zeit*, 29 June 1984, 9–10.

[13] Jürgen Habermas, "Die Moderne — ein unvollendetes Projekt," *Die Zeit*, 19 September 1980, 47–48.

[14] Michael Ende, *Die unendliche Geschichte* (Stuttgart: Thienemanns Verlag, 1979), 144.

[15] Erhard Eppler, Michael Ende, Hanne Tächl, *Phantasie, Kultur, Politik* (Stuttgart: Thienemanns Verlag, 1982), 33. Further citations given in parentheses.

[16] Peter Schneider, "Keine Lust aufs grüne Paradies," in *Deutsche Ängste* (Darmstadt and Neuwied: Luchterhand, 1988), 41–53, here 51.

[17] Gerhard Zwerenz, "Deutschland, automatisiertes Schlachtfeld," *die tageszeitung*, 22 April 1983, 10.

[18] See Ingrid Krüger, ed., *Mut zur Angst: Schriftsteller für den Frieden* (Darmstadt, Neuwied: Luchterhand, 1982), 18–19, here 18.

[19] Heinrich Böll, "Auf traurige Weise friedlos," in Krüger, *Mut zur Angst,* 48–53, esp. 49.

[20] Dieter E. Zimmer, "Deine Angst und meine Angst," *Die Zeit,* 13 November 1981, 10–12.

[21] Horst Eberhard Richter, "Der Aufstand der Gefühle," *Die Zeit,* 26 June 1981, 52.

[22] Erwin K. Scheuch, "Die Arroganz der Ängstlichkeit," *Die Zeit,* 13 November 1981, 11.

[23] Gerd Bucerius, "Schwelgt nicht in Angst," *Die Zeit,* 26 July 1981, 35.

[24] Helmut Schmidt, "'Fürchtet Euch nicht,'" *Die Zeit,* 23 December 1983, 1.

[25] *Berliner Begegnung zur Friedensförderung* (Darmstadt and Neuwied: Luchterhand, 1982), 82. Further citations given in parentheses.

[26] *Zweite Berliner Begegnung: Den Frieden erklären* (Darmstadt and Neuwied: Luchterhand, 1983), 37. Further citations given in parentheses.

[27] Günter Grass, "Den Widerstand lernen, ihn leisten und zu ihm auffordern," in *Widerstand leisten,* Günter Grass (Darmstadt and Neuwied: Luchterhand, 1984), 91–96, here 95. The Heilbronn Appeal is to be found on 97–98 of this volume.

[28] Günter Grass, "Offener Brief an die Abgeordneten des Deutschen Bundestags," in *Widerstand,* Grass, 84–90.

[29] Franz Alt, *Frieden ist möglich* (Munich: Piper, 1983).

[30] Hans-Adolf Jacobsen, "Vom Vergleich des Unvergleichbaren," *Die Zeit* 9 December 1983, 51.

[31] Jürgen Fuchs, *Einmischung in eigene Angelegenheiten* (Reinbek: Rowohlt, 1984), 157.

[32] Martin Walser, "Über den Leser — soviel man in einem Festzelt darüber sagen soll," in *Wer ist ein Schriftsteller* (Frankfurt am Main: Suhrkamp, 1979), 94–101, 100. The texts that make up "Ein deutsches Mosaik" are found in Martin Walser, *Erfahrungen und Leseerfahrungen* (Frankfurt am Main: Suhrkamp, 1965), 7–28.

[33] Martin Walser, "Händedruck mit Gespenstern," in *Stichworte zur "Geistigen Situation der Zeit,"* ed. Jürgen Habermas (Frankfurt am Main: Suhrkamp, 1979, vol. 1), 39–51, here 49.

[34] Dieter Wellershoff, "Deutschland ein Schwebezustand," in *Stichworte,* ed. Habermas, 77–114, here 88. Further citations given in parentheses.

[35] Peter Schneider, *Der Mauerspringer* (Darmstadt and Neuwied: Luchterhand, 1984), 109.

[36] Peter Schneider, "Geschichte einer Trennung," in *Deutsche Ängste,* Schneider, 19–29, here 28.

[37] Günter Grass, *Kopfgeburten oder Die Deutschen sterben aus* (Darmstadt and Neuwied: Luchterhand, 1980), 121.

[38] Peter Paul Zahl, "Die andauernde Ausbürgerung," in *Tintenfisch 15: Thema: Deutschland,* ed. Hans Christoph Buch, 95–104, here 98.

[39] Hermann Peter Piwitt, "Einen Kranz niederlegen am Herrmannsdenkmal," in *Tintenfisch 15,* 17–24, here 20.

[40] See Heinrich Mann, "Die Macht des Wortes," *Die neue Weltbühne* 4:10 (1935): 285–86.

[41] Eckhard Jesse, "Die (Pseudo-)Aktualität der deutschen Frage — ein publizistisches, kein politisches Phänomen," in *Die deutsche Frage in der Weltpolitik,* ed. Wolfgang Michalka (Wiesbaden: Steiner, 1986), 51–68.

[42] Andreas Roßmann, "Die Einheit — eine (literarische) Fiktion," *Deutschland Archiv,* 14:6 (1981): 568–69.

[43] Peter Härtling, "In der Sprache bin ich zu Haus," in *Mein Deutschland findet sich in keinem Atlas,* ed. Françoise Barthélemy and Lutz Winckler (Frankfurt am Main: Luchterhand, 1990), 20.

[44] Bernd Wagner, "Blitzschlag, Angst und Vaterlandsliebe," in *Mein Deutschland findet sich in keinem Atlas,* ed. Barthélemy, 101–25, here 121.

[45] Martin Walser, "Über Deutschland reden," in *Deutsche Sorgen* (Frankfurt am Main: Suhrkamp, 1997), 406–27, here 417.

[46] Jurek Becker, "Gedächtnis verloren — Verstand verloren," *Die Zeit,* 18 November 1988, 61.

[47] Christa Wolf, *Kassandra* (Darmstadt and Neuwied: Luchterhand, 1983).

[48] Christa Wolf, *Störfall* (Darmstadt and Neuwied: Luchterhand, 1987).

[49] Peter Hacks, "Brief an eine Dame in Paris über einen Ort namens Deutschland," in *Mein Deutschland findet sich in keinem Atlas,* ed. Barthélemy, 29–30, here 29.

[50] Günter de Bruyn, "Die eine deutsche Kultur," in *Mein Deutschland findet sich in keinem Atlas,* ed. Bathélemy, 27–28, here 28.

[51] Helga Schubert, "Etwas zu dem ich gehöre," in *Mein Deutschland findet sich in keinem Atlas,* ed. Barthélemy, 26.

[52] de Bruyn, "Die eine deutsche Kultur," 27.

[53] Stefan Heym, "Die Wunde der Teilung eitert weiter," *Der Spiegel,* 7 November 1983, 66.

[54] Christoph Hein, "Die Zensur ist überlebt, nutzlos, paradox, menschenfeindlich, volksfeindlich, ungesetzlich und strafbar," in *Als Kind habe ich Stalin gesehen* (Berlin and Weimar: Aufbau, 1990), 77–104, here 84.

[55] Thomas Krüger refers to Kolbe's text in a 2001 speech in Bundeszentrale für politische Bildung, "Kultureller Widerstand heute," http://www.bpb.de/presse/ EJTQIT,O,O,Kultureller_Widerstand_heute.html. Consulted 21.09.2006.

[56] Hans Joachim Schädlich, "Versuchte Nähe," in *Versuchte Nähe* (Reinbek: Rowohlt, 1980), 7–15, here 14.

Intermezzo: Writers and the Unification Process

Political Developments

When Mikhail Gorbachev took over the reins of power in the Soviet Union in 1985, it gradually became evident that it was not just a change of generations, but also a change of direction, as exemplified by his use of the terms *glasnost* (openness) and *perestroika* (restructuring) to underline his priorities. Gorbachev also spoke of greater democracy, something that implied that the Soviet Union's allies would enjoy greater freedom and, specifically, that it would not intervene militarily if one of these countries deviated from the Soviet model. It was in keeping with this new spirit that in May 1989 Hungary began to dismantle its border fortifications with Austria and that a non-communist government was installed in Poland shortly afterwards.

All this provided a catalyst for movement in the GDR, which, under the aging Honecker, had remained rigidly set against reform. The infamous wallpaper comment by the leading cultural functionary Kurt Hager summed up the attitudes in the GDR's highest echelons. In the light of this refusal to change, those totally disillusioned with the GDR began to make their way to Hungary and other neighboring countries in the hope of being able to cross to the West, while others at home began demonstrating on the streets and organizing for change — roughly simultaneous developments that were labeled "exit" and "voice." Whereas the GDR authorities could no longer do much about those that had left the country, and even in early October allowed those who had taken refuge in the Federal Republic's embassy in Prague to leave (albeit by way of the GDR so that they could be stripped of their citizenship), their first reaction at home was to resort to repression. Violence was used against demonstrators; moreover, the attempt by dissidents to gain official recognition for their organization Neues Forum failed. The key day was 9 October. All seemed set for a violent confrontation between demonstrators and security forces in Leipzig. As it turned out, the security forces held back, with the result that the way was open for protest to intensify. Just over a week later, Honecker was forced into retirement and succeeded by Egon Krenz, a long-term functionary who had been principally involved with the ironically named Free German Youth, the only youth movement allowed in the country.

Shortly after his accession to power, Krenz was faced with the issue of freedom of movement. When plans were announced to allow travel to the west, crowds immediately began to gather at the Berlin Wall and, in somewhat confused circumstances, the gates were opened on 9 November. This put the question of unification on the agenda. Whereas demonstrators had formerly chanted "Wir sind das Volk" (We are the people), the cry now went up: "Wir sind ein Volk" (We are one people). With the GDR authorities in disarray, at the end of November Helmut Kohl put forward a ten-point plan leading to eventual German unity. One precondition for any move toward unity was the holding of free elections in the GDR. These took place in March 1990, with the victors being the CDU (still nominally separate from its Western counterpart) and other smaller parties allied with it, the losers being the SPD and the PDS (Partei des Demokratischen Sozialismus, the renamed and to a degree reformed SED).

The way was now open for negotiations both between the two German states and the four former wartime allies. The United States under George Bush Sr. were keen to achieve rapid unification, not least because it would signify the triumph of Western ideas over communism, and the Soviet Union in the Gorbachev era was no longer intent on maintaining its client state. In these circumstances, the apparent lack of enthusiasm for German unity shown, at least initially, by Britain and France was of little consequence. Equally, there was no question of the new GDR government, given its mandate under the CDU politician Lothar de Maizière, allowing the negotiations to fail. The first step was the currency union of 1 July 1990, which forestalled the threat behind one slogan of Eastern demonstrators: "Entweder die D-Mark kommt zu uns, oder wir gehen zu ihr" (Either the D-Mark comes to us or we go to it). Full political unity followed on 3 October, when the GDR ceased to exist.

Writers and Unification

When the political system of the GDR entered a state of instability in the summer and autumn of 1989, few imagined that the end of an era was approaching. Those who began to demonstrate and call for change were looking for radical reform of their state's atrophied institutions and political processes rather than a rapid unification with the Federal Republic, which, in any case, did not seem to be part of any realistic political agenda. Since this corresponded to what a large number of writers and intellectuals had hoped for over many decades, it is not surprising that many were involved in the protest movements of 1989. Some attached themselves to the burgeoning groupings that challenged the SED's monopoly hold on power; for instance, Daniela Dahn was involved in the foundation of Demokratischer Aufbruch (Democratic Renewal), which announced itself as social and ecological. The largest oppositional group, Neues Forum, was initiated by the artist Bärbel Bohley, whose dissidence over many years had at one point taken her into temporary exile in London.[1] Other intellectuals took part in the numerous gatherings that accompanied the demands for change.

One major gathering attended by writers took place in the Berlin Church of the Redemption on October 29. In her speech there, Christa Wolf identified Stalinism, which she termed "eine Krankheit unserer Gesellschaft" (an illness of our society), as the root cause of the GDR's problems.[2] A week earlier in another speech, she had bemoaned the lack of open discussion in the GDR, recalling an occasion when a woman at one of her readings had not only spoken about the difficulties she experienced stating her opinions, but even about the problem of not really knowing what her true opinion was.[3] Another speaker in Berlin was Christoph Hein. He began his remarks by saying that he had set aside his prepared text because the time had come to speak more freely. Specifically, he referred to the need to create a true public sphere, and also to ask the police, whose response to the demonstrations of 1989 was often brutal, to reflect on their actions.[4]

The largest meeting attended by many writers and artists took place on the Alexanderplatz in Berlin on 4 November 1989, less than a week before the fall of the Wall. A crowd, estimated to number around a million, heard Stefan Heym speak in praise of those who had gathered for freedom and democracy and for true socialism.[5] In similar vein, Christoph Hein, who addressed the crowd as citizens who had found their voice, spoke of GDR socialism having been disfigured by all kinds of abuses ranging from bureaucracy to surveillance and crime,[6] while expressing the hope for reform. As for Christa Wolf, she discerned a revolutionary movement and even conjured up a vision of the political leadership marching past the citizenry at a May Day demonstration.[7] More surprisingly, another speaker at the demonstration was the former spymaster Markus Wolf; however, it did transpire later that the event had been managed in part by the notorious Stasi secret police. Nevertheless, the large numbers present showed that the meeting with its emphasis on reform of the GDR was in keeping with the mood of the moment.

This was to change with the fall of the Wall. By the end of the month, the specter of unification and the end of the GDR was beginning to haunt writers and others whose desire was to reform the GDR rather than to hasten its demise. The new mood of fear among writers is caught in the petition of 28 November titled "Für unser Land" (For our country), signed quickly by, among others, Heym, Wolf, and Volker Braun. It speaks of fighting for a society based on peace, social justice, individual freedom, and care for the environment, or of facing incorporation into the Federal Republic, which would mean the end of any socialist alternative.[8] Those fighting from this corner were undoubtedly not helped by the less-than-popular Egon Krenz adding his signature to the petition. Equally, they faced a formidable foe in the person of Helmut Kohl, who by coincidence announced his ten-point plan for German unity on the same day.

Another very prominent writer to insist on the importance of the GDR as an alternative to the Federal Republic, albeit, it would seem, for partly aesthetic reasons, was the dramatist Heiner Müller. In a long interview published in 1990, he says this is necessary as otherwise Europe would be boring, with the only alternatives to capitalism being terrorism and the mafia.[9] Elsewhere, he is very critical of the Federal Republic, saying that shopping malls in Düsseldorf show that life there is not worth living — adding that five thousand pairs of pink knickers are anything but an affirmation of life but rather invoke "Tod und Zerstörung" (death and destruction).[10] It can be pointed out that Müller, as someone who enjoyed freedom of travel, was one of the few GDR citizens under retirement age able to make firsthand judgments on the Federal Republic, a privilege he might have chosen to reflect on.

Rather than criticizing the other German state, some GDR writers looked at the opportunities the events of 1989 appeared to offer their own country. A volume of collected texts written by Helga Königsdorf carries the telling title *1989 oder Ein Moment Schönheit* (1989 or a Moment of Beauty, 1990). In it, her mood varies between sadness over mistakes made by the GDR authorities in the past and enthusiasm over the opportunities for change. This enthusiasm can be seen in a speech on 8 November 1989, the day before the fall of the Wall, in which she stresses that the demonstrators who had used their free time to protest should not be robbed of the fruits of their labors.[11] Despite her criticisms, Königsdorf remained in the SED/PDS until January 1990 and continued to hope for a future for left-wing politics, as a piece written shortly after the March elections in the GDR shows.[12]

At least two collections published during the period of transition reflect in their titles the same enthusiasm as that shown by Königsdorf. The editor of *Aufbruch in eine andere DDR* (Onwards to a New GDR, December 1989), Hubertus Knabe, at the time a lecturer in West Berlin, sums up the mood in his introduction by saying that most contributions reflect a wish that the GDR should not merge with its neighbor but be an alternative to the Federal Republic's consumer society.[13] Another Westerner, Michael Naumann, later to be Chancellor Schröder's first secretary of state for culture, edited the second, which appeared in January 1990. It bore the title *"Die Geschichte ist offen"* (History Remains Open), which suggested that there was still time for the GDR to develop a new identity. Indeed, this idea is incorporated into the subtitle *DDR 1990: Hoffnung auf eine neue Republik* (GDR 1990: Hope for a New Republic). Belief in a socialist alternative is expressed nowhere more strongly than in Fritz Rudolf Fries's ringing declaration that the dream of communism, a world of justice, is not over because of previous corruption.[14] Others are more circumspect. The poet Heinz Czechowski doubts whether it will be possible to create a new GDR-consciousness,[15] while, along with Sarah Kirsch, who left the GDR in the wake of the Biermann affair, he also doubts the SED's willingness to give up power.[16] Another writer who left the GDR at the same time, Hans Joachim Schädlich, expresses sorrow about the senselessness of the years of confinement behind the Wall, although he shows an awareness of the absurdities of history by quoting anonymously someone who pointed out that the Wall was built because too many people were leaving the GDR and opened for precisely the same reason. He concludes by saying that any true revolution in the GDR is still for the future, and expresses his hope that a democratic society might emerge.[17]

In the end, there was no reason to worry about the ability of the SED to maintain its previous grip on power. At the same time, a new GDR consciousness — that is to say, one that insisted on the continued existence of the state — did not emerge. A hint of why this was the case may be inferred from the contribution of one of the Prenzlauer Berg poets, Rainer Schedlinski, to the first of the two volumes discussed above. He speaks of a new experiment to see whether it would be possible to reconcile socialism and democracy.[18] The idea of utopia, in fact, recurred frequently at this time, with those supporting the continued existence of the GDR maintaining that the concept had not been destroyed by the previous forty years. Having been materially deprived in comparison with their Western neighbors for forty years, the population of the GDR, however, was not in a mood for experiments or for utopian dreams of the kind implied by Fries's comment above. Authors who had supported the continuing existence of the GDR were left to reflect ruefully on the course history did take. Volker Braun provides a case in point in his poem "Das Eigentum" (Property), which picks up on both the move of so many GDR citizens to the West in the autumn of 1989 and the demonstrators' cry "Wir bleiben hier" (We're staying here) in its first line: "Da bin ich noch: mein Land geht in den Westen" (I'm still here: my country goes to the West).[19]

Reactions to the events of 1989 were of course not restricted to the GDR. Although some in the Federal Republic — not least the wife of Willy Brandt, the historian Brigitte Seebacher — complained about the silence of intellectuals, there was in fact a variety of responses.[20] Not surprisingly, immediately on the fall of the Wall Martin Walser rejoiced that German history could go well for once.[21] Although he does not claim that unification is the only acceptable conclusion to what he saw as a revolution in the GDR, he does say, picking up Mikhail Gorbachev's much-quoted metaphor of the common European house, that any two German rooms would have to be more closely linked than any others. He also demands that matters German must now take precedence over Europe, ignoring the fact that German unity could only be agreed to within an international context that, in fact, went well beyond Europe.

At the other end of the scale was Günter Grass, who in a series of interventions starting in late 1989 and going up to the time of unification expresses his dissatisfaction about the way events were developing. In an interview that first appeared in *Der Spiegel* shortly after Walser's comments, he castigates his colleague for showing "Viel Gefühl, zu wenig Bewußtsein" (A lot of emotion, too little consciousness).[22] He also holds out hope for the creation of a democratic form of socialism in the GDR. Grass makes clear one major reason for his rejection of German unity at the December 1989 SPD party conference in Berlin, by which time his political mentor Willy Brandt had expressed his pleasure over what was happening by famously saying that what belonged together was now growing together. Grass, on the other hand, sees any move for unity ending in tears, expressing the traditional suspicion of political power through the claim that nothing would be gained except "einer beängstigenden Machtfülle, gebläht vom Gelüst nach mehr und mehr Macht" (a worrying mass of power, bloated by the desire for more and more power).[23] He also claims that the incorporation of the GDR into the Federal Republic would destroy the new sense of national identity gained by its citizens. This prophecy did turn out to be correct, as will be seen in the next chapter, insofar as many Easterners, including prominent intellectuals, did resent what they saw as a western takeover.

The all-pervading historical reason for Grass's rejection of unification became clear in his February 1990 speech "Kurze Rede eines vaterlandslosen Gesellen" (Short Speech of a Fellow Without a Fatherland), the title of which refers back to Kaiser Wilhelm the Second's dismissal of Social Democrats as unpatriotic. German unity, as created in 1871 under Prussian dominance, had, he claimed, only brought misery, culminating in the horrors of National Socialism. Grass expresses his view most starkly in claiming that those who think about the German Question must also include Auschwitz, adding that Auschwitz excludes any thought of unity.[24] This stands in contrast to Walser's view, referred to earlier, that Germany had served its sentence for Nazi crimes. Grass continued his warnings on the eve of unification with a speech to the parliamentary group of the Greens, seeing — in the words of his title — the GDR as a *Schnäppchen* (steal) for Western companies intent on increasing their economic power. Justifiably, as events sadly proved, he warns against increasing xenophobia in the East, while also castigating the process by which unity was achieved.[25] This refers to the decision to incorporate the GDR into the existing structures of the Federal Republic rather than, for example, adopting a new constitution.

Grass's dislike of the unification process is also powerfully expressed in fictional form in his novel *Ein weites Feld* (Too Far a Field, 1995). The main character, Theo Wuttke, is an amateur expert on the nineteenth-century author Fontane, which has earned him the sobriquet Fonty. With his knowledge of Fontane and, through him, of the course of German history following the 1871 unification, he is in a position to make comparisons between that era and the immediate post-1989 situation when the novel is set. This is because he is now working in the Treuhand agency, which was set up to privatize the GDR's state-owned assets — more or less the whole industrial and commercial sectors. Controversy over the book started with its condemnation in the magazine *Der Spiegel* by Marcel Reich-Ranicki, who was portrayed, no doubt with the aid of computer technology, on the cover of the 21 August edition ripping the book apart. Opinions on its literary merit varied and do not form part of the present discussion. At the political level, Grass found himself in hot water for his references to the terrorist murder of the first head of the Treuhand Detlev Karsten Rohwedder in 1991. In the novel there is a conversation between Fonty and Rohwedder, who complains about the way Chancellor Kohl gives his dirty work to others.[26] In a letter to his illegitimate French daughter — another thing shared with the historical Fontane — he writes about Kohl's mediocrity, suggesting, apparently with regret, that he will not be a terrorist target (626).

Ein weites Feld provoked the biggest controversy over a work of fiction since Böll's *Die verlorene Ehre der Katharina Blum* a good two decades earlier. As with the earlier work, there was enough argumentative material to spawn a volume — indeed, a 495-page volume to complement the 781-page novel.[27] The documentation shows that Grass came under fire from leading members of both major political parties. The general secretary of the CDU, Peter Hintze, finds Grass's attitude to Kohl tasteless and embarrassing, going on to accuse the author of the basest of motives by asking rhetorically: "Wie tief muß dieser Mann sinken, um seine Auflage zu steigern?" (How deep must this man sink, in order to raise his sales figures?).[28] The SPD politician Klaus von Dohnanyi, in an open letter, appears to doubt Grass's competence to intervene in political matters. Just as politicians' advice on such issues as sonnet form would be unacceptable to writers, Grass's unfounded *Pauschalkritik* (sweeping criticism) is unacceptable to politicians.[29] The question of intellectuals' competence to intervene in political matters will be discussed in the conclusion of this book; here, however, Dohnanyi seems to want to have his cake and eat it, too. It is not clear if it is the fact of criticism or its unfounded nature that is the issue. How would he and his colleagues react to unjustified praise, one wonders? Grass also found himself attacked in more surprising quarters. Reviewing the novel for the alternative *tageszeitung*, Jörg Lau sees the implication of the Rohwedder episode as being that Grass would not have minded if Chancellor Kohl had been the terrorists' victim, rather than Rohwedder.[30] Grass's justifiable reply on this point is that he had wanted to show how it might come to such a terrorist attack and, no doubt in a mood of resignation, that the insinuation that the author sympathizes with the action he describes is "normal." In the same statement, however, he does not help his case by launching into a crude diatribe against Chancellor Kohl, calling him both a liar and a *Wahlbetrüger* (electoral fraudster).[31] Another literary presentation of Rohwedder's murder had already caused controversy. Rolf Hochhuth's play *Wessis in Weimar* (Westerners in Weimar, 1993) includes a conversation between a young woman and a Rohwedder figure called simply the President, in which the young woman accuses him of a war of conquest.[32] At this point, somewhat melodramatically, a shot rings out. Hochhuth, too, found himself in hot water for justifying terrorism. In this case, the criticism was voiced before the text of the play was known. His reply, in a similar vein to that of Grass, was that he was making it comprehensible,[33] a distinction that had not only escaped some of Grass's critics but also those of Böll's two decades earlier.

With the fall of the Wall and the movement toward unity, Hans Magnus Enzensberger adopted a stance that was somewhere between those of Grass and Walser. He expresses joy at what has happened, but refuses to accept that it has a great historical significance. Specifically, he dissociates himself from the reactions of elite groups, whether or not these have expressed pleasure or displeasure about the unfolding events. Instead, he praises the people for their skepticism and their concern with everyday matters. The Brandenburg Gate, rather than being a national symbol, is good for a *kollektive Besäufnis* (collective booze-up); moreover, people are not interested in intellectual ideas but everyday issues such as work, housing, and pensions.[34] This was an original stance, especially from someone who three decades earlier had viewed the majority of the people in Germany as living nearer to a state of idiocy than ever before;[35] it can additionally be criticized as highly disingenuous. The process of unification was for most Germans a major political and historical event, not just because it inspired intellectual conflict, but also because everyday issues of the kind highlighted by Enzensberger formed part of that conflict, as the second part of this volume will show.

Notes

[1] For a fuller survey of the oppositional groups of the autumn of 1989, see Erhard Neubert, *Geschichte der Opposition in der DDR* (Bonn: Bundeszentrale für politische Bildung, 2 ed., 1998), 857–64.

[2] Christa Wolf, "'Wider den Schlaf der Vernunft,'" in *Im Dialog*, Christa Wolf (Frankfurt am Main: Luchterhand, 1990), 98–100, here 98.

[3] Christa Wolf, "'Das haben wir nicht gerlernt,'" in *Im Dialog*, Wolf, 93–97, esp. 93.

[4] See *DDR-Journal zur Novemberrevolution: documentation published by die tageszeitung* (1989) 74.

[5] See Franz Josef Görtz, Volker Hage, Uwe Wittstock, eds., *Deutsche Literatur 1989* (Stuttgart: Reclam, 1990), 115.

[6] Christoph Hein, "Der alte Mann und die Straße. Ansprache zur Demonstration der Berliner Kulturschaffenden," in *Als Kind habe ich Stalin gesehen*, 175–77, here 176.

[7] Christa Wolf, "Sprache der Wende," in *Im Dialog*, 119–21, here 119.

[8] See *DDR-Journal* (see note 4), 154.

[9] Heiner Müller, "Dem Terrorismus die Utopie entreißen," in *"Zur Lage der Nation"* (Berlin: Rotbuch, 1990), 9–24, here 17.

[10] Heiner Müller, "Da trinke ich lieber Benzin zum Frühstück," in *"Zur Lage der Nation,"* 45–58, here 57.

[11] Helga Königsdorf, *1989 oder Ein Moment Schönheit* (Berlin and Weimar: Aufbau, 1990), 84.

[12] Helga Königsdorf, "Gedanken nach der Wahl," in *1989*, Königsdorf, 145–47.

[13] Hubertus Knabe, "Die deutsche Oktoberrevolution," in *Aufbruch in eine andere DDR*, ed. Hubertus Knabe (Reinbek: Rowohlt, 1989), 9–23, here 19.

[14] Fritz Rudolf Fries, "Braucht die neue Republik neue Autoren," in *"Die Geschichte ist offen,"* ed. Michael Naumann (Reinbek: Rowohlt, 1990), 53–58, here 56.

[15] Heinz Czechowski, "Euphorie und Katzenjammer," in *"Die Geschichte ist offen,"* ed. Naumann, 31–43, here 43.

[16] Sarah Kirsch, "Kleine Betrachtungen am Morgen des 17. November," in *"Die Geschichte ist offen,"* ed. Naumann, 79–81.

[17] Hans Joachim Schädlich, "Traurige Freude," in *"Die Geschichte ist offen,"* ed. Naumann, 159–64, esp. 161–64.

[18] Rainer Schedlinski, "Gibt es die DDR überhaupt?," in *Aufbruch*, ed. Knabe, 275–84, here 279.

[19] Volker Braun, "Eigentum," in *Die Mauer fiel, die Mauer steht*, ed. Hermann Glaser (Munich: DTV, 1999, 63–64), here 63.

[20] For a full review of responses, see Helmut Peitsch, "West German Reactions on the Role of the Writer in the Light of Reactions to 9 November 1989," in *German Literature at a Time of Change 1989–1990*, ed. Arthur Williams, Stuart Parkes, and Roland Smith (Bern: Peter Lang, 1991), 155–86.

[21] Martin Walser, "11. November 1989," in *Über Deutschland reden* (Frankfurt am Main: Suhrkamp, erweiterte Neuauflage, 1989), 115.

[22] Günter Grass, "Viel Gefühl, wenig Bewußtsein," in *Deutscher Lastenausgleich*, Günter Grass (Frankfurt am Main: Luchterhand, 1990), 13–25, here 22.

[23] Günter Grass, "Lastenausgleich," in *Deutscher Lastenausgleich*, Grass, 7–12, here 11.

[24] Günter Grass, "Kurze Rede eines vaterlandslosen Gesellen," in *Ein Schnäppchen namens DDR*, Günter Grass (Frankfurt am Main: Luchterhand, 1990), 7–14, here 13.

[25] Günter Grass, "Ein Schnäppchen namens DDR," in *Ein Schnäppchen*, Grass, 39–60.

[26] Günter Grass, *Ein weites Feld* (Göttingen: Steidl, 1995), 621. Further citations given in parentheses.

[27] Oskar Negt, ed., *Der Fall Fonty* (Göttingen: Steidl, 1996).

[28] Peter Hintze, quoted in Negt, *Der Fall Fonty*, 37.

[29] Klaus von Dohnanyi, "'Du verspielst jeden Respekt als Figur des öffentlichen Dialogs,'" in Negt, *Der Fall Fonty*, 161–66, here 163.

[30] Jörg Lau, "Schwellkörper Deutschland," in Negt, *Der Fall Fonty*, 141–47, here 143.

[31] Günter Grass, quoted in Negt, *Der Fall Fonty*, 36.

[32] Rolf Hochhuth, *Wessis in Weimar* (Berlin: Volk & Welt, 1993), 31.

[33] See Franz Josef Görtz, Volker Hage, and Uwe Wittstock, eds., *Deutsche Literatur 1992* (Stuttgart: Reclam, 1993), 49–50, here 50.

[34] Hans Magnus Enzensberger, "Gangarten," *Kursbuch 100* (1990), 1–9, here 9.

[35] Hans Magnus Enzensberger, "Das Plebiszit der Verbraucher," in *Einzelheiten I* (Frankfurt am Main: Suhrkamp, 1964), 167–78, here 171.

Part 2:
Writers and Politics after Unification

Segue: Political and Literary Developments Since Unification

Political Developments

SINCE UNIFICATION IN OCTOBER 1990, the new Federal Republic has established a political life comparable in many respects to that of most Western democracies. Following the election in 1998, there took place for the first time the kind of change of government that is normal in such democratic societies when the electorate, grown weary with Helmut Kohl, made possible a new coalition between the SPD and the Greens, a decision confirmed by a hair's breadth in 2002. Unlike previous occasions, there was in 1998 a complete break, with no element of continuity in the shape of the FDP, as when the main government party changed from CDU to SPD in 1969 or vice versa in 1982. However, this element of continuity was restored following the very tight election of 2005 when the only practical solution was a Grand Coalition between the two major parties, albeit under a CDU chancellor — Angela Merkel, the first woman to hold this office.

Regardless of who was in government, following unification the Federal Republic faced a variety of issues, the difficulties of which helped to bring down Kohl and thereafter made life far from easy for his successor Gerhard Schröder. One of the most pressing undoubtedly was that of unemployment. By early 2005, the official figure for unemployment stood at over five million, with the full employment associated with the economic miracle seemingly only a distant memory. Subsequent improvements in 2007 and 2008 have been welcome, even if figures remain high. Nevertheless, it is important to note in this connection that economic problems, despite some successes for right-wing extremist parties at regional level, have not led to massive disillusionment with democracy as happened in the Weimar Republic, a specter that haunted the Federal Republic in earlier decades.

In the area of foreign policy, postunification Germany has been faced with finding a new role in a changed world. Prior to unification, both German states had, albeit to different degrees, arguably been client states of their respective superpower allies, on which they depended for support and, in the case of the GDR, for its very existence. For many years, at least until about 1970, the idea that the Federal Republic was an economic giant but a political dwarf was current. Despite its treaty commitments, united Germany was freer, for instance, to suggest it merited a permanent place on the United Nations Security Council. These aspirations, however, were rebuffed in 2005 when the United Nations was unable to agree on major reforms to its structures.

In the Federal Republic, the issues referred to above go far beyond humdrum daily politics, even, in many cases, raising fundamental questions about the identity of the state and its citizens. Much of the unemployment problem lies in the East, where the successor party of the once all-powerful SED, the PDS, subsequently renamed Die Linke, retained a strong presence. Indeed, thanks to its links and subsequent 2007 merger with the Wahlinitiative Soziale Gerechtigkeit (Electoral action for social justice), a group founded by dissident Social Democrats before the 2005 election, it has gained strength in the western part of the country, gaining seats in state parliaments in 2008. Such developments inevitably raise the question of the successes and failures of unification and, specifically, of how far the country feels united. For many years, a large majority of Easterners regarded themselves as second-class citizens, while Westerners baulked at the cost of financing improvements in the East. As for the area of foreign policy, moves to play a more active role in world affairs by, for example, sending troops to the former Yugoslavia in the mid-1990s, invariably involve discussions of the German past — specifically, what lessons should be learned from the debacle of National Socialism. More generally, there is also the question of how the whole Nazi era should be retained in the public memory, now that those with firsthand experience of it are becoming fewer. Not surprisingly, these have been issues on which writers and intellectuals have had much to say. Their comments on such questions will form the basis of the second chapter in this part of this volume.

Literary Developments

With the demise of the GDR, one parameter that had influenced German literature over forty years disappeared: the need for writers in the Eastern part of the country to use fictional works as a substitute for the lack of a public sphere, represented by mass media with more than one ideological leaning. Many writers greeted this with relief, not least Christoph Hein, who said that it was now possible to concentrate on literature, which he defined as the sort of profound aestheticism found in Proust's descriptions of drinking tea.[1] In the event, he did continue to write novels that might well be classed as political, publishing, for example, *Von allem Anfang an* (From the Very Beginning, 1997), which describes a childhood in the early years of the GDR and suggests, at least in the title, that the seeds of that state's destruction were already present, and more recently *In seiner Kindheit ein Garten* (In His Childhood a Garden, 2005), which deals with the theme of terrorism. The same can be said of Christa Wolf, who, in the tradition of her earlier *Kassandra,* made use of a mythological setting for her work *Medea: Stimmen* (Medea: Voices 1996), in which the contrast between the worlds of Greece and the eponymous heroine's native Colchis invokes the differences between the Federal Republic and the GDR, not to the advantage of the former.

Political themes, too, continued to play a significant role in Western literature, with, unsurprisingly, Martin Walser being one of the first to turn his attention to the themes of German unity and disunity. Walser's *Die Verteidigung der Kindheit* (In Defense of Childhood, 1991) portrays the life of Alfred Dorn, born in Dresden but spending his adult life in West Berlin and Hessen. His life's work is to preserve in the form of artifacts and documents memories of his childhood and youth in Dresden, the city destroyed both by the Allied bombing of February 1945 and the policies of the GDR. The novel contains many references to the stupidity of the years of division and is thus very different in tone from Grass's already discussed *Ein weites Feld.* The problems of incorporating unification into literature is the subject of Joachim Lottmann's novel *Deutsche Einheit* (German Unity, 1999). Here the main character is given a grant to write on that topic but makes scant progress.

If some established writers, such as Grass and Walser, have at least on occasion continued on previously trodden political paths, then other, mainly younger authors have sought new directions. In the late 1990s especially, a feeling developed that German literature was heavy and dull, thus driving readers toward foreign literature in translation, which indeed has generally continued to dominate bestseller lists. Maxim Biller, especially, called for more readable literature, having described most German literature as being as sensuous as a street map of Kiel.[2] Certainly, around the time of his complaints a development dubbed "pop literature" attracted a great deal of attention, with its protagonists happy to announce that their writing was the exact opposite of Martin Walser's.[3] It was, however, to prove an ephemeral phenomenon, at least as far as wide public attention was concerned. Nevertheless, that it is possible to combine humor with serious political themes has been shown by some younger writers. The Easterner Thomas Brussig's *Helden wie wir* (Heroes Like Us, 1995) links with considerable originality the fall of the Berlin Wall with sexual perversion, while the novels of Rafael Seligmann treat the post-Holocaust Jewish experience in Germany with both humor and poignancy. Other writers, for example, Bodo Kirchhoff, have given their work an international dimension by setting some of their novels outside Germany, something that was quite rare in postwar decades. A new generation of women writers, such as Karen Duve and Judith Herrmann, have also come to prominence, with their advent giving commentators the chance to reuse the postwar coinage *Fräuleinwunder* — this time applied to young female writers rather than young German women in general.

One of the few works by a German author to achieve international success in the last decades is Bernhard Schlink's work *Der Vorleser* (The Reader, 1995). It is initially the story of a relationship between a teenager and a woman approximately two decades older. Besides the sexual dimension, the relationship consists of a reading ritual whereby the young man reads aloud to his mistress. The reason for this ritual becomes clear later when the woman is on trial because of her past as a concentration camp guard. Her erstwhile lover discovers that she is illiterate but he does not reveal this to the court. Since she, too, continues to cover up the fact to her own detriment, she ends up being given a lengthy prison sentence. One possible implication is that Schlink is turning a war criminal into a victim and, because of her lover's silence, making a member of the postwar generation the guilty party.

The related question of German suffering is a theme in other postunification works — for example, Hans-Ulrich Treichel's *Der Verlorene* (The Lost, 1998), where the person lost is the brother of the main character, who disappeared among the mass of German refugees fleeing the advancing Soviet armies in 1945. The emergence of such works, along with the growing preeminence of writers such as Botho Strauß and Peter Handke, whose stances seem far removed from that of, for example, Günter Grass, raise the question whether German literature has entered a new phase. What this means for writers' relationship with politics will be discussed below; suffice it to say here that German literature has become more varied in recent years.[4]

Whether it has entered a new era of quality is not easy to determine. The publishing industry was hit by the protracted economic recession at the beginning of the new millennium. The atmosphere at the various book fairs, if newspaper reports are to be believed, seems to change from one event to another. A report on the Leipzig Book Fair in March 2005 speaks, for instance, of regression to the atmosphere of the early 1990s having followed the end of the brief pop literature era, and it castigatesGerman literature in general for timidity and a lack of courage.[5] Even if this were to be accepted as a true picture, it certainly does not follow that there has ever been a lack of issues for debate among writers and intellectuals since the heady days of 1989/90. As with Mark Twain's premature obituary, reports of the death of German literature are much exaggerated.

Notes

[1] See Franz Josef Görtz, Volker Hage, Uwe Wittstock, eds., *Deutsche Literatur 1991. Jahresüberblick* (Stuttgart: Reclam, 1992), 271.

[2] Maxim Biller, "Soviel Sinnlichkeit wie der Stadtplan von Kiel. Warum die neue deutsche Literatur nichts so nötig hat wie der Realismus. Ein Grundsatzprogramm," in *Maulhelden und Königskinder,* ed. Andrea Köhler and Rainer Moritz (Leipzig: Reclam, 1998), 62–71.

[3] See Johannes Ullmaier, *Von Acid nach Adlon und zurück* (Mainz, Ventil, 2001), 12.

[4] A comprehensive study of post-1990 German literature can be found in Stuart Taberner, *German Literature of the 1990s and Beyond: Normalization and the Berlin Republic* (Rochester, NY: Camden House, 2005).

[5] Gerrit Bartels, "Wer die Zeitenwende kennt, weiß noch nicht, wohin die Reise geht," *die Tageszeitung,* 17 March 2005, 14.

7: East and West

T HE EVENTS OF 1989/90 OFFERED WRITERS the opportunity not just to comment on the unfolding unification process, but also to review the previous structures that had lasted since 1949 and, only slightly previously, had seemed set in stone. The result was something that became known as the *Deutsch-deutscher Literaturstreit* (the Intra-German literature quarrel), even though the argument was not principally about literature, but rather politics, and the two sides were not simply East and West Germans. At least the bone of contention was clear: attitudes to the GDR, as adopted by writers and intellectuals in both German states.

The arguments came to a head with the publication in early 1990 of Christa Wolf's story *Was bleibt* (What Remains). This work, which is clearly autobiographical, describes the surveillance of a GDR writer by the Stasi secret police, something to which Wolf herself was subject almost constantly from 1969 onward. What provoked a storm on the publication of the book was the fact that it had been almost entirely written in the 1970s, but only submitted for publication when political conditions in the GDR had changed. One of the first critics to launch into Wolf was the literary editor of *Die Zeit*, Ulrich Greiner. He castigated Wolf as the *Staatsdichter* (state poet) of the GDR, thus associating her by implication with the many sordid features of the Ulbricht and Honecker regimes.[1] Significantly, he did not mention her various difficulties with the GDR authorities, some of which have been referred to earlier in this volume. His other major accusation was that the publication of *Was bleibt* at this particular time showed a lack of sensitivity and honesty. Ironically, in claiming this, he was following the example of Wolf's Stasi pursuers, who adopted the codename *Doppelzüngler* (forked tongue) for their campaign of surveillance. In reality, Wolf's text is in many respects honest to the point of leaving herself vulnerable to attacks for moral coward-ice. When the main character is visited by a young author — widely believed to be based on Gabi Kachold — who is set on confrontation with the auth-orities, she realizes that this is something she herself is incapable of. Greiner was backed up in his accusations by the leading critic of the *Frankfurter Allgemeine Zeitung*, Frank Schirrmacher. His review amounted to an attempt to evaluate Wolf's personality. He concluded that her experience of National Socialism had contributed to the formation of an authoritarian personality, with her subsequent opposition to Nazism taking an equally rigid form as her previous childish enthusiasm. In his role as amateur psychologist, Schirrmacher perceived a kind of displacement as having taken place. After the war, Schirrmacher claimed, Wolf rejected the authentic bourgeois family as a point of identification and replaced it with unconditional loyalty to the state.[2] Schirrmacher extended this critique to other postwar German authors, claiming that the view that, after National Socialism, intellectuals possessed a stable, unswerving, antiauthoritarian personality is a myth entertained by many German writers, artists, and scholars (89). Since no names were mentioned, it is hard to take this criticism too seriously. It would certainly be hard to apply it to many leading Western writers and intellectuals like Böll and Enzensberger.

Greiner continued his attacks on Wolf and German literature in general by popularizing the term *Gesinnungsästhetik* (conviction aesthetics) to characterize much of postwar German literature. By invoking Max Weber's idea of *Gesinnungsethik* as the characteristic of the intellectual, this term suggested that literature in both German states had been too concerned with political issues such as restoration, fascism, clericalism, and Stalinism, to the detriment of literary quality.[3] As for Wolf herself, Greiner criticized her reflections on the Chernobyl explosion in her *Störfall* (Accident: A Day's News, 1987), as *Gesinnungskitsch* (conviction kitsch). Whatever the merits of Greiner's arguments, it is worth noting that he was to a large extent mirroring what was said by those holding official positions within the cultural life of the GDR. The president of the GDR Writers Association, Hermann Kant, for instance, spoke of inferior works gaining credibility in the Federal Republic because they could be presented as examples of political dissidence. During the witch-hunt against Stefan Heym in 1979, Kant spoke of manuscripts undergoing a process of *Veredelung* (ennoblement) on the way from East to West.[4]

The debates on the role of writers in the GDR were intensified by the attention soon given to the role of the Stasi in cultural life. The issue came sharply into public view with the publication of memoirs by authors who had suffered from its surveillance and interference before they left the GDR. One of the first to gain access to material that had been stored about him was Reiner Kunze, who had left the GDR in 1977 in the wake of the Biermann affair. The volume *Deckname «Lyrik»* (Code Name "Poetry," 1990) consists of excerpts from these documents that reveal, among other things, that his neighbors allowed their flat to be used for surveillance, including the boring of a hole in the dividing wall.[5] The following year Erich Loest published a similar volume with the title *Die Stasi war mein Eckermann* (The Stasi Was My Eckermann, 1991), which refers not only to Goethe's famous amanuensis, but also to a song by Wolf Biermann.[6] These volumes with their frequent references to the organization's myriad of unofficial informants undoubtedly reinforced the image of the Stasi as an all-powerful organization that pervaded all areas of life in the GDR.

The next stage in the Stasi debate was brought about by the increasing number of revelations about writers who had cooperated with the organization and/or acted as informants. Names that entered the frame were Hermann Kant, Heiner Müller, and — most significantly of all — Christa Wolf. It transpired that Wolf had worked unofficially for the Stasi from 1959 to 1962 under the code name "Margarete." However, it also quickly transpired that the information she had given was not highly valued and also that one of the writers she reported on, Walter Kaufmann, was not unduly worried about her previous activities.[7] Nevertheless, she was strongly criticized by Erich Loest, who by contrast was much more indulgent with Müller, whose contacts with the Stasi he saw as typical of that author's game-playing.[8] What arguably created an even greater shock than the revelations about Wolf and Müller was the slightly earlier discovery that two of the leading figures of the alternative Prenzlauer Berg scene of the 1980s, Sascha Anderson and Rainer Schedlinski, had also worked with the Stasi. This provoked the damning epithet "Sascha Arschloch" from Wolf Biermann, who had always had no truck with the kind of literature, which, in his view, consisted of nothing more than obscure word games.[9] At the same time, his harsh condemnation represented a volte-face in the light of what he had written a year earlier, when he admitted that during his period as a convinced communist, he, too, would have collaborated with the Stasi if asked.[10]

The full extent of the Stasi's involvement with the world of literature was made clearer with the publication of fuller documentation in 1996, compiled by the Eastern novelist Joachim Walther.[11] What this volume reveals undoubtedly sheds a bad light on the GDR as a state and on those who were willing to cooperate with such an organization, even if it is important not to exaggerate the number of collaborators. The co-editor of another book on the subject concludes in an accompanying essay that the overall penetration of literature was relatively slight.[12] Nevertheless, it is sad to report that few, if any, of those who collaborated were willing to do anything but play down their role — including Monika Maron, who had subsequently left the GDR and condemned her erstwhile colleagues root and branch. As far as she was concerned, any criticism they directed at the GDR was shallow and the popularity they enjoyed too easily earned.[13] Nevertheless, her criticisms show how important the comments of those authors who had left the GDR were in the debates of the 1990s. Not surprisingly, given their treatment, many showed scant sympathy for their former country and those in the West who appeared to have sympathized with it. An example of this attitude is provided by Günter Kunert, who also left the GDR in the wake of the Biermann affair. At the time of unification, he spoke of wanting to have nothing more to do with professional liars masquerading as presidents of writers associations.[14] Despite the use of the plural, it would seem that he had Hermann Kant clearly in mind. As early as November 1989,

Kunert dismissed all hope of creating a renewed GDR by suggesting that the concept of democratic socialism was based on the false premise that man was a rational being.[15] Equally scathing was Hans Joachim Schädlich, who condemned those Western intellectuals who had preferred to relate to communists ideologues and to those in power rather than to dissidents.[16] How difficult relations were between writers in the newly united Germany is proved by the difficulties experienced in uniting parallel cultural institutions. In addition to the PEN club referred to earlier, the East and West German Academies of Arts were not united until 1993, while it took until 1994 to unite the Eastern and Western writers associations.

In the light of all the criticisms of GDR authors made at the time of unification, the question has to be asked whether they had betrayed their profession and only produced inferior literature. In other words, as seemed to be implied at the time, were they comparable to those writers condemned by Thomas Mann in 1945 for having remained in Nazi Germany? The answer has to be that no general answer is possible. Clearly, some did associate themselves largely uncritically with the regime and all its works, including the Stasi. At the other extreme, there were out-and-out opponents who did seek to have their work published in the GDR. This was by no means dishonorable, but does show that they were prepared to work to some extent within the rules of the society where they lived. Most controversial are those, such as Christa Wolf and Volker Braun, who hoped for reform within the socialist system. If it is claimed that they should have realized that no significant reform was possible, then the question arises of when they should have realized this. When Wolf speaks of her first meetings with communist opponents of Nazism, she describes her sense of inferiority in the face of those who appeared to have been on the correct side of history.[17] This must be seen as an entirely understandable reaction from a member of a generation that, although too young to have been involved with the worst atrocities, was to some degree tainted by Nazism. It also has to be remembered that the GDR, despite its failings, did not indulge in the same murderous policies as Nazism. As for Kunert's criticisms, which go back to the time before unification and are based on a negative view of unchanging human character, it can only be said that his kind of pessimism has never been universal.[18] In fact, the events of 1989 would not have been possible without some degree of optimistic belief in the possibility of change for the better. Many GDR writers contributed to this movement, and they deserve credit rather than wholesale opprobrium.[19]

Debates about the East at or shortly after unification went beyond the re-evaluation of the role of GDR literature. Some Western writers adopted the role of anthropologists and observed at closer quarters their new compatriots. One of these, not surprisingly, was Peter Schneider, who in a collection of essays written at the time of unification even coined the term *DDR-*

Spezies (GDR species).[20] One example of this race was, in Schneider's view, the typical GDR male, who retained all the characteristics of the traditional macho-type, while the GDR woman, because of the tradition of being part of the labor force, had achieved a degree of emancipation. Schneider asks, in apparent bewilderment, how beautiful, desirable, emancipated women could waste their time on this "Ladenhüter der Gattung" (throwback of the genus; 154). Schneider also contributed to a volume with the telling title *Der rasende Mob* (The Raging Mob, 1993), a reference to the xenophobic violence shown in the East following unification. In his contribution, Klaus Bittermann refers to the attack on a home for asylum seekers in Rostock-Lichtenhagen in 1992. In fact, a notorious picture from this incident — a man in a replica German soccer shirt who has urinated into his trousers giving a Nazi salute — adorns the front cover of the book. Bittermann speaks of this *Vorzeigeossi* (representative Easterner), who always denied that he was a Nazi and claimed he was only someone who wanted foreigners to behave decently. Bittermann also points out that these words about decency were uttered when the man was confronted with the picture that achieved worldwide distribution.[21] The repeated use of the popular abbreviation *Ossi* reflects the tone of Bittermann's essay and that of much of the book: half serious and half jocular. Indeed, the book forms part of a series entitled *Critica Diabolis,* which suggests that tongue-in-cheek exaggeration was part of the concept. Nevertheless, the proverb "Many a true word spoken in jest" does spring to mind, in connection with both this volume and that of Schneider's.

In their criticisms of ordinary East Germans, writers were arguably reflecting the views of their fellow Westerners, who were unhappy about having to foot the bill for unification and who felt that the recipients of their largesse were not being duly grateful. They were certainly questioning the discourse that saw GDR citizens as emerging triumphantly through their protests from decades of oppression. However, criticism was not restricted to Easterners. It was, for example, not just Eastern writers who found themselves in the firing line at the time of unification, as has been seen from the comments by Kunert and Schädlich. The essence of the criticism aimed at Western writers and any others who appeared to show sympathy or understanding for the GDR was contained in the title of a 1992 volume edited by Cora Stephan *Wir Kollabateure.* Given the odium attached to the term "collaboration" in relation to the Nazi occupation of Europe during the Second World War, there was again the implication that the GDR was comparable in its iniquity to the Nazi era, while the use of "we" was no doubt intended to strengthen the overall argument of the book by a dose of self-criticism. In her introduction, Stephan launches a forceful polemic against those Western circles that supported the GDR, attacking the idea of a socialist utopia and the idealization of the GDR's antifascism. She extends her attack by excoriating what she calls the "protestantischen Bußpredigern" (protestant repentance preachers), who compared human closeness and modesty in the GDR favorably with the "freiflottierenden Single-Dasein" (free-floating singles' existence) and the consumerist egoism of Western society.[22] Of the contributors to Stephan's volume, one of the most hard-hitting was Chaim Noll, a GDR dissident, who lambastes not only his erstwhile Eastern colleagues, but also those in the West, in particular the 1968 generation, who enjoy high salaries and own their own homes but still see themselves as possessing "ein zwar in Sofakissen schlummerndes, in Wohlstand verdämmendes, doch bei Gelegenheit revolutionaries Potential" (on occasion a revolutionary potential, which was admittedly slumbering among the sofa cushions and drowsing in prosperity).[23]

In the face of this powerful rhetoric, it is as well to recall the nature of any collaboration between East and West, as discussed in earlier parts of this volume. In reality, relations between writers often mirrored those between politicians, with the 1950s and early 1960s, particularly the time around the building of the Berlin Wall, seeing very restricted contacts. Although in the 1970s many Western writers, including Martin Walser, seemed close to the DKP or even joined it, the limits to their influence became apparent when, a decade later (as seen in chapter 6), there were mass resignations from the VS at the time DKP influence seemed strong. As for the discussions over peace in the 1980s, the loan arranged by Franz Josef Strauß at around the same time was much more significant for the GDR than any perceived moral support from intellectuals.

This is not to deny the existence of such support or to exonerate individuals. However, a more valid charge against Western writers might be that they increasingly ceased taking any interest in what was happening to the east of the Federal Republic. Peter Schneider had complained in a 1985 essay about the gradual disappearance of a point on the compass.[24] What he meant was that Western intellectuals were no longer interested in what was going on to their east and had simply accepted the status quo despite its injustices. Indeed, writing at the time of unification, Patrick Süskind praises the preunification Federal Republic and admits that the East was never of much interest to him.[25] Although he concedes that he felt happy when the Berlin Wall fell, he speaks of having had a much-greater attachment to such far-flung parts of Europe as Crete and the Outer Hebrides than to the areas that made up the GDR.

Indifference of the kind admitted by Süskind would be an entirely inappropriate term to apply to the reactions of many Eastern writers to the attacks on the GDR made at the time of unification. Many, including some who had left the GDR but remained attached to it in various ways (for example, by not giving up citizenship), sought to defend or at least show understanding for the behavior of their colleagues and for GDR citizens in general. Günter de Bruyn, for example, who enjoyed a great deal of respect because of his history of opposition to the GDR regime, welcomed unity, but was quick to defend Christa Wolf in particular. He also warned against comparisons between the GDR and the Nazi period, seeing the danger that in this way the horrors of Nazism would unintentionally be made to look harmless.[26] Rolf Schneider, who left the GDR in the late 1970s but retained residence rights, defended ordinary citizens against criticisms of passivity, pointing out that showing any initiative in the GDR was pointless, up to the point of being suicidal.[27]

In this essay, Schneider also touched on the topic that came more and more to the fore after unity: the unhappiness of Easterners about the effects of unity on their everyday life. Westerners were increasingly regarded as the causes of increased rents and insecurity of tenure, as well as arrogant, unscrupulous salesmen. On a similar theme, a story "Heute kommt Westbesuch" (A Western Visitor Is Coming Today) by Erich Loest, who also left the GDR in the 1970s, captures the feelings of inferiority and helplessness of a middle-aged Eastern woman as she prepares for a visit from her Western sister-in-law.[28] The Western woman will look younger and be smartly dressed and *au fait* with all recent developments. By contrast, she faces unemployment and feels shame about her GDR job: distributing the rare commodity of the automobile to those who had been on the waiting list for years. She had once shown initiative, or at least independent thinking, when she suggested that Soviet cars were unpopular, but this had landed her in hot water and almost worse for denigrating the leading socialist state.

Despite his many problems with the GDR authorities, Stefan Heym both refused to abandon his socialist ideals (he was briefly a member of the PDS group in the federal parliament) and was quick to criticize the activities of Westerners in the East following unification.[29] His story "Auf Sand gebaut" (Built on Sand) is admittedly a satire on Easterners, who are now seeking to profit from capitalism, but also on Westerners seeking to profit from the East — specifically, to take advantage of the decision of the federal government to restore Eastern property to former Western owners rather than merely pay compensation.[30] The narrator is the somewhat naïve husband of a woman who believes that, in the changed times, her house is now worth a fortune. Her dreams are in danger of being shattered by two grotesquely named Westerners with designs on the house: the claimant Prottwedel and his lawyer Schwiebus. However, at the end of the story, another claimant appears — the Israeli Frau Rothmund. Her grandfather was obliged to sell the house to an SS man Dietmar Prottwedel, who did not even pay the ridiculously low price fixed at the time. The end of the story leaves the outcome of these particular events open; what is beyond doubt is that the case of Herr Prottwedel, and by implication that of all Westerners seeking to take advantage of the changed situation in the East, is flawed, at least morally and in this case legally as well.

Another writer who refused to go into raptures over unification was Klaus Schlesinger. This was somewhat surprising since, like so many others, he had left the GDR in the wake of the Biermann affair. Like Heym, he had harsh words for the apparent takeover of the GDR by Western interests. He begins a 1993 piece by stating that he had always seen the choice between the two German states as one between plague and cholera. He goes on to say that he would not bother writing about the GDR if it were not for the *geleckte Affen* (smart Alecs) from the West who, having previously taken no interest in the place, are suddenly omniscient in all things relating to it.[31] He then goes on to criticize the Western desire to demolish half of the GDR when the Federal Republic is equally, if not more, disfigured by architectural monstrosities. Schlesinger does not spare Easterners either, accusing them of sucking up to Westerners before ending his polemic with a series of somewhat direct sexual metaphors. Unification is compared to a marriage based on money. While he speaks of the possibilities of orgasms during the wedding night, it would seem that two and a half years later, the offense of rape within marriage has been committed (13).

That Christa Wolf has responded to her critics is less of a surprise. She, too, makes use of the topos of ignorance when it comes to Western criticism of the GDR and, in particular, the literary life of that country. In the introduction to a volume of her correspondence with her colleague Franz Fühmann, she justifies their publication by reference to the widespread ignorance about the concrete circumstances in which GDR literature was written and about the relations between writers.[32] She goes on to speak of continuing prejudices before coining the word *Nach-Urteile* (post-judices, 62) to describe attitudes toward those writers who chose to stay in the GDR. Wolf also criticizes aspects of life in the Federal Republic. A speech made to mark the eightieth anniversary of the birth of Heinrich Böll gave her the opportunity to stress what she considered to be the continuing relevance of his criticisms of the Federal Republic. She highlights in particular Böll's concern about unemployment and his belief that only a shorter working week can solve the problem. In the meantime, she points out, unemployment has more than doubled, while the link between mass unemployment and a possible endangering of the foundations of democracy remains.[33]

As noted above, Wolf's novel *Medea: Stimmen* must also be read as a critique of the Federal Republic and a partial defense of the GDR. Following her role in Jason's quest for the Golden Fleece, Medea has moved westwards to Corinth, where she becomes increasingly isolated. One thing that she dislikes about her new home is the lust for wealth and the way the value of a citizen is determined by the amount of gold he possesses.[34] It is true, the picture of her native Kolchos is less than positive, with its obdurate rulers failing to respond to the needs of the citizens; however, women seem to be treated more as equals — that is to say, as if their opinions were of some consequence, as the chauvinistic Jason puts it (59). In his review of the novel, Volker Hage sees such passages as calendar verses,[35] while a more recent review in the right-of-center *Die Welt* of a collection of Wolf's essays not only suggests that she no longer has anything worthwhile to say, but that, despite her willingness to dissociate herself from the GDR, she has still failed to grasp the true nature of communism.[36] It is clear that long after unification she remains for some a highly controversial figure.

Equally controversial has been the Eastern political author Daniela Dahn, who has expressed strong criticism of many of the consequences of unification and because of this acquired from her detractors the spiteful sobriquet "die heilige Johanna des Ostens" (the Joan of Arc of the East).[37] Matters came to a head in 1998 when she was put forward by the PDS for the position of lay judge at the constitutional court of the state of Brandenburg. A particularly vitriolic attack was launched against her by the former permanent representative of the Federal Republic in East Berlin, Klaus Bölling, who, while conceding that she was a gifted writer, saw her as an unrepentant apologist for the GDR whose hatred for the Federal Republic was clear from her writing and whose appointment to a judicial position would be nothing less than scandalous.[38] By contrast, Dahn was defended by her colleague Volker Braun[39] and also in the conservative *Frankfurter Allgemeine Zeitung,* where Franziska Augstein reminded readers that her work had been praised even by members of the CDU.[40] As it turned out, Dahn was not elected, as the SPD withdrew its support.

The comment that precipitated the controversy concerned the judicial treatment of former Nazi lawyers in the early years of the GDR — specifically, what have become known as the Waldheim trials. Following unification, these trials were seen in some quarters as proof that the GDR system of justice did not conform to the principle of a fair trial. In her comments, Dahn concedes that the trial was flawed — for example, that the accused were not allowed defense lawyers until the appeal process and that punishments were imposed on the basis of statutes that did not exist at the time of the crime, something always seen as against the principles of the rule of law. On the other hand, she points out that the involvement of the accused in equally dubious processes of law is beyond doubt and that the arguments being advanced to exonerate Nazi lawyers amount to the claim that applying Nazi justice was in no sense a crime.[41] In fact, such arguments are more or less the same as those so disastrously advanced by Filbinger in the 1970s. Dahn also suggests that the trials have to be seen in the context of a time when, following liberation from Nazism, a large number of countries gave severe sentences to those deemed to have collaborated with the enemy. It may, however, have been the comments at the end of the essay that provoked the most ire. Dahn launches a swinging attack on the anticommunism that still prevails in the Federal Republic, concluding by saying that unless it changes, there will be no internal unity in the new Germany (200).

It is this refusal to accept everything Western that has characterized most of Dahn's writing since unity — in particular, what might be regarded as her major work *Westwärts und nicht vergessen* (Westwards But Let's Not Forget, 1996). Six of the eight chapters contain in their subtitle the word *Unbehagen* (disquiet), referring to some aspect of the unification process. Indeed the volume's subtitle is *Vom Unbehagen in der Einheit* (On Disquiet in Unity). The bases for the disquiet, as expressed in the chapter headings, include the author's position as an author, a woman, and a leftist. The starting point is visible in the first chapter — ironically entitled "Osttrotz wider die neue Herrlichkeit" (Eastern Defiance Against New Splendor), with the second term conjuring up images of Prussian militarism — which consists of a dialogue between the author and her publisher. She states her aim as being to combat the current vilification of the GDR and the glorification of the Federal Republic by pointing to the "bescheidenen Vorteile der DDR und die mehr als unbescheidenen Nachteile der Bundesrepublik" (modest advantages of the GDR and the more than immodest disadvantages of the Federal Republic).[42] Obviously, opinions will differ about the points she raises; nevertheless, the frequently negative reactions to Dahn's work show the difficulties of adopting such a stance in postunification Germany.

If intellectuals have ever been the mouthpiece of wider feelings held in society, then this is surely the case in relation to both the unification process and the postunification situation in Germany as a whole. This was underlined at the time of the 2005 election, when the differences between the two parts of the country once again came to the fore. When it was discovered that a woman in the East had murdered each of her nine babies, this was blamed on the "proletarization" of life in the GDR by the Western CDU politician Jörg Schönbohm. The Bavarian first minister Edmund Stoiber expressed the hope that the election would not be decided in the East, a view that suggested that he would have preferred it if East Germans had not had the vote. Such statements, both referred to critically in an interview with Christa Wolf in *Die Zeit,* were not only likely to have encouraged *Osttrotz,* but also contributed to a final outcome that confirmed that voting habits in the East remained different from those in the West.[43]

In addition to the issues discussed above, there is the economic dimension, with the eastern part of Germany still lagging behind the west. At the time of the fifteenth anniversary of unification, this was accepted as inevitable by the journalist Uwe Rada in an article in the *tageszeitung,* which proclaimed simply that attempts to revive the East had failed.[44] By contrast, at around the same time, the German-Turkish writer Zafer Şenocak stressed the psychological dimension: the inability of the German soul to see anything positive in the country's situation. For him, the peaceful unification of Germany is a second German miracle, but nobody is willing to realize it.[45]

In fact, as the twentieth anniversary of unification approaches, the issue of the GDR past remains capable of stirring passions. It was only after a prolonged period of uncertainty, in which the SPD prevaricated, that Wolf Biermann was awarded honorary citizenship of Berlin in 2007. In an interview shortly after the award, Biermann castigated the party for its coalition with the PDS-Linke — specifically, for what he described as climbing into the bed of power with the successors of the *nomenklatura*.[46] He also claimed that the same ruling class of the GDR was doing better in the new Germany than its victims. While the issue of honorary citizenship was still under discussion, Biermann found an ally in Gert Loschütz, an author born in the GDR who moved to the Federal Republic as a child. He also launched an attack on Volker Braun, who had just been elected chair of the literature section of the Academy of Arts. The starting point of his criticism was Braun's poem "Die Mauer" (The Wall), on the basis of which he implied that Braun would never have lifted a finger to support Biermann. The poem, published in the Federal Republic in 1966, juxtaposes official GDR stances about the Wall (it had prevented war, all those who sought to leave the GDR had been misled by Western propaganda) with Western-style invective culminating in the demand that the piece of *Dreck aus Beton* (concrete filth) be torn down.[47] Braun's aim was undoubtedly to question the propaganda being emitted in both German states, as well as the crude language in which it was framed. However, Loschütz fails to refer to Braun's provocative juxtaposition, which could have had serious consequences in that the GDR's legal authorities, not famed for their aesthetic sensibilities, might well have reacted unfavourably to any quotation of western standpoints regardless of context, preferring to see him as an out-and-out GDR apologist who had produced the "widerlichsten Hervorbringungen" (most repulsive outpourings).[48] Given this ridiculously one-sided attitude, it is small wonder that even the conservative *Frankfurter Allgemeine Zeitung* leapt to Braun's defense.[49]

In the light of this kind of polemic, it might seem that little has changed since the early 1990s. That would certainly be exaggerated, both in the case of writers and the wider Germans citizenry, even if the GDR past, like Nazism and terrorism, can continue to stir passions. Moreover, one writer at least, Reinhard Mohr, has detected and praised a change of mood, as the title of his essay "Ostneid, Westneid? Es geht uns gut" (Western Envy? Eastern Envy? We're Fine) shows.[50] While he acknowledges that there is still a gap between the two parts of the country, not least economically, he believes that difference is something that should be celebrated. This is a kind of optimism of which not just Şenocak might approve, even if it would disprove his assertion, referred to above, about German inability to see things positively.

Notes

[1] Ulrich Greiner, "Mangel an Feingefühl," in *Es geht nicht um Christa Wolf,*" ed. Thomas Anz (Munich: edition spangenberg, 1991), 66–70, here 66.

[2] Frank Schirrmacher, "Dem Druck des härteren, strengeren Lebens standhalten," in *"Es geht nicht um Christa Wolf,*" ed. Anz, 77–89, here 81. Further citations given in parentheses.

[3] Ulrich Greiner, "Die deutsche Gesinnungsästhetik," in *"Es geht nicht um Christa Wolf,*" ed. Anz, 208–16, here 213.

[4] See Joachim Walther et al., eds., *Protokoll eines Tribunals* (Reinbek: Rowohlt), 103.

[5] Reiner Kunze, *Deckname "Lyrik"* (Frankfurt am Main: Fischer, 1990), 73–74.

[6] Erich Loest, *Die Stasi war mein Eckermann* (Göttingen: Steidl, 1991).

[7] See Hermann Vinke, ed., *Akteneinsicht Christa Wolf* (Hamburg: Luchterhand, 1993), 158.

[8] See Vinke, ed., *Akteneinsicht,* 151.

[9] Wolf Biermann, "Der Lichtblick im gräßlichen Fatalismus der Geschichte," *Die Zeit* 25 October 91, 73–74.

[10] Wolf Biermann, "Auch ich war bei der Stasi," *Die Zeit,* 4 May 1990, 73–74.

[11] Joachim Walther, *Sicherungsbereich Literatur* (Berlin: Links, 1996).

[12] Klaus Michael, "Feindbild Literatur. Die Biermann-Affäre, Staatssicherheit und die Herausbildung einer Alternativkultur," in *Aus Politik und Zeitgeschehen (Das Parlament),* 28 May 1993, 23. The co-edited volume is *MachtSpiele: Literatur und Staatssicherheit,* ed. Peter Böthig, Klaus Michael (Leipzig: Reclam, 1993).

[13] Monika Maron, "Der Schriftsteller und das Volk," *Der Spiegel,* 12 February 1990, 68–70.

[14] Günter Kunert, "Was erwarten Sie von Deutschland? Was wünschen Sie dem vereinten Land?," *Die Zeit,* 5 January 1990, 52.

[15] See Franz Josef Görtz, Volker Hage, and Uwe Wittstock, eds., *Deutsche Literatur 1989: Jahresüberblick* (Reclam: Stuttgart, 1990), 121.

[16] Hans Joachim Schädlich, "Das Fähnlein der treu Enttäuschten," *Die Zeit,* 26 October 1990, 68.

[17] See Vinke, *Akteneinsicht,* 166.

[18] See, for example, the stance taken by Wolf Biermann in a discussion that appeared in *Die Zeit:* Wolf Biermann, "'Wenn ich so dächte wie Kunert, möchte ich lieber tot sein.' Ein ZEIT-Gespräch zwischen Wolf Biermann, Günter Kunert und Fritz J. Raddatz," *Die Zeit,* 14 November 1980, 41–42.

[19] For a wider discussion of these issues, see Peter Peters, "We Are One Book. Perspectives and Developments of an All-German Literature," in *The Individual, Identity and Innovation,* ed. Arthur Williams and Stuart Parkes (Bern: Lang, 1994), 297–314.

[20] Peter Schneider, "Gibt es zwei deutsche Kulturen; Die Kühlschranktheorie und andere Vermutungen," in *Extreme Mittellage,* Peter Schneider (Reinbek: Rowohlt, 1990), 120–57, here 136. Further citations given in parentheses.

[21] Klaus Bittermann, "Die Geisterwelt der Ossis," in *Der rasende Mob,* ed. Klaus Bittermann and Henryk M. Broder (Berlin: Verlag Klaus Bittermann, 1993), 104–38, here 128.

[22] Cora Stephan, "Vorwort," in *Wir Kollaborateure,* ed. Stephan (Reinbek: Rowohlt, 1992), 7–10, here 7.

[23] Chaim Noll, "Treue um Treue," in *Wir Kollaborateure,* ed. Stephan, 90–106, here 101.

[24] Peter Schneider, "Über das allmähliche Verschwinden einer Himmelsrichtung," in *Deutsche Ängste,* Schneider, 54–65.

[25] Patrick Süskind, "Deutschland, eine Midlife-Crisis," *Der Spiegel,* 17 September 1990, 116–25.

[26] Günter de Bruyn, "Jubelschreie, Trauergesänge," *Die Zeit,* 37/7 September 1990, 61–62, here 61.

[27] Rolf Schneider, "Die heilsame Entfremdung," *Der Spiegel,* 24 September 1990, 54.

[28] Erich Loest, "Heute kommt Westbesuch," in *Von Abraham bis Zwerenz,* vol. 2, ed., Bundesministerium für Bildung, Wissenschaft, Forschung und Technologie (Berlin: Cornelsen, 1995), 1198–1206.

[29] See the interview with Stefan Heym: "Ich kann doch nicht mein ganzes Leben wegwerfen," *Die Zeit,* 6 December 1991, 64–65.

[30] Stefan Heym, "Auf Sand gebaut," in *Auf Sand gebaut,* Stefan Heym (Frankfurt am Main: Fischer, 1993), 26–36.

[31] Klaus Schlesinger, "Sehnsucht nach der DDR?," in *Von der Schwierigkeit, Westler zu werden,* Klaus Schlesinger (Berlin: Aufbau, 1998), 11–14, here 11. Further citations given in parentheses.

[32] Christa Wolf, "Nirgends sein o Nirgends du mein Land," in *Hierzulande. Andernorts,* Christa Wolf (Munich: DTV, 2001), 61–68, here 61. Further citations given in parentheses.

[33] Christa Wolf, "'Mitleidend bleibt das ewige Herz doch fest.' Zum 80. Geburtstag Heinrich Bölls," in *Hierzulande,* Wolf, 175–94, here 180.

[34] Christa Wolf, *Medea: Stimmen* (Munich: Luchterhand, 1996), 38. Further citations given in parentheses.

[35] Volker Hage, "Kein Mord. Nirgends," in *Deutsche Literatur 1996,* ed. Franz Josef Görtz, Volker Hage, and Hubert Winkels (Stuttgart: Reclam, 1997), 268–73, here 272.

[36] Tilman Krause, "Christa steht auf Obstsalat," *Die Welt,* 16 July 2005. http://www.welt.de/print-welt/article682742/Christa_steht_auf_Obstsalat.html. Consulted 13 October 2008.

[37] Dahn herself refers to being characterized in this way. See Daniela Dahn, *In guter Verfassung* (Reinbek: Rowohlt, 1999), 7.

[38] Bölling's comments originally appeared in *Welt am Sonntag* and are included in the documentation section of *In guter Verfassung,* Dahn, 128–29, here 128.

[39] See Dahn, *In guter Verfassung,* 141.

[40] See Dahn, *In guter Verfassung,* 172–73.

[41] Daniela Dahn, "Eine beispiellose Tragödie," in *Vertreibung ins Paradies,* Daniela Dahn (Reinbek: Rowohlt, 1998),188–200, here 190. Further citations given in parentheses.

[42] Daniela Dahn, *Westwärts und nicht vergessen* (Reinbek: Rowohlt, 1997), 10.

[43] Christa Wolf, "Bei mir dauert alles sehr lange," *Die Zeit,* 7 October 2005. http://www.zeit.de/text/2005/40/Wolf-Interview. Consulted 1 October 2005.

[44] Uwe Rada, "Sonderwohlfahrtszone Ost," *die tageszeitung,* 24 September 2005. http://taz.de/pt/2005/09/24/a0202.nf/textdruck. Consulted 24 September 2005.

[45] Zafer Şenocak, "Dunkle deutsche Seele," Die Welt, 7 October 2005. http://www. welt.de/print-welt/article169207/Dunkle_deutsche_Seele.html. Consulted 13 October 2008.

[46] Wolf Biermann, "'Berlin zottelt an meinem Herzen,'" Berliner Zeitung, 10 April 2007. http://www.berlinonline.de/berliner-zeitung/archiv/.bin/dump.fcgi/2007/ 0410/feuilleton/0009/index.html. Consulted 13 October 2008.

[47] Volker Braun, "Fünf Gedichte auf Deutschland," Kursbuch 4 (1966): 64–72, here 65.

[48] "Gert Loschütz über Biermann und andere Dichter," Deutschlandradio, 22 January 2007. http://www.dradio.de/dkultur/sendungen/politischesfeuilleton/ 584711/. Consulted 2 October 2007.

[49] igl, "Die Mauer," Frankfurter Allgemeine Zeitung, 29 January 2007, 33.

[50] Reinhard Mohr, "Ostneid? Westneid? Es geht uns gut," Die Welt, 4 May 2007, http://www.welt.de/kultur/article850776/Ostneid_Westneid_Es_geht_uns_gut. html. Consulted 7 May 2007.

8: New Views on the Past

ATTITUDES TO GERMANY'S NAZI PAST have been a recurring theme throughout this volume, with reference being made, for example, to the immediate postwar debates around the comments by Thomas Mann about German literature written during the Third Reich, to concerns about "restoration" in the early years of the Federal Republic, and to the worries about democracy at the time of the Grand Coalition when for the first time a former member of the Nazi party became federal chancellor. The overall consensus, at least among writers and intellectuals, was that during the first decades of the existence of the Federal Republic there had been a political failure to face up to the past. This idea found expression in the phrase *unbewältigte Vergangenheit* (unmastered past), a term that came to be used more widely in society. More recently, it has become normal to speak of *Vergangenheitsbewältigung*, which implies that the necessary process of coming to terms with the past has at least begun. At the same time, as noted earlier, writers' and intellectuals' efforts (or lack of them) to confront the past have come under scrutiny, with both the Gruppe 47 and the 1968 generation being subject to a reassessment of their roles.

Two works written in the preunification Federal Republic arguably stand out as prime examples of the expression of concern about society's failure to deal with the Nazi past. The first, *Die Unfähigkeit zu trauern* (The Inability to Mourn), written by the psychologists Alexander and Margarete Mitscherlich, dates from 1967. The authors speak of a denial of the past, which led in the postwar period to an absence of signs of melancholy or mourning among the great mass of the population.[1] The rapid removal of ruins immediately after the end of the war is thus to be seen as a sign of a manic desire to remove all signs of Nazism. Nevertheless, despite such efforts, which persist in what is seen as a lack of emotional response to the events of the war years, the past lives on as a problem that, in the view of the Mitscherlichs, society still has to face. Their ideal, as expressed in the introduction to the paperback edition, is *Trauerarbeit* (the work of mourning) — incidentally, a term that entered the language to describe a process that can lead to a healing — and a society that is "höflich, anteilnehmend, rücksichtsvoll" (polite, sympathetic, caring; 10).

The second work to be considered in this context, Ralph Giordano's *Die zweite Schuld* (The Second Guilt, 1987), appeared two decades after the Mitscherlichs's study, with the paperback edition describing it on its back cover as a critical analysis of West German "inability to mourn." The author was himself a victim of Nazi racial policies, an experience that he describes in his autobiographical novel *Die Bertinis* of 1982. What, then, is the nature of the second guilt Giordano speaks of? It is the failure by the relevant generations honestly to confront either the Nazi past or their own role in it, and the concomitant attempt to suppress oppressive memories and "sich aus einem kompromittierenden Abschnitt selbsterlebter und mitgestalteter Nationalgeschichte davonzustehlen" (to steal away from a compromising segment of history they experienced and helped to create).[2] In this, they were helped by a majority of politicians, whose priority was to gain votes rather than talk about the past. The results of such behavior by older generations are, according to Giordano, a sense of disorientation among the young and a society in which, despite all the progress made, democracy and freedom cannot be taken as matters of course (26).

If the works of the Mitscherlichs and Giordano remain seminal to the discussion of the Nazi past in the preunification era, then it is possible to see a change since unification. This is not surprising given the changed context. German unification put an end to a political situation that resulted directly from the end of the war and the Nazi period and was thus a constant reminder of this past. Accordingly, the return of what, with the end of division, was frequently seen as normality potentially allowed a different kind of debate, one that was less influenced by present political realities. As was seen in the previous section, the end of the GDR meant that all aspects of that state came under scrutiny, including its attitude to the Nazi past. Particularly, the claim that official antifascism meant that the evil of Nazism had been eradicated proved to be highly dubious once xenophobic, and in some cases neo-Nazi, disturbances started in the East. The undoubted hollowness of official GDR claims then led, in turn, to a general questioning of left-wing antifascism.

Beyond this political dimension, other factors also played a part. With the passage of time, those with a direct experience of the Nazi period were inevitably becoming fewer. As a result, personal memories of this era were giving way to public memory, provided primarily by books, films, the media, museums, and the education system. Thus, the issue was how to retain a memory of the past for generations with no direct implication in the events. Added to this was the internationalization of the Holocaust — that is to say, the increasing interest, backed by the expressed desire to learn from the past, being taken in numerous countries in what had happened at Auschwitz and elsewhere. A Holocaust Museum opened in Washington, DC, in 1993, while 24 January, the anniversary of the liberation of Auschwitz, has become an official day of memory in a number of countries.

Changes in perceptions of history do not of course coincide strictly with political developments. Shortly prior to unification, in 1986, a dispute over the singularity of Nazi crimes — known as the *Historikerstreit* (historians' quarrel), even if not all the participants were historians — attracted much public attention. The specific issue was whether Nazi genocide was a unique event in history, a question that also became linked with Hitler's declaration of war against the Soviet Union in 1941. The first shot was fired by Ernst Nolte, a philosopher turned historian, who argued not only that Nazi genocide was not unique but also that it was a reaction to the Soviet gulag system and thus a kind of Asiatic import foreign to Europe. The related argument was that the war against the Soviet Union was a preemptive strike against a country that itself had plans to attack Germany. The counterattack was launched by the philosopher Jürgen Habermas, who insisted on the unique nature of Nazi genocide. As in all such disputes, it is difficult to assess how far perceptions were changed. If such processes could be assessed on the basis of the amount of interest shown, then the characterization by the then-federal president Richard von Weizsäcker of the end of the war in 1945 as liberation rather than capitulation certainly would be a case in point. His groundbreaking speech marking the fortieth anniversary of the end of the war achieved a rapid circulation in printed form of 650,000, another sign of a renewed interest in the recent past.

Given the way that the Nazi past has become increasingly a question of public memory, it is not surprising that one of the major disputes since unification has been over the Holocaust Memorial in Berlin, which finally opened in 2005.[3] The idea for such a memorial came in 1988 from the television journalist Lea Rosh, while the creation of a *Förderkreis* (official support group) predated the fall of the Berlin Wall by two days. One member of the support group was the novelist Siegfried Lenz. The project gained the backing of the federal government under Chancellor Kohl, as well as acceptance by the CDU-led Berlin government, although Berlin's Governing Mayor Diepgen showed a distinct lack of enthusiasm, as did Chancellor Schröder initially following his accession to power.[4] Among writers and intellectuals, there was considerable support, for example from Günter Grass. However, the same cannot be said of Jewish circles. The novelist Rafael Seligmann, as late as 2003, spoke of an act of political correctness by the curatorium and its acceptance by politicians, "die auf die Weltmeinung schielen" (squinting at world opinion).[5] The Hungarian writer György Konrád, now resident in Berlin, objected to the monumentality of the project, which he declared a waste of money. He would have preferred the money to have been used for something that would have given pleasure, that the murdered Jews, too, might have enjoyed.[6] Particularly blunt, as ever, was the journalist Henryk M. Broder, who stated in 1997:

> Es geht nicht an, dass Menschen, die sich selbst als Nachkommen der Täter bezeichnen, darüber verfügen, welche Opfer ein Denkmal ver-

dienen und welche nicht. Die Sonderbehandlung der Juden darf nicht unter einem positiven Vorzeichen fortgesetzt werden.[7]

[It is not acceptable that people, who describe themselves as the successors of the perpetrators, determine which victims deserve a monument and which do not. The special treatment of the Jews must not be continued, even under a positive sign.]

This comment, which incorporates the Nazi euphemism for mass murder *Sonderbehandlung,* refers to the question of whether the memorial should have been exclusively for Jewish victims of the Nazis or should have included others, such as gypsies and homosexuals. Such views did not represent all Jewish opinion. The head of the Jewish community Ignatz Bubis was in favor, as was the architect and leading member of the Jewish community Salomon Korn, who played a major part in the debate. Although he unreservedly supported the memorial, he expressed concerns about whether resources were being directed to it at the expense of other sites, such as former concentration camps. He was also concerned that the scale of the project might have negative consequences, as had happened in his view with the memorial in the Berlin Neue Wache, opened in 1993. This memorial was controversial because it referred to all victims of war and violence, arguably without much discrimination; indeed, that the Holocaust Memorial was dedicated solely to Jewish victims was possibly a reaction to this, conceded Ignatz Bubis.[8] There have also been doubts about the way the Neue Wache memorial was created. At its center stands an enlarged version of a Käthe Kollwitz *Pietà;* in Korn's view, a subtle work of art had been expanded out of all proportion.[9]

Doubts about the monumentality of the project, indeed, about the possibility of any kind of presentation of the Holocaust with an aesthetic dimension, caused a change of mind in the case of Walter Jens, at that time president of the Academy of Arts. In a 1998 text entitled "Widerruf in letzter Minute" (Retraction at the Last Minute), he claimed that monumental art could not capture the horrors of the Holocaust.[10] Jens was not the only person to change his mind. Among the signatories of an open letter that appeared in *Der Tagesspiegel* on 4 February 1998 was Günter Grass. This letter, too, expressed doubts about the size of the site and the possibility of modern art being able to provide the right context for the reflection the monument should inspire.[11]

Most of the objections against the memorial were answered in a long essay by Jürgen Habermas in *Die Zeit,* which appeared in March 1999. For him, the memorial is inextricably linked with emphasizing the identity of a nation that history requires should pay special attention to civil rights.[12] In this context, he attacks Chancellor Schröder for his superficial desire to "dispose of" (*entsorgen*) history (42). As for the aesthetic question, he concedes that it might be difficult, if not, impossible, to present the breakdown of civilization through art (43). Habermas justifies the restriction of the memorial to the Jewish victims of the Nazis by stressing the major role Jews had played in German culture and society, although all victims must retain society's respect (44). He also answers those who fear that the memorial will attract protest and vandalism from extremists. Such an argument is dismissed as pusillanimous. Any such protests will show the state of society and thus the nature of problems still to be faced (44). When the memorial finally opened, the consensus, at least in the printed media, seemed to be that what many had deemed impossible had been achieved. Writing in *die tageszeitung,* the writer and journalist Stefan Reinecke expressed a kind of surprised delight at the paradox that the memory of something horrendous had been turned into something pleasing without what was being commemorated having been devalued. The title of his article, "Ein Skandal, der gefällt" (A Scandal That Pleases), captures his feelings.[13] The exception to the rule remained Henryk M. Broder. In a debate with the television author Wolfgang Menge, he retained his implacable opposition, speaking of his hatred of suggestive architecture.[14]

One of those to object to the memorial was Martin Walser, arguably the writer at the center of the debates about attitudes to the Nazi past following unification. In his speech on being awarded the Peace Prize of the German Book Trade in 1998, which he used to criticize prevailing attitudes toward the past, he describes the planned memorial as a "fußballfeldgroßer Alptraum" (nightmare the size of a football field).[15] For his detractors, this statement was proof that someone who had once been at the forefront of progressive intellectual concern about the Nazi past had relapsed into viewpoints more associated with the conservative Right, with some claiming that he had never been on the Left.[16] This concern with issues relating to Nazism goes back at least to the 1960s. The play *Eiche und Angora* (Oaks and Rabbits, translated as *The Rabbit Race,* 1962), for instance, which is set over a period of some fifteen years after the 1945 defeat, contrasts the fortunes of the former Nazi official Gorbach, who is able to keep pace with the changing political climate, with his factotum Alois, who has always been one step behind. What is particularly interesting in this play, however, is the way that Nazis are not portrayed as larger-than-life monsters but as very ordinary people. This idea resurfaces in Walser's essay on the Auschwitz trials of the 1960s, the event that to a large degree turned the name Auschwitz into a metonym for all the horrors of National Socialism. According to this text, casting the guards on trial as inhuman monsters, as was the practice in parts of the media, provides comfort to the many, who are happy to believe that they as "normal people" would have been incapable of any acts of bestiality and are thus able to dissociate themselves from what happened and, in the words of the title, create only "our Auschwitz." Against this, Walser sets collective responsibility, even collective guilt, suggesting that if nation and state are still significant concepts, all Germans are implicated.[17] Walser's views and presentation of Nazis at that time contrast starkly with that of Rolf Hochhuth, in whose play *Der Stellvertreter* (The Representative, 1963) the doctor, a Mengele-type figure, is presented as a monster. Walser's presentation is much closer to that of other writers of his generation, such as Grass, who, according to the poet and critic Michael Hamburger, seek to "de-demonize" the past and show in their works set in the Nazi era "the banality of millions of ordinary men who differed from Eichmann only in being differently employed."[18] In other words, given a position of authority, they would have behaved in the same way as Eichmann.

Walser continued to stress the relevance of Auschwitz in later works, beginning, for example, a 1979 speech with the bald assertion: "Seit Auschwitz ist noch kein Tag vergangen" (Still not a day has passed since Auschwitz).[19] It is not surprising therefore that his 1998 speech, which to some seemed a demand that less attention be paid to Auschwitz, should arouse a major controversy, which was dubbed (although many others took part) "Die Walser-Bubis-Debatte."[20] Two passages in particular attracted attention. The first is Walser's admission that he has frequently turned his head away when presented with horrific media images of Nazi crimes.[21] The second is the claim that Auschwitz is instrumentalized by intellectuals for present purposes (12). The result, in his view, of constant reference to the Nazi past is not true concern with what happened but only lip service (13). Against this he sets the importance of individual conscience against public memory as epitomized in the Holocaust Memorial. At the political level, he suggests that the Germans are now a normal people, living in an ordinary society (13).

If there is a link between this and his earlier comments, it is found on at least two levels. One has to do with the importance Walser continues to attach to the collective of the German people. The other is his desire to challenge the prevailing discourse — in the current context, the endless references to the Nazi past even as the events themselves recede further into the past. Walser was to go even further in this provocative direction in his novel *Tod eines Kritikers* (Death of a Critic, 2002), a work that led him to be branded as an anti-Semite. In this novel, a literary critic — who is regarded as a Jew, although this idea may be based more on rumor than fact — is apparently murdered by a writer whose work he has severely criticized. Although in the end it transpires that no murder has taken place, the fact that the doyen of German literary critics, Marcel Reich-Ranicki, who has been often far from enamored by Walser's work, is Jewish was enough to suggest to some that the latter harbored feelings of anti-Semitic hatred toward his tormentor.[22]

This was not the first time that Walser had raised the issue of German-Jewish relations in his work since unification. The novel *ohne einander* (without each other, 1993), initially set in a news magazine based, it would appear, on *Der Spiegel*, recounts how rational thought disappears once the Jewish issue surfaces. The owner is worried lest a particular article appears anti-Semitic. However, once its author claims Jewish forebears, the objection vanishes, although a balancing article is then commissioned from the novel's protagonist Ellen Kern-Krenn. As she struggles, despite many misgivings, with this task of writing a positive review of the film *Hitlerjunge Salamon* (The Hitler Youth, Salamon, translated as *Europa Europa*, 1991), a colleague quotes Karl Kraus's dictum that philo-Semites are really anti-Semites who have not yet realized this fact.[23] Since this aphorism is more or less repeated, albeit without the attribution to Kraus, in *Tod eines Kritikers*, it can be assumed that it is close to Walser's own view.[24] What seems beyond doubt is that Walser seeks a change in what might be dubbed pathological German attitudes toward Jews. Such attitudes are satirized in the play *Kaschmir in Parching* (Cashmere in Parching, 1995) where a mysterious outsider immediately gains status once he is taken for a Jew. Against this unhealthy attitude, Walser sets the ideal of a German-Jewish symbiosis as exemplified by the academic Victor Klemperer, the author of the famous study into the language of the Third Reich. In a speech on Klemperer delivered in 1995, he stresses how, despite the Nazi terror, he remained true to his *Deutschtum* (German identity),[25] while in his 1998 speech he underlines his refusal to accept that the German-Jewish relationship inevitably had to end with Auschwitz.[26] The problem with Walser's stance is, of course, that this relationship did lead to Auschwitz and that all attempts to seek a less-charged German-Jewish relationship create an outcry that suggests that the achievement of normality remains something of a dream. There may, however, be some comfort for Walser in comments made in the novel *Der Musterjude* (The Exemplary Jew, 1997) by Rafael Seligmann. The Jewish hero Moische Bernstein loses his position as a journalist because he attacks capitalism, while his adversary Wimmer loses his because he is accused of anti-Semitism, which is in the eyes of Moische's lawyer the equivalent of a death sentence in post-Nazi Germany.[27] Moreover, Walser himself showed a degree of flexibility when, a year after the opening of the Memorial, he was quoted as approving of it, stating that the danger of creating a monstrosity had been avoided. At the same time, he maintained his insistence on the personal dimension of remembrance of the past, saying that the Memorial invited internal reflection.[28]

The comment in Seligmann's novel about the dangers of being perceived as anti-Semitic in postwar Germany also finds expression in Friedrich C. Delius's story *Die Flatterzunge* (The Loose Tongue, 1999). Based on a true event, it recounts how a trombonist loses his livelihood when, during an orchestral tour to Israel, he signs a bar chit with the name Adolf Hitler. He rebels against this professional death sentence by questioning the, in his view, overzealous attempts by his fellow citizens to make amends for the Nazi past. He mocks, for instance, the way a Berlin bus stop is called "German Resistance" to prove that some Germans resisted Nazism. That the signs in the buses indicate this by the abbreviation "Dt. Widerstand" makes this even more ludicrous in his eyes.[29] It would be dangerous to infer that Delius is entirely in sympathy with his character; nevertheless, he does offer him something of a way out: an invitation from Israel to play there, accompanied by the advice, written in English: "Just be the German you are" (140).

Much more explicit are the comments made by Bodo Morshäuser in a long essay *Hauptsache Deutsch* (Main Priority German, 1992) published in 1992. He comes close to Walser on the issue of instrumentalization, with his target both sides of the political spectrum. His argument is that all sensible dialogue between the political Left and Right is made absurd by endless reference to the past and, specifically, Auschwitz. With Auschwitz occupying center stage, extreme views take over, with dialogue giving way to conflict between systems of belief.[30] Morshäuser's suggestion that everyone on the Right denies Auschwitz is somewhat odd; what is important to note in this context, though, is that his comments did not cause the same stir as those of Walser.

The only work to have come close to doing so is Schlink's *Der Vorleser* (The Reader, 1995), although in this case much of the debate has taken place outside Germany.[31] As noted above, this work raises the issue of Germans as victims, an issue that resurfaced following an intervention by the England-based German author W. G. Sebald, by no means someone in sympathy with crude ideas of German victimhood. In lectures given in Zurich in late 1997, Sebald suggested that, almost without exception, postwar German literature had failed to portray the Allied bombing of Germany, while those who had experienced the events also retained a wall of silence. Sebald's thesis, which he did not modify after initial responses to his comments, was that German writers were unable or unwilling to describe the experience of bombing raids on German cities.[32] These comments sparked a major debate about why this should be the case and whether indeed it was the case. The critic Joachim Güntner, for instance, suggested that the books were there but that they had found few readers, a view that at least reinforces Sebald's claim that lack of interest in the bombings was prevalent throughout society (91). The ever-forthright Maxim Biller used the occasion to damn more or less all postwar German literature that deals with the war. For him, this literature concentrated on the sufferings of German soldiers, while the victims of the soldiers were largely forgotten.[33] Clearly, this view seems at odds with that of Sebald, even if the latter is primarily concerned about the portrayal of civilians affected by war.

What is beyond doubt is that the theme of German suffering has returned to German literature. One earlier work describing Allied bombing,

Gerd Ledig's *Vergeltung* (Retribution, 1956) was reprinted in 1998 by Suhrkamp, while a 2002 work on the subject by the historian Jörg Friedrich became an immediate bestseller.[34] Nevertheless, it would be an oversimplification to speak of a return to the frequently held view of the 1950s that Germans were the victims of the war, and that events such as the expulsion of Germans from the eastern territories were major injustices that could be considered without reference to earlier Nazi acts of barbarism. A work like Treichel's *Der Verlorene*, mentioned above, with its concentration on the feelings of the brother of the lost boy, does not come into this category. In the case of Uwe Timm's autobiographical novel *Am Beispiel meines Bruders* (Taking the Example of My Brother, 2003) — which deals, again from the point of view of a sibling, with a brother, a volunteer for the Waffen SS killed in the war — there have been accusations of a lack of sympathy for the person killed. In the title of a polemic published in *Der Spiegel,* Timm's fellow author Günter Franzen accuses him of being "Links, wo Kein Herz ist" (Left, Where No Heart Is), a charge he extends to a 1968 generation characterized by "pausbäckiger Selbstzufriedenheit" (chubby-cheeked smugness).[35]

Franzen also refers in his essay to the idea put forward in 2000 by the official representatives of Germans expelled from their former homelands in the east of a *Zentrum gegen Vertreibungen* (center against expulsions). Given its source, this idea unsurprisingly did not meet with comprehension in Poland and the Czech Republic, as Daniela Dahn points out in an essay rejecting the idea. While accepting that suffering was inflicted on those expelled, she is unwilling to see them all as victims, asking whether the promoters were more interested in reapportioning guilt away from Germany toward Eastern Europe than expressing either personal sorrow or any desire for reconciliation.[36] It was only in the autumn of 2007 that it was agreed by the federal government to go ahead with the center, with a concrete proposal being accepted in early 2008. It remains to be seen how far the center will concentrate on the German experience. As Dahn points out, Hitler's plan for a new European order led in the early years of the war to the displacement of some 16 million people.

Given his own biography, it is not surprising that Günter Grass should have returned to the theme of expulsion and German suffering in his 2002 work *Im Krebsgang* (Crabwalk, 2002).[37] To be exact, the story recounted is not one of expulsion but of what happens when, in the face of the advancing Soviet army, Tulla Pokriefke, a fictional character from Grass's Danzig Trilogy, sets out to cross the Baltic on the ill-fated ship *Wilhelm Gustloff.* The death toll on this all-too-real ship, which was sunk by Soviet submarine action on 30 January 1945, surpassed that on the much-better-known *Titanic.* In Grass's story, Tulla gives birth to a son during the disaster; however, it is to her grandson she turns to keep alive the memory of her experiences. In that part of the narrative set in the present, the boy, a neo-Nazi, kills a young Jew with whom he has corresponded electronically. The blame for his anti-Semitic act is laid at the door of his father, a member of the 1968 generation who, as a self-styled antifascist, has swept his mother's and similar fates under the carpet. Grass is certainly not going to the other extreme, presenting the Germans as innocent victims. His point is that, if German suffering is ignored or not put into historical context, the consequences are likely to be political extremism of the type found in his young character, and that has scarred the Federal Republic, especially in the 1990s.

The lessons to be learned from the Nazi past in the area of foreign policy have also been the subject of much discussion since unification. The slogan associated with the 1968 generation, and thus with many of the authors referred to in this book, was *Nie wieder Auschwitz, nie wieder Krieg* (Never again Auschwitz, never again war). However, the validity of this dictum came into question with the end of the Cold War, as the threat of global nuclear destruction gave way to the reality of regional conflicts. The first conflict to provoke major controversy was the First Gulf War of 1991. How strong postwar pacifism remained throughout German society became evident with the protests against this war at many German universities. At the same time, some writers spoke in favor of the war, with differences of opinion between colleagues reputedly leading to the termination of a number of personal friendships.

A number of essays in favor of the war — or of at least attacking the *"edle Seelen"* (noble spirits) of the peace movement, as the volume's subtitle puts it — are found in a book with the telling title *Liebesgrüße aus Bagdad* (From Baghdad with Love). One of the most trenchant contributions is that of Hans Magnus Enzensberger, who compares Saddam with Hitler. His piece is essentially a psychological portrait of Saddam, who is seen as having the same characteristics as Hitler. This, in Enzensberger's view, renders armed conflict inevitable, because such a person always achieves his ambition of unleashing war.[38] Another writer to come out unreservedly in favor was Wolf Biermann, who in his essay on the subject baldly states that he is for the Gulf War.[39] One of his main concerns is the potential vulnerability of Israel to attack from Iraq, an issue that was bound to be very important in Germany. That Germany had supplied Saddam Hussein with the means of creating weapons with such a capability, without there being much public protest, is the topic of Ralph Giordano's piece in the *Liebesgrüße* collection.[40]

Whether Enzensberger's references to Hitler amount to an instrumentalization of the Nazi past for present purposes of the type castigated by Walser is a matter of debate. Suffice it to say that Walser himself was an opponent of the war, seeing it as a relapse into atavistic habits when sanctions, given time, might have worked. A similar belief in nonviolent methods was to be found in a VS resolution.[41] A volume that collected antiwar sentiments (though not exclusively) had the telling title *Ich will reden von der Angst meines Herzens* (I Will Speak of the Anxiety in My Heart, 1991), with the unorthodox word order in German intended to show the urgency of the issue.[42] The same intensity of feeling was generally not engendered by the Second Gulf War, even if Enzensberger reinforced his pro-war stance, with the main interest being in debates between German and American intellectuals over the concept of a just war.[43] This may have been because between these two conflicts lay the event that added a different dimension to debates over war and peace: the civil war in Yugoslavia.

At the time of the First Gulf War, there was no question of the involvement of German troops, as this was felt to be rendered impossible by the Basic Law. At the time of the Second Gulf War, Chancellor Schröder immediately refused to send troops, thus removing that question from the debate. By contrast, the conflict in the much-closer Yugoslavia made the question of German military involvement much more relevant. In the end, the constitutional barriers were overcome and German troops have been active in former Yugoslavia, as well as elsewhere — for example, Afghanistan. When conflict broke out in Yugoslavia, the issue of the lessons to be learned from the past surfaced especially when it became clear that the Serbs were confining people in what amounted to concentration camps. One writer who urged an end to what might be called the traditional pacifistic stance was Peter Schneider. In a 1995 essay, he castigated the failure of the European countries and the European public to respond to Serb atrocities in Bosnia. For him, the issue was simple: without an effective military response to Serb aggression, there could be no political response either.[44] Arguably the major figure to accept the need for military action, albeit "mit Bauchschmerzen" (with stomach pains), was Jürgen Habermas, who signed an international petition for military action initiated by artists at the 1995 Avignon Festival.[45]

The intellectual debate over Yugoslavia intensified with the public adoption of a strongly pro-Serbian stance by the Austrian Peter Handke, whose fame meant that the stir created went far beyond his native country to Germany and Europe as a whole. What was ostensibly a report on a visit to Serbia became for some an apology for the Milošević regime and a questioning of the extent of Bosnian suffering. In his text, Handke shows sympathy for the simpler life he finds in Serbia as well as distrust for the media reporting of the war in the Balkans. Whereas such distrust might be understandable, the tone chosen by Handke to attack those who criticize Serbia is certainly open to criticism. The French philosopher Alain Finkielkraut, for example, is described as "ein unbegreiflicher Plapperer" (an incomprehensible babbler).[46] Not surprisingly, Handke's stance attracted strong criticism, not least from Peter Schneider. In particular, Schneider takes exception to Handke's questioning of the authenticity of pictures of Bosnians rounded up in camps. He describes this as *Niedertracht* (despicableness), accusing Handke of turning his anger on the victims rather than the torturers and killers.[47] Although a good decade has now elapsed, the issue has not gone away, with Handke maintaining his position publicly by visiting the imprisoned Milošević, attending his funeral, supporting Serbian nationalist politicians, and refusing to take back what he said or even, as he put it in a 2006 interview with *Die Zeit*, to acknowledge there was anything to take back.[48] Later in the same year, Handke suffered for this stance, when the city of Düsseldorf withdrew its initial offer of the Heinrich Heine prize.

The arguments over war and peace since unification are just one example of how much the Nazi era remains a point of reference in debate in Germany. There seems little prospect of that changing in the foreseeable future. Sometimes debate is occasioned by publications originating in other countries — for example, in the 1990s Daniel J. Goldhagen's *Hitler's Willing Executioners*, and more recently the publication in Germany of Jonathan Littell's *The Kindly Ones*. However, it is only proposed here to look at two controversies from 2006 and 2007, both directly concerning major German writers who have been frequently referred to in this volume.

In 2006, Günter Grass published his autobiographical *Beim Häuten der Zwiebel* (On Peeling the Onion), in which he admitted membership in the Waffen SS in the last part of the war.[49] This provoked major controversy, given Grass's reputation as someone whose political commitment was based on high moral principle. Not surprisingly, Jewish opinion was shocked. The president of the Council of Jews in Germany, Charlotte Knoblauch, spoke of Grass's behavior invalidating his previous political activity, a view only partially modified by her deputy Dieter Graumann, who accepted that the late confession did not render wrong certain stances Grass had taken previously.[50] For Henryk M. Broder, however, the occasions when Grass had been on the right side of the argument were few and far between. For him most of what Grass has said is low-grade nonsense. The only concession he makes is that those he calls Grass's interpreters, prophets, and apologists are as much to blame as the man himself.[51]

Some of Grass's colleagues were also quick to condemn, with Peter Handke quoted as seeing Grass as bringing shame on the world of literature.[52] Another to pronounce harsh words was Walter Kempowski shortly before his death in 2007. He found Grass's delayed admission of his wartime role "ein starkes Stück" (hard to swallow).[53] On the other hand, Grass had many defenders — in his own generation, for example, Walser and Christa Wolf, and among younger writers, Burkhard Spinnen, who suggested that his youthful failings had led to his later efforts to improve society.[54] This stance was similar to that of Grass himself, who has always conceded his youthful infatuation with Nazism and based much of his writing on the wish to expiate this. As for the issue of SS membership, he asked in a 2007 interview for perspective, that he be viewed in totality.[55]

Clearly, it is difficult to mediate between such different standpoints. Grass was certainly on weak ground when it transpired that in 1969 he had advised the SPD politician Karl Schiller to tell the whole truth about his involvement with Nazism, something he himself was singularly failing to do. On the other hand, the criticism directed at him seems out of all proportion when it is borne in mind that the issue at hand was the behavior of a seventeen year old, who additionally never became involved in any war crimes and whose involvement in the SS was at a time when, as Germany's defeat approached, it was no longer any kind of Nazi elite. The propensity to exaggerate over issues relating to the Nazi past was underlined a year later when it was suggested that Martin Walser and Siegfried Lenz had been youthful members of the Nazi party, a claim both denied. Since in this case the documentary evidence was flimsy, with no signed application forms being produced, the affair quickly fizzled out. Nevertheless, the issue remains of why such affairs (Walter Jens was under fire in 2004 over membership of the Nazi party, the GDR writer Erwin Strittmatter posthumously in 2008 over SS links) have come to occupy so much public space. In an essay about scandals surrounding Grass, Walser, and Handke, Günther Nickel puts most of the blame upon the media, while acknowledging that writers do seek to exploit the same media for their own ends, especially when a new work is about to be published.[56] What is incontestable is that the traditional press, in Germany as in other countries, is under increased pressure from newer media. One way to counter this is arguably to give a high profile to potentially scandalous stories about figures in the public eye. Another aspect to be considered is the frustration of younger colleagues with the continued prominence of Grass, Walser, and their contemporaries. The Berlin-based writers Eva Menasse and Michael Kumpfmüller have spoken of a gerontocracy,[57] while the journalist Ulrich Greiner has questioned what he calls the "geistigen Nutzen" (intellectual benefit) bestowed upon German culture by the generation in question.[58] Finally, there is the issue of a change of mood since unification. Grass, Walser, and their contemporaries were leading figures in the preunification Federal Republic that, although less intensively than the GDR, has also come under scrutiny since 1989 and 1990. How far the intellectual climate has changed, with the result that those who once enjoyed iconic status have become vulnerable to criticism, is a subject for the next chapter.

Notes

[1] Alexander and Margarete Mitscherlich, *Die Unfähigkeit zu trauern* (Munich: Piper, 20.ed, 1988), 40. Further citations given in parentheses.

[2] Ralph Giordano, *Die zweite Schuld oder Von der Schwierigkeit, Deutscher zu sein* (Munich: Knaur, 1990), 12. Further citations given in parentheses.

[3] For a full account of how the memorial came to be built, see Claus Leggewie and Erik Meyer, *"Ein Ort, an den man gerne geht": Das Holocaust-Mahnmal und die deutsche Geschichtspolitik seit 1989* (Munich and Vienna: Hanser, 2005).

[4] See Leggewie, "Ein Ort, an den man gerne geht," 167–68.

[5] Rafael Seligmann, quoted in Leggewie, "Ein Ort, an den man gerne geht," 291.

[6] György Konrád, "Abschied von der Chimäre," in *Das Holocaust-Mahnmal*, ed. Michael S. Cullen (Zurich: Pendo, 1999), 191–97, here 196.

[7] Henryk M. Broder, "'Auf der Höhe der Zeit,'" in *Das Holocaust-Mahnmal*, ed. Cullen, 186–90, here 190.

[8] See the chronicle of events in *Das Holocaust-Mahnmal*, ed. Cullen, 283.

[9] Salomon Korn, "Monströse Platte," in *Das Holocaust-Mahnmal*, ed. Cullen, 36–41, here 39–40.

[10] Walter Jens, "Widerruf in letzter Minute," in *Das Holocaust-Mahnmal*, ed. Cullen, 206–10, here 207.

[11] See Cullen, *Das Holocaust-Mahnmal*, 290.

[12] Jürgen Habermas, "Der Zeigefinger. Die Deutschen und ihr Denkmal," *Die Zeit*, 31 March 1999, 42–44, here 43. Further citations given in parentheses.

[13] Stefan Reinecke, "Ein Skandal, der gefällt," *die tageszeitung*, 10 May 2005. http://www.taz.de/pt/2005/05/10/a0170.nf/textdruck. Consulted 10 May 2005.

[14] "'Das ist die Fortsetzung des Dritten Reiches,'" *Der Tagespiegel*, 9 June 2005, 29. Available online at http://www.zeitgeschichte-online.de/201/_rainbow/documents/pdf/presse_holocaust_mahnmal.pdf. Consulted 13 October 2008.

[15] Martin Walser, "Erfahrungen beim Verfassen einer Sonntagsrede," in *Die Walser-Bubis-Debatte*, ed. Frank Schirrmacher (Frankfurt am Main: Suhrkamp, 1999), 7–17, here 13.

[16] See, for example, Wolfram Schütte, "Der Sommer des Ressentimentalisten," *titel-magazin*, 2002. Now available in shortened form on http://www.fritz-bauer-institut.de/texte/essay/10-02_schuette.htm.

[17] Martin Walser, "Unser Auschwitz," in *Deutsche Sorgen* (Frankfurt am Main: Suhrkamp, 1997), 187–202, esp. 200.

[18] Michael Hamburger, *From Prophecy to Exorcism* (London: Longmans, 1965), 144.

[19] Martin Walser, "Auschwitz und kein Ende," in *Deutsche Sorgen*, 228–34, here 228.

[20] See the volume referred to in note 15 above and Johannes Klotz and Gerd Wiegel, eds., *Geistige Brandstiftung? Die Walser-Bubis-Debatte* (Cologne: Papyrossa, 1999).

[21] Walser, "Erfahrungen beim Verfassen einer Sonntagsrede," 8. Further citations given in parentheses.

[22] For a review of the reception of *Tod eines Kritikers*, see Stuart Parkes, "Tod eines Kritikers. Text and Context," in *Seelenarbeit an Deutschland: Martin Walser in Perspective*, ed. Parkes and Fritz Wefelmeyer (Amsterdam and New York: Rodopi, 2004), 447–68.

[23] Martin Walser, *ohne einander* (Frankfurt am Main: Suhrkamp, 1993), 59.

[24] Martin Walser, *Tod eines Kritikers* (Frankfurt am Main: Suhrkamp, 2002), 144.

[25] Martin Walser, "Das Prinzip Genauigkeit," in *Deutsche Sorgen*, 565–92, here 573.

[26] Martin Walser, "Erfahrungen beim Verfassen einer Sonntagsrede," 12.

[27] Rafael Seligmann, *Der Musterjude* (Munich: DTV, 2. ed 2002), 386.

[28] Harry Nutt, "Ach, Walser!," *Frankfurter Rundschau*, 11 May 2006, 17.

[29] Friedrich Christian Delius, *Die Flatterzunge* (Reinbek: Rowohlt, 1999), 133. Further citations given in parentheses.

[30] Bodo Morshäuser, *Hauptsache Deutsch* (Frankfurt am Main: Suhrkamp, 1992), 116.

[31] For an overview of the controversy and more detailed discussion of the novel, see William Niven, "Bernhard Schlink's *Der Vorleser* and the Problem of Shame," *MLR*, 98:2 (2003): 381–96.

[32] W.G. Sebald, *Luftkrieg und Literatur* (Munich and Vienna: Hanser, 1999), 91. Further citations given in parentheses.

[33] Manfred Biller, "Unschuld mit Grünspan," in *Deutsche Literatur*, ed. Hage, 1998, 278–83, here 278.

[34] Jörg Friedrich, *Der Brand* (Munich: Propyläen Verlag, 2002).

[35] Günter Franzen, "Links, wo kein Herz ist," *Der Spiegel*, 27 October 2003, 216–18, here 218.

[36] Daniela Dahn, "Da liegt kein Segen darauf," *Süddeutsche Zeitung*, 6 February 2004. Now available online at http://www.danieladahn.de/index.php?section=texte.

[37] Günter Grass, *Im Krebsgang* (Göttingen: Steidl, 2002).

[38] Hans Magnus Enzensberger, "Hitlers Wiedergänger," in *Liebesgrüße aus Bagdad*, ed. Klaus Bittermann (Berlin: Edition Tiamat, 1991), 44–52, here 51.

[39] Wolf Biermann, "Kriegshetze Friedenshetze," *Die Zeit*, 1 February 1991, 59–60, here 59.

[40] Ralph Giordano, "Menetekel Saddam Hussein," in *Liebesgrüße*, ed. Bittermann, 74–85.

[41] For an overview of writers' opinions on the First Gulf War, see *Fachdienst Germanistik* 9:3 (1991): 1–2.

[42] *Ich will reden von der Angst meines Herzens* (Frankfurt am Main: Luchterhand, 1991).

[43] For an overview of the debate, see Joachim Günter, "Die deutsch-amerikanische Verständigung," *Neue Zürcher Zeitung*, 26 September 2002. http://www.nzz.ch/2002/09/26/fe/page-article8F9VE.html. Consulted same day.

[44] Peter Schneider, "Bosnien — ein Kommunikationsfehler?," *Die Zeit*, 4 August 1995, 37–38, here 37.

[45] Jürgen Habermas, "'Ein Abgrund von Trauer,'" *Der Spiegel*, 7 August 1995, 34.

[46] Peter Handke, *Eine winterliche Reise zu den Flüssen Donau, Save, Morawa und Drina oder Gerechtigkeit für Serbien* (Frankfurt am Main: Suhrkamp, 1996), 23.

[47] Peter Schneider, "Der Ritt über den Balkan," *Der Spiegel*, 15 January 1996, 163–65, here 165.

[48] See Peter Handke, "Ich komme aus dem Traum," *Die Zeit*, 11 February 2006. http://zeus.zeit.de/text/2006/06/L-Handke-Interv_. Consulted 2 February 2006.

[49] Günter Grass, *Beim Häuten der Zwiebel* (Göttingen: Steidl, 2006).

[50] Dieter Graumann "Großartig, kleinmütig," *Frankfurter Rundschau*, 18 August 2006. This interview contains the reference to Charlotte Knoblauch.

[51] Henryk M. Broder, "Der Herr der Binse," *SPIEGEL ONLINE*, 14 August 2006. http://www.spiegel/de/kultur/gesellschaft/0,1518,431695,00.html. Consulted 16 August 2006.

[52] "Handke: Grass 'eine Schande für das Schriftstellertum,'" *FAZ.Net*, 13 September 2006. Consulted 11 November 2006. Now available online through http://www.faz.net/IN/INtemplates/faznet/default.asp?tpl=common/zwischenseite.asp &dox={B13E6D20-9263-F513-2451-EE466A862D56}&rub={CF3AEB15-4CE6-4960-822F-A5429A182360}. Alternatively, see "Handkes Grass-Kritik: 'Schande für das Schriftstellertum,'" http://www.spiegel.de/kultur/literatur/0,1518,436864,00. html. Consulted 13 October 2008.

[53] Walter Kempowski, "Ich bin vergiftet worden," *Frankfurter Rundschau*, 4 August 2007.

[54] Burkhard Spinnen, "Bitte, seid behutsam. In jeder Beziehung," *Die Welt*, 14 August 2006. http://www.welt.de/print-welt/article235502/Bitte_seid_behutsam_In_jeder_ Beziehung.html. Consulted 13 October 2008.

[55] Günter Grass, "Selbstbildnisse eines Dichters," *Frankfurter Rundschau*, 4 October 2007.

[56] Günther Nickel, "Die medialen Kampagnen gegen Günter Grass, Martin Walser und Peter Handke," *titel-magazin* (2007). http://www.titel-magazin.de/print.php? sid=6282&POSTNUKESID=7cdd73c156f3bb. Consulted 5 October 2007.

[57] Eva Menasse, Michael Kumpfmüller, "Wider die intellektuelle Gerontokratie," *Süddeutsche Zeitung*, 17 August 2006, in Goethe-Institut Dossier, "Günter Grass in der Kritik — Ausgewählte Pressestimmen."

[58] Ulrich Greiner, "Es ist nun wirklich genug!," *Die Zeit*, 24 August 2006. http://zeus.zeit.de/text/2006/35/L-Taeter. Consulted 24 August 2006.

9: A Swing to the Right?

CRITICISMS OF THE FEDERAL REPUBLIC'S leftist intellectuals, who are alleged to have had a detrimental stranglehold on the discourse of the public sphere, have been referred to frequently in the course of this volume — in particular, those criticisms made in the 1970s against the background of Red Army Faction terrorism. A similarly intensive period of criticism has followed unification. This time, however, the emphasis has been less on the dangers to democracy posed by strident political ideology than on the problems caused by a failure to face up to the real political issues of the day — specifically, those created by unification. At the same time, the different kinds of attitudes adopted have created a different kind of discourse that can no longer be considered peripheral, but rather raises the question whether the overall intellectual climate of the Federal Republic has swung markedly to the Right.

One example of the new kinds of poses being struck is provided by Cora Stephan's work *Der Betroffenheitskult* (The Cult of Consternation, 1993). In it, she criticizes German society for a woolly moralism that manifests itself especially in antinational feelings and a refusal to accept responsibility. Instead of considering what realistic actions a given situation may demand, many Germans lapse into a helpless *Betroffenheit* (feeling of concern). Accordingly, Stephan speaks of the public sphere in Germany being unreal and of a desire for provincial innocence.[1] More specifically, she detects a lack of a self-confident, enlightened national identity that might help to provide a sense of orientation in face of current problems (52). It has to be pointed out that Stephan is not speaking specifically about intellectuals, but of society as a whole. Nevertheless, her critique can be linked to the influence of intellectuals in society, with the concluding part of her text containing numerous negative comments on Jürgen Habermas, the intellectual often seen, along with Grass, as representing the spirit of the preunification Federal Republic.

By contrast, Gerhard Henschel, in a work entitled *Das Blöken der Lämmer* (The Bleating of the Lambs, 1994), directs his fire directly at left-wing writers and intellectuals with the pointed satirical tone typical of the volumes published in the *Edition Tiamat* collection. Much of the text consists of quotations from the most celebrated postwar authors, including Böll and Grass, that in Henschel's eyes, fall into the category of left-wing kitsch. Indeed, the subtitle of the book is *Die Linke und der Kitsch*" (Leftists and

Kitsch). That the two are all too frequently linked by an umbilical cord is the thesis of the postscript by the novelist Eckhard Henscheid, who claims that left-wing writing almost invariably fails at the aesthetic level. Equally dubiously, such writing often claims to represent the interests of the Enlightenment and the working class — in his view, "ein doppelt uneingelöster Anspruch" (a doubly unredeemed claim).[2] Admittedly, Henscheid is equally critical in passing about the conservative intellectual milieu; nevertheless, the book as a whole, as the title makes clear, is an indictment of the allegedly naïve stances adopted by left-wing writers.

Another two volumes in the same series widen the attack by targeting the *Gutmenschen* of the Federal Republic, a coinage that has entered the language and to which the English "good person" does not do justice. Once again, as with Stephan, the target is the person who, having learned, at least in his or her own mind, the lessons of the German past, now sees everything in moral terms and seeks to tread the path of political virtue, especially when it comes to defending democracy against any re-emergence of right-wing extremism. While here, too, the critique is not exclusively aimed at writers and intellectuals, it is clear from the two volumes that substantial numbers of them are seen as falling into the category of the *Gutmensch*. Each of the two books takes the form of a dictionary of such people — that is to say, a compilation of the topics or arguments they raise, along with a text explaining how they are misused. One example, which clearly has to do with writers, is the habit of referring to the Nazi book-burning ceremony of 1933. The writer Simone Borowiak in her entry *Bücherverbrennung* (book burning) refers to the tendency of some colleagues, when they are subjected to harsh criticism, to compare the fate of their works to that suffered by so many books in 1933. She describes this comparison as the fashionable reference for those who cannot tell the difference between a book review and a pyre or between a holiday camp and Buchenwald.[3] As if to forestall the kind of criticism this kind of comment might provoke, the same volume also has an entry under the heading *Geschmacklos* (tasteless), which is described as the adjective the *Gutmenschen* use when they are subject to satirical or polemical attack (85).

The question of the changing status of intellectuals in society is tackled more analytically in a collection of essays that appeared in 1992. At the same time, the chosen title *Intellektuellendämmerung* (Twilight of the Intellectuals) suggests that an era is over, a point taken up by Martin Meyer in his introduction. He speaks of the loss of utopian hopes after the disasters of the twentieth century having led to a general sense of melancholy and resignation, which has been reinforced by the massive changes that have taken place in the public sphere.[4] While Meyer does not refer specifically to the Federal Republic, his comments, particularly on the loss of utopian visions, can be linked to the German situation following unification. There is certainly no contradiction between them and Christian Meier's characterization in one of the volume's essays of the changed situation of (West) German intellectuals. He sees intellectual life in the preunification Federal Republic as having been linked to the existence of the two power blocs and the belief in a socialist alternative against a background of increasing prosperity, conditions that no longer apply.[5] Nevertheless, he does go on to suggest that this paradigm might be replaced by a different one. Whether this has been the case and whether it is a rightist current will be discussed below.

For those who detected a move to the right among intellectuals, 1993 was a decisive year. Three essays by established writers, all of which first appeared in *Der Spiegel,* suggested, at least at first sight, that a change of paradigm had occurred. The first to appear in February was Botho Strauß's subsequently much-anthologized "Anschwellender Bocksgesang" (The Swelling Song of the Goat), which created an initial stir almost on the level of that occasioned by Böll's Baader-Meinhof essay two decades earlier and which has retained its seminal status. On this occasion, critical voices were moved to regard Strauß as a dangerous right-winger, as was the case with the SPD politician and leading thinker Peter Glotz, who, addressing unnamed friends with a rhetorical flourish, warned of a dangerous situation.[6]

When the essay appeared, Strauß was already well-established as a leading member of the post-Gruppe 47 generation of writers. He was regarded as a stern critic of the superficial nature of much of modern society; this time, however, as his title indicated, he appeared to be predicting a forthcoming catastrophe for the society of the Federal Republic, the word *Bocksgesang* being a literal translation of the word "tragedy" in the original Greek. Although the text begins with what appears to be praise for the modern pluralist society, it quickly suggests that such a society is not sustainable, as the ecological crisis shows. There follows a denunciation of German society as one lacking a sense of history ever since the 1968 generation destroyed previously important taboos. The nature of the loss of values is explained in the following sentence, which is remarkable for its archaic language and for its generalized claim: "Daß ein Volk sein Sittengesetz gegen andere behaupten will und dafür bereit ist, Blutopfer zu bringen, das verstehen wir nicht mehr und halten es in unserer liberal-libertären Selbstbezogenheit für falsch und verwerflich" (That a people wishes to maintain its moral law against others and is prepared to make blood sacrifices for it — that we no longer understand and consider it in our liberal, libertarian egoism wrong and reprehensible).[7] It is in keeping with this that Strauß should also at this point castigate the way the soldier is now scorned. Thus, it seems that for Strauß the enemy is not the German military tradition so strongly linked with its history until 1945. In fact, another enemy is identified: the mass media, which are blamed for the regretted loss of values. Strauß's criticism of these culminates in the astonishing and somewhat paradoxical claim that the rule of what he calls the "telekratische Öffentlichkeit" (telecratic public sphere) is, even without being bloody, the most all-embracing totalitarianism in history (68). Even if it is accepted that there are other than physical forms of violence, one wonders if the use of the term totalitarianism is appropriate in a context without such physical violence.

For the political scientists Martin and Sylvia Greiffenhagen, Strauß's polemic is a classical example of conservative thought, characterized, among other things, by ethnocentricity and xenophobia.[8] Strauß himself, in response to such criticism, felt obliged to add a postscript that rejected any link between his ideas and right-wing extremism. In what seems nothing less than a piece of self-congratulation, he also suggested that the scandal caused by the essay may be to do with its manneristic style and language, which differentiated it from run-of-the-mill journalistic writing.[9] It remained a moot point whether this style was a strength or a weakness. In his response to Strauß in *Die Zeit*, Ulrich Greiner (one of the main critics of Christa Wolf in 1990, it will be recalled) suggested that political essays, unlike fictional works of literature, should avoid ambiguity.[10]

There is no similar lack of clarity for readers to wrestle with in Hans Magnus Enzensberger's *Der Spiegel* piece "Ausblicke auf den Bürgerkrieg" (Outlook on the Civil War), a much-condensed version of his book *Aussichten auf den Bürgerkrieg* (Prospects of Civil War, 1993) that appeared in the same year. There is also a very different view from Strauß concerning those who seek to preserve what they consider to be their core identity. They are regarded as indulging in acts of collective madness that will most likely destroy what they seek to preserve. Enzensberger also detects a similar capacity for self-destruction among young rioters and hooligans in Germany, claiming, somewhat melodramatically, that when hooligans get to work any subway car can turn into a mini-Bosnia.[11] He also stresses the economic dimension ignored by Strauß: Both civil war and rioting destroy any hope of economic recovery in the areas affected.

Enzensberger also draws general conclusions from his diagnosis. In the face of the phenomena he describes, it would be impossible for anyone to resolve all the world's crises. At first sight, this view would seem to run counter to his stance on Iraq described above. In fact, he is not entirely negative. He accepts the responsibility of Germany for right-wing extremism within its own borders, as well as the need for the international community to respond to the aggression of Saddam Hussein and his ilk. Equally, he praises the Czech student Jan Palach, who set fire to himself out of true conviction in protest following the 1968 Soviet invasion, comparing him favorably with what he calls "wirre Fanatiker" (confused fanatics; 35). The problem with such distinctions is that they inevitably involve personal judgments, which are bound to be open to question. Moreover, Enzensberger also falls victim to the kind of exaggeration usually associated with the popular press when he claims that the favorite victims of today's civil warriors are women and children (21). In fact, it was men and male adolescents who were massacred in Srebreniča in 1995, while young men are statistically more likely to fall victim to street violence.

Unsurprisingly, Martin Walser's 1993 essay, which first appeared shortly after that of Enzensberger, links with his national concerns, as the title "Deutsche Sorgen" (German Worries) shows. His main concern is the growth of extreme right-wing violence and society's inadequate response to it. Singled out for blame are those intellectuals who, in his view, have excluded right-wing thought from mainstream discourse. It is this that he blames for the violence, saying that a particular group of young people have been dubbed antisocial simply because their right-wing discourse is not deemed acceptable.[12] This statement is another example of Walser's belief that dialogue is the best way to prevent violence. Responding to the criticism caused by his essay, he claimed that he was attempting to stimulate such dialogue, pointing out that nobody ever invited skinheads to discuss their concerns.[13] Whether this belief in dialogue, also expressed at the time of the First Gulf War, is naïve or realistic in light of the given circumstances is again a matter of opinion. It is also possible to question whether skinhead discourse can be described as merely right of center, rather than odiously extreme.

As this book has shown, questions relating to Germany and the Germans have never been far below the surface of intellectual debate since 1945, even if Walser claims in the essay discussed above that the word "nation" had been expunged from the vocabulary of large sections of society.[14] Unsurprisingly, these questions came very much to the fore at the time of unification, with many prominent figures expressing their views. *Nachdenken über Deutschland* (Reflections on Germany) was the title of a five-volume series based on lectures given in Berlin, to which, among others, politicians from different parties, such as Rita Süssmuth (CDU), Antje Vollmer (Greens), and Hans Modrow (PDS) contributed, as well as writers including Günter Grass, Rolf Hochhuth, and Walter Jens.[15] The continuity of the issue of Germany can be seen from the way that the same title had been used five years earlier for another volume that included essays by writers and academics.[16] According to the blurb, the questions to be considered were: "Who are we? Where do we come from? Where are we going?"

For those writers with openly rightist views, the answer to the last question was simple now that Germany was united, at least as far as their aspirations were concerned: namely, a new direction. These aspirations were encapsulated in the concept of a "Berlin Republic," by which they meant a self-confident state that was freed from its obligations as a defeated country and that had turned its back on the diffidence of its predecessor based in Bonn. It goes without saying that for those with a different political standpoint, the idea was repugnant. Hence, considerable controversy was caused when in 1994 a volume edited by the poet Ulrich Schacht, a former GDR dissident, and the journalist Heimo Schwilk appeared with the title *Die selbst-bewusste Nation* (The Self-Confident Nation).[17] Moreover, pride of place was given to Strauß's essay from the previous year. Three years later, the two produced a joint volume, *Für eine Berliner Republik* — a title that could not have been much clearer. The authors' views are made immediately clear in their joint introduction. The enemy is the 1968 generation, with the year itself standing for the start of a process leading to the wilful destruction of the political and moral base of the Federal Republic.[18] Moreover, the CDU government of Helmut Kohl is seen as having done nothing to stop the rot. The text is at its most demagogic with its dismissal of Jürgen Habermas as someone who despises Germany (12). It ends with a plea for a return to the antitotalitarian spirit of the Basic Law.

That this project, or at least a significant part of it, of a different kind of Federal Republic as embraced by Schacht and Schwilk failed to establish itself was clearly shown by the events of May 1995. To mark the fiftieth anniversary of the end of the war, a number of public figures — mainly rightists, but including the former SPD minister Hans Apel — published a manifesto "Gegen das Vergessen" (Against Forgetting), in which the term "liberation," as used by Federal President Weizsäcker in 1985 to describe the end of the war, was called into question. For the exact anniversary on 8 May, a rally was planned at which Schacht was due to speak. As it turned out, this meeting was called off following pressure from the Kohl government on CDU speakers, especially the veteran right-winger Alfred Dregger. Schacht was at least able to publish his speech, with its references to innocent German victims of bombing attacks and expulsion, a generalization that ignores, for instance, that one victim of bombing was the chief Nazi judge at the notorious People's Court, Roland Freisler.[19] Nevertheless, the events of 1995 suggested that the Berlin Republic, as imagined by Schacht and Schwilk, was still some way off. Ten years later, the situation did not seem to have changed, with the anniversary attracting less attention from writers and intellectuals.

This does not mean that discussion of national topics has come to an end. At times, it has taken on a personal dimension, as when in late 2004 *Die Zeit* asked a number of prominent and somewhat less prominent people for their thoughts on Germany. The only writer to contribute was Martin Walser, whose text begins with an account of how he was helped by a young man when recently lost in Osnabrück. This helpfulness leads him to draw the conclusion that a country with such citizens is saved rather than lost.[20] He then goes on to contrast this personal experience with comments about how Germans are invariably portrayed negatively in films, something that saddens him even if the memory of the young man remains something of a comfort. Once more, Walser is putting a premium on personal experience over media or similar representations.

Another, less famous contributor to *Die Zeit* on this occasion was a Turkish tailor, who had taken German nationality in 1996 and who expressed his pleasure at living in the country.[21] During the years of the Schröder chancellorship, such naturalizations were made easier with the relaxation of the principle that nationality depended on having German forebears. However, this liberalization of stringent nationality laws does not appear to have coincided with easier relations between Germans and immigrants, especially in the most recent years, with aspects of the debate again raising the question of whether the intellectual climate has moved to the right. In previous decades, many intellectuals had shown sympathy with minority ethnic groups, who had moved to Germany either to take up employment as *Gastarbeiter* (guest workers), as such migrants were initially called, or as asylum seekers. In the case of the former, there was an awareness of the harsh working conditions they frequently suffered and their isolation in society because of the discrimination they were subjected to. In this connection, the seminal text dates from 1965 and was written by the Swiss author Max Frisch. Although he was writing specifically about Italian immigrants in Switzerland, many of his comments could be increasingly applied to the Federal Republic and to the people of various nationalities who moved there after the supply of labor from the east had dried up following the construction of the Berlin Wall. It was his epigrammatic statement: "Man rief Arbeitskräfte, und es kamen Menschen" (Labor was called for, and people came) that struck a cord, as well as the characterization of the indigenous people as "ein kleines Herrenvolk" (a small master race), a term that could raise an ironic smile when referring to the Swiss but, with or without the adjective, invoked unpleasant memories and a sense of guilt in Germany.[22]

It was a piece of investigative journalism by Günter Wallraff in the 1980s that suggested to a broader public how badly outsiders were frequently treated in the Federal Republic. In keeping with his usual practice, Wallraff had disguised himself, this time concealing his identity under that of a Turkish laborer. In this guise, taking on casual work through an agency for temporary labor, he experienced a variety of unpleasant and potentially dangerous jobs. Outside the workplace, too, he experienced discrimination — for example, when he tried to approach the Catholic Church. His record of these experiences appeared under the title *Ganz unten* (Way Under, 1985, translated as *The Lowest of the Low*) and was immediately a bestseller.[23] How far sympathy with outsiders could go in certain quarters was shown at the time of unification when, in response to the attacks on non-Germans referred to above, some demonstrators paraded with such slogans as "Ausländer, lasst uns mit diesen Deutschen nicht allein!" (Foreigners, do not leave us alone with these Germans!).

If an example of comparable sentiments expressed by a writer is sought, then the example of Günter Grass springs to mind. In a 1992 speech, the printed version of which is dedicated to the three Turkish women who died as a result of the arson attack in Mölln in 1992, Grass concludes with a hymn of praise to gypsies, a group that not only suffered terribly under the Nazis but has also been the victim of discrimination in the Federal Republic as in other European states. In contrast to the political agenda of restricting immigration, Grass proclaims his belief that the Germans urgently need half a million or more Roma and Sinti living among them.[24] Grass was also prominent in the controversy over government asylum policy in the early 1990s, going as far as resigning from the SPD when the party decided to support the amendment of the Basic Law's blanket acceptance of the right to asylum for those suffering political persecution. Around 70 writers and artists published a manifesto in November 1992 defending this right, with Walter Jens, for example, explaining its historical significance. For him, the constitutional right to asylum was an expression of gratitude to those who had sheltered Germans who had fled Nazism, a promise to redeem in the future other victims of, for example, torture, persecution and racism.[25]

What was called the "Hamburg Manifesto" did not meet with universal approval. Among those who refused to support it or expressed skepticism were Peter Schneider and the critic Marcel Reich-Ranicki. In the same year, Hans Magnus Enzensberger published an essay entitled *Die große Wanderung* (The Great Migration, 1992), in which he expresses major doubts about the possibility of immigration without difficulties in any context. He claims simply that every migration leads to conflict, whether it is undertaken voluntarily or under coercion, and regardless of the numbers involved.[26] As for the situation in Germany, he, in contrast to Grass, expresses doubt whether past crimes are an adequate justification for allowing mass immigration, while also impishly suggesting that the Germans are not a people to accept outsiders, since they do not even like each other and are thus unlikely to love their "Nicht-Nachbarn" (non-neighbor; 12).

If Enzensberger's comments frequently consist of assertions and generalizations, more recent debates have focused on specific issues like the position of the Turkish community in German society. With the growth of Islamic fundamentalism and terrorism, there has been concern that a substantial minority of people living in the Federal Republic have not been integrated into their German environment, but are living in a parallel society. At the same time, politicians such as the CDU's Friedrich Merz have introduced into the debate the concept of a *Leitkultur* (dominant culture), meaning that German values should pertain throughout society. Among writers, one of the major contributors to the debate has been Peter Schneider, who in December 2005 published two long pieces on successive days in *Die Welt*. He begins by referring to the way that some members of the Turkish community showed pleasure at the events of 11 September 2001. He then goes on to speak of honor killings carried out against women who refuse to accept conventions such as arranged marriages. Although Schneider criticizes the host community, both for its failure to integrate immigrants and for its turning a blind eye to negative developments within the Turkish community, he also picks out what he calls "die aktive Haltung der Verweigerung" (the active attitude of refusal) on the part of some Moslems in Germany. He goes on to stress the inalienable nature of universal human rights, saying that tolerance toward another culture reaches its limits if part of that culture involves the infringement of these rights.[27] Despite such comments, Schneider did not escape criticism for retaining the outdated ways of thinking of the 1968 generation — specifically, when he expressed doubts about plans by the Baden-Württemberg state government (subsequently adopted by other states ruled by the Christian Democrats) to subject those seeking German citizenship to a test of their democratic attitudes. The author of detective stories Thea Dorn accused him and his ilk of preferring to bask in the eternal traditions of antifascism, antitotalitarianism, and anti-German feelings.[28]

Controversy over how to react to Islamic extremism came even more to a head in 2006 with the publication in Denmark of cartoons depicting the prophet Mohammed. The journalist Frank Schirrmacher shows himself to be particularly skeptical about any possible resolution of the problem, suggesting that the very existence of Western culture was unacceptable to Islamists.[29] Botho Strauß, too, stresses the potential for conflict, actually using that word for the title of his piece in *Der Spiegel*. At the same time, he does suggest some ways of alleviating the conflict — for example, by making the injuring of what he calls people's sacred feelings a criminal offense.[30] He is also able to discern possible positive consequences across society arising from Moslems' strong code of values. His hope is that Western society will rediscover some of the values it has lost in the secular age of indifference. Clearly, there are echoes here of the criticisms of modern society found in "Anschwellender Bocksgesang." By contrast, Peter Schneider finds comfort in the potential strength of liberal values. While acknowledging moral weaknesses in the West, he does not see this situation as irreversible, believing that the struggle for individual self-determination and freedom from religious control to have had a sublime, almost holy dimension.[31] In an interview given at the time of the debate, Günter Grass, by contrast, does not indulge in either subtle argument or exalted rhetoric. Referring, as many did in this connection, to Samuel Huntington's thesis of a clash of civilizations, he speaks not of a clash of cultures, but of a dispute between two *Unkulturen*, by which he means both Islamic extremism and Western arrogance.[32] As for the cartoons themselves, he finds a resemblance between them and those published by the Nazis to vilify Jews. Reference to the Nazi past is also to be found in the comments of the Romanian-born writer Richard Wagner, who refers to Iranian denials of the Holocaust. He suggests that no apologies for these remarks will be forthcoming in the way that the Danish authorities apologized for the cartoons. He sees a worldwide conflict taking place between Western values and those seeking to combat these achievements with an understanding of religion that he describes as premodern.[33]

It is small wonder that, in this atmosphere, the German-Turkish writer Zafer Şenocak, writing in *Die Welt* in 2006, does not see any easy solutions. Like Grass, he is critical of both Moslem extremism and Western Islamophobia.[34] Earlier in August 2005, he had described the relationship between Germans and Turks as being like that of a couple trapped in a loveless marriage. Using the word *Lager* (camp), he speaks of an entrenched mentality within both population groups, with any hope of a rapprochement having to be left to later generations.[35] Given such pessimism, the time when immigrant populations enjoyed some kind of bonus, at least within certain more liberal sections of the population, seems to be receding.

This was confirmed by subsequent developments. In 2007, a controversy broke out over the building of a large mosque in Cologne, with Ralph Giordano taking the lead in the opposition to the project, believing the sponsors to represent values at odds with the Federal Republic's Basic Law. In a statement published in June 2007, Giordano speaks of the failure of integration[36] and, in a discussion with a Moslem representative held slightly earlier, of the difficulties of Islamic society in adapting to the modern world.[37] At the same time, he does lay some of the blame at the door of the Federal Government's failed immigration policies. Giordano's intervention provoked demonstrations and, by his own account, death threats against him, while in the discussion referred to above he himself raised the specter of civil unrest if the mosque were to be built.

This controversy rumbled on into 2008, with the increasingly strident Giordano, in a debate published in the *Frankfurter Allgemeine Sonntagszeitung*, accusing the usually hardline Federal Minister of the Interior Wolfgang Schäuble of complacency when it came to what he perceived as the gradual Islamization of Germany.[38] By contrast, Günter Wallraff, who because of *Ganz unten* enjoyed prestige among Moslems, sought dialogue with Islam, although his attempts to have extracts of Salman Rushdie's *Satanic Verses* read in a mosque did not meet with success.[39] Nevertheless, he remained optimistic about the future, seeing younger generations of people in Germany with a Turkish background breaking down entrenched positions in their community. The same optimism was shared by the German-Turkish writer Feridun Zaimoğlu in an interview conducted during the 2008 Leipzig Book Fair.[40]

Despite such optimism, the problem of violence in the name of Islam remains an issue of concern, with Şenocak claiming that terror is at the heart of Islam, in that it originates directly in the Koran.[41] The general issue of violence is also at the center of an essay by Hans Magnus Enzensberger, *Schreckens Männer* (Men of Terror, 2006). His starting point, as the subtitle makes clear, is the concept of the *radikalen Verlierer* (radical loser), a phenomenon that goes beyond the world of politics to include, for instance, the adolescent who arms himself (Enzensberger stresses that it is almost exclusively males who fall into the category) and runs amok. Politics only enters the equation when the loser attaches himself to a cause. This approach allows him to list together 59 groups, including the IRA, PKK, and ETA. He also includes the Nazis in his loser category, underlining in them what he sees as one of the loser's main characteristics: the desire to die in an orgy of killing. He says the Nazis' real goal was not victory, but "Ausrottung, der Untergang, der kollektive Selbstmord, das Ende mit Schrecken" (extermination, downfall, collective suicide, a horrific ending).[42] The major part of the essay, however, is devoted to Islamic extremism. He describes in some detail the decline of Arab societies since the Middle Ages in such areas as science and technology, something that is seen to have provoked the sense of humiliation that is a feature of the radical loser. Moreover, such a person is immune to rational argument, with the liberal hope of dialogue being seen by Enzensberger as a piece of self-delusion (43). Nevertheless, Enzensberger's conclusion is quite sanguine: Islamic terrorism is unlikely to bring Western countries to their knees but will only provoke inconveniences of the type now experienced by airline passengers.

Many of Enzensberger's arguments are reminiscent of those found in the 1993 essay discussed above — for example, the emphasis on the self-destructive urge and the idea that violence can erupt without warning among the people being categorized. The real issue is, however, whether such seemingly different phenomena as individual gun violence and Islamic terrorism, not to mention Nazism, can all be explained in psychological terms. Discussion of phenomena such as Nazism often includes a psychological dimension, especially when it comes to the person of Hitler, but other social science disciplines, such as politics and sociology, are usually seen as providing important contributions to any attempts at explanation. By contrast, Enzensberger rejects such explanations, seeing the social situation of terrorists as irrelevant and pointing out that they are frequently from privileged rather than dispossessed backgrounds (46). Such a point is well-made, but the conclusion must surely be that it is impossible to subsume all acts of senseless violence, whether they claim a political dimension or not, under a single concept. What is more, in the case of such movements as Nazism and the Taliban, victory is part of the agenda. Newsreels of Hitler in France in 1940 following victory do not show someone whose immediate priority is self or collective destruction. Enzensberger would be on stronger ground if he spoke of a refusal to compromise.

Does all this amount to a swing to the Right among intellectuals and those generally sympathetic to their views? Such a view would undoubtedly be too simplistic. In his analysis of the New Right, as represented by Schwilk,

Schacht and cohorts, Roger Woods convincingly shows that their ambition for hegemony has not been achieved in either the political and cultural field. This is seen as due in part to their own recognition that many of the old shibboleths of the Right, such as nationalism and traditional religion, cannot be resurrected in today's world. As for the specific case of Botho Strauß, Woods notes that his writing does not lend itself to being harnessed for political purposes, as no political movement is going to base its program on dark forebodings.[43] In his essay, quoted earlier, Christian Meier speaks of a change of paradigm following the events of 1989/1990. With intellectual life no longer being dominated by the influence of the Cold War, he foresees the end of dominating intellectual currents, suggesting that they will be replaced by *Einzelgänger* (lone voices) and a greater emphasis on analysis.[44] This idea of the lone voice would seem to apply to Strauß and to another voice from the conservative Right, Martin Mosebach.

In 2007, Mosebach was awarded the prestigious Büchner Prize. He used his speech — provoked no doubt by the association of the name of Büchner with revolution through his political activity and his most famous play *Dantons Tod* — to create a very individualistic link between the French Revolution, specifically the discourse of Saint-Just, and the ideas expressed by Heinrich Himmler in his infamous speech to members of the SS in Posen in 1943.[45] The heated reaction this caused certainly showed that there were still plenty of defenders of the ideals of the Enlightenment associated with revolutionary France. For example, the critic Wolfram Schütte acknowledges the brilliance of Mosebach's speech, but describes his argument as disgracefully dishonest given the differences between the positive ideals of the French Revolution and the evil ideology of Nazism.[46] The vehemence of this and other reactions again makes talk of a new right-wing hegemony appear premature. More generally, Mosebach's comments show the dubious tendency, found in all parts of the political spectrum, to compare anything disliked with some aspect of Nazism.

There is another point to consider. In the complex post–Cold War era, it is often difficult to employ a traditional left-right scale with arguments like Peter Schneider's comments on immigration, referred to above. The only term that might be appropriate is normalization. Just as the end of the Cold War has brought greater political freedom by putting an end to the abnormal division of Germany and Europe, intellectual life in Germany, as Meier suggests, is now freed of the previous constraints brought about by that state of affairs. The result is that in Germany as elsewhere, there is now a vast variety of competing intellectual voices with no group enjoying a near-monopoly esteem, as was the case with the Gruppe 47.

Notes

[1] Cora Stephan, *Der Betroffenheitskult* (Berlin: Rowohlt, 1993), 168. Further citations given in parentheses.

[2] Eckhard Henscheid, "Nachwort," in Gerhard Henschel, *Das Blöken der Lämme* (Berlin: Tiamat, 1994), 149–61, here 151.

[3] Droste Wiglaf and Klaus Bittermann, eds., *Das Wörterbuch des Gutmenschen II* (Berlin: Tiamat, 1995), 32. Further citations given in parentheses.

[4] Meyer, Martin, "Intellektuellendämmerung," in *Intellektuellendämmerung* (Munich: Hanser, 1992), 1–12, esp. 9.

[5] Christian Meier, "Nicht Zerstörung, sondern neue Herausforderung der Vernunft," in Meyer, *Intellektuellendämmerung*, 77–95, here 85.

[6] Peter Glotz, "Freunde, es wird ernst," in *Deutsche Literatur 1993*, ed. Franz Josef Görtz, Volker Hage, and Uwe Wittstock (Stuttgart: Reclam, 1994), 273–74.

[7] Botho Strauß, "Anschwellender Bocksgesang," in *Der Aufstand gegen die sekundäre Welt* (Munich: Hanser, 1999), 55–78, here 59. Further citations given in parentheses.

[8] Martin and Silvia Greiffenhagen, *Ein schwieriges Vaterland* (Munich and Leipzig: List, 1993), 280–83.

[9] Strauß, "Anschwellender Bockgesang," 77.

[10] Ulrich Greiner, "Der Seher auf dem Markt," *Die Zeit*, 25 April 1994, 53.

[11] Hans Magnus Enzensberger, *Aussichten auf den Bürgerkrieg* (Frankfurt am Main: Suhrkamp, 1993), 30. Further citations given in parentheses.

[12] Martin Walser, "Deutsche Sorgen II," in *Deutsche Sorgen*, 453–67, here 460.

[13] See Görtz et al., *Deutsche Literatur 1993*, 76.

[14] Martin Walser, "Deutsche Sorgen II," 456.

[15] The volumes edited by Dietmar Keller were published in 1990/1 by Verlag der Nation, Berlin and are based on speeches/debates held over the reunification period.

[16] Werner Weidenfeld, ed., *Nachdenken über Dutschland* (Cologne: Verlag: Wissenschaft und Politik, 1985).

[17] Heimo Schwilk and Ulrich Schacht, eds., *Die selbstbewußte Nation: "Anschwellender Bocksgesang" und weitere Beiträge zu einer deutschen Debatte* (Frankfurt am Main: Ullstein, 1994).

[18] Heimo Schwilk and Ulrich Schacht, "Die Berliner Republik und das Grundgesetz," in *Für eine Berliner Republik*, ed. Schwilk and Schacht (Munich: Langen-Müller, 1997), 8–14, here 8. Further citations given in parentheses.

[19] Ulrich Schacht, "Das Maß der Erschütterung," in Schwilk, *Für eine Berliner Republik*, 47–60, esp. 48.

[20] Martin Walser, "Der hilfreiche Radfahrer oder Warum das Land gerettet ist," *Die Zeit*, 6 December 2004, 13.

[21] Ayhan Gecay, "Ich bin gerne deutscher Bürger," *Die Zeit*, 6 December 2004, 14.

[22] Max Frisch, "Überfremdung I," in *Die Schweiz als Heimat* (Frankfurt am Main: Suhrkamp, 2nd ed., 1991), 219–21, here 221.

[23] Günter Wallraff, *Ganz unten* (Cologne: Kiepenheuer und Witsch, 1985).

[24] Günter Grass, *Rede vom Verlust* (Göttingen: Steidl, 1992), 57.

[25] See Franz Josef Görtz, Volker Hage, and Uwe Wittstock, eds., *Deutsche Literatur 1992* (Stuttgart: Reclam, 1993), 92.

[26] Hans Magnus Enzensberger, *Die große Wanderung* (Frankfurt am Main: Suhrkamp, 1992), 13. Further citations given in parentheses.

[27] Peter Schneider, "'Erziehung zum Haß,'" *Die Welt*, 9 December 2005. http://welt.de/data2005/12/09/814871html?prx=1. Consulted 10 December 2005. The first article "'Wir brauchen die Deutschen nicht'" appeared the previous day. http://www.welt.de/data/2005/12/08/814524.html?prx=1. Consulted 10 December 2005.

[28] Thea Dorn, "Wie gefährlich ist der deutsche Staat?," *Die Welt*, 11 January 2006. http://www.welt.de/data/2006/01/11829523.html?prx=1. Consulted same day.

[29] Frank Schirrmacher, "Vorbereitungsgesellschaft," *Frankfurter Allgemeine Zeitung*, 13 February 2006, 37.

[30] Botho Strauß, "Der Konflikt," *Der Spiegel*, 13 February 2006, 120–21, here 121.

[31] Peter Schneider, "Das Versprechen der Freiheit," *Der Tagesspiegel*, 23 February 2006. http://www.tagesspiegel.de/kultur/;art772,2180386. Consulted same day.

[32] Günter Grass, "'Kein Kampf der Kulturen, sondern zweier Unkulturen,'" *Die Welt*, 10 February 2006. http://www.welt.de/data/2006/02/10/843397.html? prx=1. Consulted same day.

[33] Richard Wagner, "Kampf gegen die Menschenrechte," *Berliner Zeitung*. http://www.berlinonline.de/print.php.Berliner-zeitung/feuilleton/523452.html. Consulted 5 March 2008.

[34] Zafer Şenocak, "Krieg der Ignoranten — Gastkommentar," *Die Welt*. http://welt.de/data/2006/02/10/843575.html?prx=1. Consulted 12 February 2006.

[35] Zafer Şenocak, "Eine auswegslose Ehehölle," *Die Tagezeitung*, 2 August 2005, 9.

[36] Ralph Giordano, "Nein und dreimal nein," *FAZ Net*, 1 June 2007. http://www.faz.net/s/Rub594835B672714A1DB1A121534F010EE1/Doc~E87EE751. Consulted 2 June 2007.

[37] "'Stoppt den Bau dieser Moschee,'" *Kölner Stadt-Anzeiger*, 31 May 2007. http://www.ksta.de/servelet/OriginalContentServer?pagename=ksta/ksArtikel/Druckfas. Consulted 31 May 2007.

[38] Ralph Giordano, Wolfgang Schäuble, "'Mir macht Angst, dass Sie so viel Verständnis haben,'" *Frankfurter Allgemeine Sonntagszeitung*, 2 March 2008, 7.

[39] Günter Wallraff, "'Raus aus den Hinterhöfen,'" *Die Zeit*, 27 March 2008, 18.

[40] Feridun Zaimoğlu, "'Liebe ist reaktionär,'" *SPIEGEL ONLINE*, 13 March 2008. http://www.spiegel.de/kultur/literatur/0,1518,druck-541282,00.html. Consulted 14 March 2008.

[41] Zafer Şenocak, "Der Terror kommt aus dem Herzen des Islam," *Die Welt,* http://www.welt.de/politik/article500196/Der Terror_kommt_aus_dem_Herzen des_Islam.html. Consulted 31 December 2007.

[42] Hans Magnus Enzensberger, *Schreckens Männer: Versuch über den radikalen Verlierer* (Frankfurt am Main: Suhrkamp, 2006), 22. Further citations given in parentheses.

[43] Roger Woods, *Germany's New Right as Culture and Politics* (Basingstoke: Palgrave, 2007), esp. 113.

[44] Meyer, "Nicht Zerstörung," 86.

[45] Martin Mosebach, *Ultima ratio regis* (Munich: Hanser, 2007), 21–22.

[46] Wolfram Schütte, "Katholik: 1x vom Teufel geritten," *titel-magazin.* http://www.titel-forum.de/modules/php?. Consulted 18 April 2008.

Conclusion

URING ALL THE DISCUSSION in the previous chapters on the political activities of writers, the question of how to judge their efforts has remained largely unresolved. One obvious reason for this is that it is difficult to provide a simple answer. Any attempt to determine whether they were right or wrong is likely to carry a subjective element, even if some issues — the need to fight any resurgence of Nazi ideology and the obligation to oppose terrorist violence, for example — do seem clear cut. Equally, any judgment based on success seems simplistic in that it runs the risk of debasing intellectual debate by applying criteria more applicable to economic and business activities. Equally, any success is ultimately impossible to quantify; all that can be stated with confidence is the aim of any contribution to political debate.

One possible answer might seem to present itself, if the following question is answered in the affirmative. Have German writers fulfilled the social role of intellectuals? Unfortunately, this immediately raises another question of what such a role might be, a subject that has occasioned debate over centuries. Opinions have varied on this, from the view that they have no contribution, or at least no positive contribution, to make, to the claim that they have a special role. In his work *Capitalism, Socialism and Democracy,* the political scientist Joseph A. Schumpeter speaks, in a manner reminiscent of Max Weber, of the lack of "direct responsibility for practical affairs,"[1] thus suggesting they have a parasitic role in society. By contrast, the sociologist Karl Mannheim speaks of "watchmen in what would otherwise be a pitch-black night."[2]

Mannheim's comment implies that intellectuals are the guardians of something worthwhile. Using images from a similar area, Bernard-Henri Lévy suggests what this might be, saying that the presence of intellectuals in the modern city is one of the keys of democracy[3] and that where such a presence is removed this, at least in France, has led to disaster. In other words, intellectuals have the role of defending the values associated with democratic society. For Lévy, this means fighting the "dictatorship of opinion" (61), while the philosopher Ortega y Gasset states that for the intellectual, the world only seems to exist in order to be questioned.[4] This kind of critical stance is widely accepted as appropriate for intellectuals — indeed, it is seen as part of their duty — whereas bowing to political power means abandoning this requirement. This is also the view of Theodor Geiger, who warns against intellectuals aligning themselves with those in power, because power will always take its own course. The result would be a loss of intellectual substance and a betrayal of their role.[5] It is such a betrayal that East German writers found themselves accused of, justifiably in certain cases, at the time of unification.

The idea of intellectuals betraying their calling is found in one of the most well-known books on their role, Julien Benda's *La Trahison des clercs.*[6] Here, the accusation is that betrayal means espousing extreme political views. As seen in chapter 5, this was part of the accusations made by Sontheimer and Schelsky against certain West German writers and intellectuals in the 1970s. By contrast, as was seen in chapter 3, Hans Dieter Zimmermann excludes writers associated with the Gruppe 47 from his strictures against intellectuals, seeing them as having made a constructive contribution to the history of the Federal Republic. What is more, the situation is complicated by the refusal of certain writers, frequently referred to in this volume, to accept the role of public intellectual. This is the case with Enzensberger, as the title of his 1995 interview with *Die Zeit* — which colorfully expresses his refusal to be a washcloth with which to polish the world — shows.[7] Walser has also consistently adopted a similar stance, even if he expresses his position less colorfully. In 1966, he warned against commitment being like a compulsory school subject for writers,[8] while four decades later he told the journalist Martin Doerry, whose grandmother was murdered in Auschwitz, that he rejected any such role, not wishing to persuade and teach anybody.[9] Despite such protestations, given their prominence, it is hard not to conclude that there is a degree of disingenuousness in the stances of both Enzensberger and Walser.

It is clearly very difficult to mediate between the different views referred to above. In general terms, most of the comments quoted suggest a legitimate role for intellectuals in political debate, however unwilling some have been to accept such a role. As for the specific case of Germany, it is hoped that what is contained in this volume shows that since 1945 there have been enough issues in the realm of politics to warrant the intervention of writers and intellectuals. Whether all these interventions have been well-judged is ultimately often a matter of opinion. One generalized comment is perhaps possible. Where writers, especially those of the postwar generation, have criticized political power as such, they often appear to exclude the possibility of the benign use of power. As even democratic politics involves power, the question is surely how it is used. Despite this reservation, however, I have tried to show that writers helped to establish the democracy of the Federal Republic and sought to make improvements to the political system established in the GDR, while also, through their criticisms, contributing to the mood that led to the downfall of that state when it showed itself incapable of reform. This does not mean that writers did not at times commit errors of judgment.

A recent novel by Friedrich Christian Delius, *Mein Jahr als Mörder* (My Year as a Murderer, 2004), can in part be read as going to the heart of the matter. Like many of his works, it is linked to real events and people — in this case, the execution of the doctor Georg Groscurth, who had once been the personal physician of Rudolf Hess, for his opposition to the Nazis. When the first-person narrator, a student of literature in West Berlin and thus at least prospectively a literary intellectual, hears in 1968 that a judge engaged in the show trial against Groscurth has been acquitted and also learns how badly Groscurth's widow has been treated after the war because of her refusal to accept the prevailing mood of anticommunism, he determines to murder the judge. This never seems likely to happen and is in fact rendered impossible by the judge's death from natural causes. The nearest the young man gets to violence is a long, open-air diatribe against Germans in general and Berlin in particular that begins: "Verfluchte Stadt der Sklaven da unten, Sklaven der Kaiser, der Hitlers, der Russen und selbst der Amis" (Cursed city of slaves down there, slaves of emperors, of Hitlers, of the Russians and even the Yanks).[10] It is followed by a short paragraph that concludes with the narrator realizing that he is making a fool of himself (285). Like Delius's hero, writers had good reason to be unhappy at certain aspects of postwar Germany; however, not least at the time of the student movement, some of them did make fools of themselves. One example that could be said to come into this category is the essay on cultural revolution by Peter Schneider that appeared in 1968. Most of it consists of stilted prose worthy of the most blinkered ideologue. One specific example of what, at the least, seem eccentric views is the claim that petrol tankers are more beautiful than the cars they service, because the forms of the latter have been corrupted by the obsession of capitalism with marketing. All they invite, according to Schneider, is a desire to commit arson; in fact, they only realized their utility value when burning as part of the May 1968 events in Paris.[11] It is small wonder that his memoir of 1968, referred to in chapter 4, should contain the word *Wahn* (delusion) in its title.[12]

What is the situation some forty years later? As has been seen, later generations of writers have not felt the same need to intervene as regularly in political debates as those who either experienced the horrors of National Socialism or whose childhood and youth were most affected by the shadows the Nazi era cast. This tendency has been particularly marked since unification in 1990, which put an end to what in historical terms was an artificial situation, even allowing for the disunity that was a feature of German history until the latter part of the nineteenth century. A book that appeared in early 2005 confirms what has happened. In it, the economist Max A. Höfer quantifies the prominence of writers and intellectuals in the print media. Unsurprisingly, the top place is occupied by Grass, with Walser and Enzensberger close behind in third and sixth positions respectively.[13] Why this should be so is suggested in a 2005 piece by the writer and translator Michael Kleeberg.[14] His simple answer is that his generation does not feel any need to intervene in matters political. He is also concerned how writers, if they involve themselves in politics, sacrifice the aesthetic quality of their writing. According to Kleeberg, today's writers cannot be blamed for not wanting to sink below their artistic level.

It has to be agreed that Kleeberg has a point, at least in relation to Grass, although hardly in the cases of Walser and Enzensberger. Böll, too, wanted his political writing to be at the same level as his literary work, saying in a 1976 interview that, when writing a political essay, he did not wish to sacrifice the intellectual level he demanded of himself elsewhere.[15] Whether he always lived up to this aim, for instance, in his Baader-Meinhof essay, remains a matter for debate. However, at the end of his essay, despite what has gone before, Kleeberg does suggest that writers have a role in defending society's values of freedom, equality, and the rule of law, but also implies he does not know how to proceed. Indeed, the question of aesthetics in political writing remains a difficult subject. In a 2008 discussion about political writing between the authors Ulrich Peltzer and Michael Kumpfmüller, both of whom have been labeled political writers, the main issue is the relation between politics and aesthetics. For Peltzer, political writing is more a question of aesthetics, whereas Kumpfmüller stresses the continuing importance of social issues.[16]

One example of how politics and aesthetics might be reconciled is provided by a brilliant piece of writing by Joseph von Westphalen that appeared in 2005. It followed a minor scandal concerning the Federal Republic's then–foreign minister Joschka Fischer, who had come under criticism from some of his diplomats, most notably from the ambassador to Switzerland, Frank Elbe. What was at issue was whether there should be official obituaries for former diplomats who had served both Nazi Germany and the Federal Republic. Rather than writing a simple polemic, Westphalen recreates his fictional character Harry von Duckwitz, an irreverent diplomat from *Im diplomatischen Dienst* (In the Diplomatic Service, 1991), his satirical novel that apparently contained enough reality for it to be read avidly by trainee diplomats. Duckwitz ruminates in free indirect style about the boring life of the diplomat and about the exaggerated reactions of the right-wing press, particularly the *Frankfurter Allgemeine Zeitung,* which had made the most fuss over the issue. For him (and no doubt Westphalen), it is all a tempest in a teacup. This is well captured by the style of the writing, as in this passage about Elbe, to whom he imputes professional frustration:

Jetzt, an der Pensionsgrenze, führte er mit Hilfe der schneidig sekundier-
enden konservativen Presse den Aufstand gegen Fischer an, weil der die
netten Nazi-Diplomaten-Opas nicht mehr würdigen lassen wollte.[17]

[Now, close to his pension, he, with the dashing aid of the conservative
press, was leading the rebellion against Fischer because he no longer
wished to honor the nice Nazi diplomat granddads.]

Obviously, not all comments by writers on political matters can follow this
example; nevertheless, it does suggest that writers can use their literary talents in such contexts.

However amusing Westphalen's text is, it deals with a topic relating to
the past. Even if, as has been seen, the past remains of particular relevance in
Germany, there is still the question of the role of intellectuals in relation to
the contemporary political system, as raised by Enzensberger in 1988 when
he suggested that the traditional dichotomy between the worlds of power
and the intellect was outdated in an advanced democratic society. Certainly,
there is plenty of evidence that there is no longer the same separation and
mutual suspicions between the two worlds. One of Chancellor Schröder's
achievements was to appoint a secretary of state for culture, an innovation
continued under Chancellor Merkel that recognizes the importance of this
area. One small sign that intellect and power could co-exist occurred in
2007 when Merkel was awarded the Leo Baeck Prize for her contribution to
German-Jewish relations. On this occasion, the laudation was held by Wolf
Biermann, who certainly did not mince words, not least in referring to her
predecessor (in the context, arguably with bad taste) as "Gasmann Schröder"
for his involvement on leaving office with the Russian natural gas industry.
Merkel herself was compared to a mature primary school teacher.[18] These
examples suggest that Biermann did not indulge in self-censorship, whereas
Merkel must have known that she would be confronted by someone who
would not respect diplomatic niceties.

Even if such signs of openness and mutual respect confirm — if such
confirmation is still needed — that democracy is as established in the Federal
Republic as elsewhere, this does not mean that the best of all possible worlds
has been achieved. There will always be concern over specific issues — for
example, Günter Grass's concern in 2007 over the danger of democracy
being compromised by policies adopted in the fight against terrorism.[19]
However, there is arguably a more insidious threat to open democratic societies in an area that should be of particular concern for writers, the misuse of
narrative techniques for purposes of manipulation. It is only necessary to
recall such expressions as "spin," "sound bites," and "line of the day" to
perceive the danger. A recent French book by Christian Salmon quotes many
examples of manipulation in the form of — in the word of the book's title —
Storytelling. President Clinton is quoted, for instance, as saying that politics

was no longer for solving economic, military, and political problems, but for enabling people to improve their "stories."[20] Clearly, Germany is not the United States or Great Britain, nor even Berlusconi's Italy or Sarkozy's France; nevertheless, it would be foolhardy to deny possible dangers. Writers and intellectuals are a prospective obvious source for a counter voice, or preferably, counter voices, in such a situation.

It is in keeping with such a view that the East German writer Thomas Brussig should have lauded what he calls the culture of debate in a 2007 essay. In contrast to Kleeberg, he does not see a blanket problem with the general level of intellectual debate in Germany. Instead, he differentiates between debates, mostly relating to the past, which are conducted at a high level, and those relating to current and future issues — he refers to food safety and issues arising from an aging population — which are not generally conducted at the same level. He also claims that the second group of topics is more important because they affect everyday life. He concludes with the hope that what he calls the beautiful debates might be more important and the more important debates more beautiful. The result would be a "Debattenkultur, um die wir zu beneiden wären. Einen unverzichtbaren Luxus" (a culture of debate in Germany, for which we should be envied. An indispensable luxury).[21]

Such a view is of course subjective and, in any case, relates to a particular time. This book has tried to show that there has been a fascinating culture of debate in Germany since 1945. What is more, in an age of manipulation, such a culture is needed on a global scale. Is it not reasonable to claim that German writers have set an example?

Notes

[1] Joseph A. Schumpeter, *Capitalism, Socialism and Democracy* (London: Unwin, 1970), 147.

[2] Karl Mannheim, *Ideology and Utopia* (London: Routledge & Kegan Paul, 1968), 143.

[3] Bernard-Henri Lévy, *Éloge des Intellectuels* (Paris: Grasset, 1987), 9. Further citations given in parentheses.

[4] José Ortega y Gasset, "Der Intellektuelle und der Andere," in *Die Intellektuellen*, ed. Wolfgang Bergsdorf (Pfullingen, Neske, 1982), 15–26, here 23.

[5] Theodor Geiger, *Aufgaben und Stellung der Intellektuellen in der Gesellschaft* (Stuttgart: Ferdinand Enke, 1949), 71.

[6] Julien Benda, *La Trahison des Clercs* (Paris: Bernard Grasset, 1928).

[7] Hans Magnus Enzensberger, "Ich will nicht der Lappen sein, mit dem man die Welt putzt," *Die Zeit*, 20 January 1995, 47–48.

[8] Martin Walser, "Engagement als Pflichtfach für Schriftsteller," in *Heimatkunde,* 103–24.

[9] Martin Walser, "Wegschauen oder Hinschauen," *Der Spiegel,* 28 January 2008, 140–43, here 143.

[10] Friedrich Christian Delius, *Mein Jahr als Mörder* (Berlin: Rowohlt, 2004), 283. Further citations given in parentheses.

[11] Peter Schneider, "Die Phantasie im Spätkapitalismus und die Kulturrevolution," *Kursbuch* 15 (1968): 1–37 here 26.

[12] Peter Schneider, *Rebellion und Wahn* (Cologne: Kiepenheuer & Witsch, 2008).

[13] Max A. Höfer, *Meinungsführer, Denker und Visionäre* (Frankfurt am Main: Eichborn, 2005).

[14] Michael Kleeberg, "Warum nicht wir," *Die Welt,* 19 March 2005. http://www.welt.de/data/2005/03/19/612334.html?prx=1. Consulted same day.

[15] Heinrich Böll, "Eine deutsche Erinnerung. Interview mit René Wintzen Oktober 1976," in *Werke. Interviews 1 1961–1978,* ed. Bernd Balzer (Cologne: Kiepenheuer &Witsch, no year) 504–665, here 646.

[16] "Über die Gegenwart nachdenken. Michael Kumpfmüller und Ulrich Peltzer im Gespräch," *Neue Zürcher Zeitung,* 26 April 2008. http://www.nzz.ch/nachrichten/kultur/literatur_und_kunst/ueber_die_gegenwart_nach. Consulted same day.

[17] Joseph von Westphalen, "Fischer — der Roman," *die tageszeitung,* 10 April 2005, 13.

[18] Wolf Biermann, "'Behutsam und beharrlich,'" *Die Welt,* 7 November 2007. http://www.welt.de_print/article1337710/Behutsam_und_beharrlich.html?print= Consulted 14 November 2007.

[19] Günter Grass, "'Wir demontieren unsere Demokratie,'" *Der Tagespiegel,* 16 October 2007. http://www.tagesspiegel.de/kultur/Literatur-Guenter-Grass;art 138,2399916. Consulted 16 October 2007.

[20] Christian Salmon, *Storytelling* (Paris: La Découverte, 2007), 128.

[21] Thomas Brussig, "Worüber wir reden," *Der Tagesspiegel,* 16 August 2007. http://www.tagesspiegel.de/kultur/Schiessbefehl;art772,23558605?_FRAME=33&_FO Consulted 16 August 2007.

Works Cited

Abromeit, Heidrun, and Klaus Burkhardt. "Die Wählerinitiativen im Wahlkampf 1972." Supplement to *Das Parlament*, 15 September 1973.

Adorno, Theodor W. *Jargon der Eigentlichkeit*. 3rd ed. Frankfurt am Main: Suhrkamp, 1967.

Agde, Günter, ed. *Kahlschlag: Das 11. Plenum des ZK der SED 1965*. Berlin: Aufbau, 2001.

Aicher-Scholl, Inge. "Wohlstand ohne Konzept?" In Walser, *Die Alternative oder Brauchen wir eine neue Regierung?*, 104–14.

Alt, Franz. *Frieden ist möglich*. Munich: Piper, 1983.

Aly, Götz. *Unser Kampf*. Frankfurt a.M: Fischer, 2008.

Amery, Carl. "Brief zur Verteidigung des Freistaates." In Duve, Böll, and Staeck, *Briefe zur Verteidigung der bürgerlichen Freiheit*, 224–29.

———. "Eine kleine Utopie." In Walser, *Die Alternative oder Brauchen wir eine neue Regierung?*, 7–13.

Améry, Jean. "In den Wind gesprochen." In *Die zornigen alten Männer*, edited by Axel Eggebrecht, 258–79. Reinbek: Rowohlt, 1979.

Andersch, Alfred. *Deutsche Literatur in der Entscheidung*. Karlsruhe: Verlag Volk und Zeit, [1947].

———. "Das junge Europa formt sein Gesicht." In Schwab-Felisch, *Der Ruf,* 21–29.

Andres, Stefan. "Warum nicht ein anderes Gesetz." In Wagenbach, *Vaterland, Muttersprache*, 92–93.

Anon. "Alltag der Ostzone." *Die Gegenwart* 4:24 (1949): 6–7.

Anon. "'Kein Mensch glaubt es.'" *Die Gegenwart* 1:2/3 (1946): 49–50.

Anon. "Rede an die deutsche Jugend. Eine Parodie frei nach Ernst Wiechert." In *Der Ruf: Unabhängige Blätter für die junge Generation,* edited by Hans A. Neunzig, 58–60. Munich: Nymphenburger Verlagshandlung, 1976.

Anz, Thomas, ed., *"Es geht nicht um Christa Wolf."* Munich: edition spangenberg, 1991.

Arendt, Hannah. *Eichmann in Jerusalem*. Munich: Piper, 1986.

———. "Organisierte Schuld." In *Bundesrepublikanisches Lesebuch,* edited by Hermann Glaser, 227–35. Frankfurt am Main: Fischer, 1980.

Arnold, Heinz Ludwig, ed., *Günter Grass — Dokumente zur politischen Wirkung*. Munich: Richard Boorberg Verlag, 1971.

Augstein, Rudolf. "Der geschundene Siegfried." In Richter, *Plädoyer für eine neue Regierung oder Keine Alternative*, 63–65.

———. "Zugebaute Scham." *Der Spiegel*, 8/16 February 1998, 29.

Bartels, Gerrit. "Wer die Zeitenwende kennt, weiß noch nicht, wohin die Reise geht." *Die Tageszeitung*, 17 March 2005, 14.

Barthélemy, Françoise, and Lutz Winckler, eds. *Mein Deutschland findet sich in keinem Atlas*. Frankfurt am Main: Luchterhand, 1990.

Baumann, Michael. *Wie alles anfing*. Frankfurt am Main: Anabas Verlag et al., 1977.

Baumert, Gerhard. "Letter to *Ost und West*." 1:4 (1947): 85–87.

Baumgart, Reinhard. "Die verdrängte Phantasie oder Sechs Thesen uber Literatur und Politik." In Kuttenkeuler, *Poesie und Politik*, 358–66.

Becher, Johannes R. "Deutschland, dich suchend." In Schwarz, *Wir heißen Euch hoffen*, 1951, 26.

———. "Die Sprache des Friedens." *Der Monat* 3:29 (1950/51): 488–89.

Becher, John T. "John T. Becher schrieb an seinen Vater." *Der Monat* 3:29 (1950/51): 488–89.

Becker, Jürgen. "Modell eines möglichen Politikers." In Richter, *Plädoyer für eine neue Regierung oder Keine Alternative*, 121–25.

Becker, Jurek. "Gedächtnis verloren — Verstand verloren." *Die Zeit*, 18 November 1988, 61.

Benda, Julien. *La Trahison des Clercs*. Paris: Bernard Grasset, 1928.

Bering, Dietz. *Die Intellektuellen: Geschichte eines Schimpfwortes*. Stuttgart: Klett/Cotta, 1978.

Berliner Begegnung zur Friedensförderung. Darmstadt and Neuwied: Luchterhand, 1982.

Biermann, Wolf. "Auch ich war bei der Stasi." *Die Zeit*, 4 May 1990, 73–74.

———. "Behutsam und beharrlich." *Die Welt*, 7 November 2007. http://www.welt.de_print/article1337710/Behutsam_und_beharrlich.html?print=. Consulted 14 November 2007.

———. "'Berlin zottelt an meinem Herzen.'" *Berliner Zeitung*, 10 April 2007, http://www.berlinonline.de/berliner-zeitung/archiv/.bin/dump.fcgi/2007/0410/feuilleton/0009/index.html. Consulted 13 October 2008.

———. "Kriegshetze Friedenshetze." *Die Zeit*, 1 February 1991, 59–60.

———. "Der Lichtblick im gräßlichen Fatalismus der Geschichte." *Die Zeit*, 25 October 1991, 73–74.

————. "'Wenn ich so dächte wie Kunert, möchte ich lieber tot sein.' Ein ZEIT-Gespräch zwischen Wolf Biermann, Günter Kunert und Fritz J. Raddatz." *Die Zeit*, 14 November 1980, 41–42.

Biller, Manfred. "Unschuld mit Grünspan." In *Deutsche Literatur 1998*, edited by Volker Hage, Rainer Moritz, and Hubert Winkels, 278–83. Stuttgart: Reclam, 1999.

Biller, Maxim. "Soviel Sinnlichkeit wie der Stadtplan von Kiel. Warum die neue deutsche Literatur nichts so nötig hat wie der Realismus. Ein Grundsatzprogramm." In *Maulhelden und Königskinder*, edited by Andrea Köhler and Moritz Rainer, 62–71. Leipzig: Reclam, 1998.

Bittermann, Klaus. "Die Geisterwelt der Ossis." In *Der rasende Mob*, edited by Klaus Bittermann and Henryk M. Broder, 104–38. Berlin: Verlag Klaus Bittermann, 1993.

Böll, Heinrich. "Auf traurige Weise friedlos." In *Mut zur Angst: Schriftsteller für den Frieden*, edited by Ingrid Krüger, 48–53. Darmstadt, Neuwied: Luchterhand, 1982.

————. "Eine deutsche Erinnerung." In *Werke: Interviews I*, 504–665.

————. "Ende der Bescheidenheit." In Kuttenkeuler, *Poesie und Politik*, 347–57.

————. "Rufschädigung ist eine ansteckende Krankreit." In *Werke: Interviews I*, 696–701.

————. *Werke: Interviews I*. Ed. Bernd Balzer. Cologne: Kiepenheuer und Witsch, n.d.

————. "Will Ulrike Gnade oder freies Geleit." In *Ende der Bescheidenheit. Schriften und Reden 1969–72*. Munich: DTV, 1985, 222–29.

Born, Nicolas. "Eines ist dieser Staat sicher nicht: ein Polizeistaat." In Duve, Böll, and Staeck, *Briefe zur Verteidigung der Republik*, 20–24.

Bräunig, Werner. *Rummelplatz*. Berlin: Aufbau, 2007.

Brandt, Willy. "Braucht die Politik den Schriftsteller?" In Lattmann, *Einigkeit der Einzelgänger*, 9–18.

Brasch, Thomas. *Vor den Vätern sterben die Söhne*. Berlin: Rotbuch, 1976.

Braun, Volker. "Eigentum." In *Die Mauer fiel, die Mauer steht*, edited by Hermann Glaser, 63–64. Munich: DTV, 1999.

————. "Fünf Gedichte auf Deutschland." *Kursbuch 4* (1966): 64–72.

Briegleb, Klaus. *Mißachtung und Tabu*. Berlin and Vienna: Philo, 2003.

Broder, Henryk M. "'Auf der Höhe der Zeit.'" In *Das Holocaust-Mahnmal*, edited by Michael S. Cullen, 186–90. Zurich: Pendo, 1999.

————. "Der Herr der Binse." *SPIEGEL ONLINE*, 14 August 2006. http://www.spiegel/de/kultur/gesellschaft/0,1518,431695,00.html. Consulted 16 August 2006.

Brussig, Thomas. "Worüber wir reden." *Der Tagesspiegel,* 16 August 2007. http://www.tagesspiegel.de/kultur/Schiessbefehl;art772,23558605?_FRAME =33&_FO. Consulted 16 August 2007.

Bucerius, Gerd. "Schwelgt nicht in Angst." *Die Zeit,* 26. July 1981, 35.

Buch, Hans Christoph. "'Herdentiere oder Einzelganger' Uber die Krise der VS und Moglichkeiten zu deren Überwindung." *Vorwärts,* 24 March 1983, 13.

————, ed., *Tintenfisch 15: Thema Deutschland.* Berlin: Klaus Wagenbach Verlag, 1979.

————. "Von der möglichen Funktion der Literatur." *Kursbuch 20* (1970): 42–52.

Chotjewitz, Peter O. "Beichte eines Staatsbürgers." In *Nicht heimlich und nicht kühl,* edited by Heiner Boehncke and Dieter Richter, 38–39. Berlin: Ästhetik und Kommunikation Verlag, 1977.

————. *Die Herren des Morgengrauens.* Berlin: Rotbuch, 1978.

Clemens, Albrecht, Günter C. Behrmann, Michael Bock, Harald Homann, and Friedrich H. Tenbruck. *Die intellektuelle Gründung der Bundesrepublik.* Frankfurt am Main: Campus, 2000.

Cofalla, Sabine. *Der soziale Sinn Hans Werner Richters.* Berlin: Weidler, 1997.

Cramer, Heinz von. "Es ist so spat, wie es schon einmal war." In Walser, *Die Alternative oder Brauchen wir eine neue Regierung,* 85–96.

Cullen, Michael S., ed., *Das Holocaust-Mahnmal.* Zurich: Pendo, 1999.

Czechowski, Heinz. "Euphorie und Katzenjammer." In Naumann, *"Die Geschichte ist offen,"* 53–58.

Dafür I and II (Magazine published by the Sozialdemokratische Wählerinitiative for 1969 election).

Dahn, Daniela. "Da liegt kein Segen darauf." *Süddeutsche Zeitung,* 6 February 2004. www.sueddeutsche.de/sz/feilleton/red-artikel769/ Consulted 6 February 2004.

————. "Eine beispiellose Tragödie." In *Vertreibung ins Paradies.* Reinbek: Rowohlt, 1998, 188–200.

————. *In guter Verfassung* Reinbek: Rowohlt, 1999.

————. "Vereintes Land — geteilte Freude." In *Wenn und aber.* Reinbek: Rowohlt, 2002, 134–58.

————. *Westwärts und nicht vergessen.* Reinbek: Rowohlt, 1997.

"'Das ist die Fortsetzung des Dritten Reiches.'" *Der Tagespiegel,* 9 June 2005, 29.

de Bruyn, Günter. "Die eine deutsche Kultur." In Barthélemy and Winckler, *Mein Deutschland findet sich in keinem Atlas,* 27–28.

————. "Jubelschreie, Trauergesänge." *Die Zeit,* 7 September 1990, 61–62.

DDR-Journal zur Novemberrevolution. Documentation published by *die tageszeitung,* 1989.

Delius, F. C. "Abschied von Willy." In*Heute — und die 30 Jahre davor,* edited by Rosemarie Wildermuth, 135. Munich: Ellermann Verlag, 3rd ed., 1979.

Delius, Friedrich Christian. *Die Flatterzunge.* Reinbek: Rowohlt, 1999.

———. *Konservativ in 30 Tagen.* Reinbek: Rowohlt, 1998.

———. *Mein Jahr als Mörder.* Berlin Rowohlt, 2004.

———. "Strickmuster einer Verstrickung." In *Vom Verlust der Scham und dem allmählichen Verschwinden der Demokratie,* edited by Heinz Ludwig Arnold, 186–98. Göttingen: Steidl, 1988.

"'Der Kanzler ist kein Volkserzieher.' Gesprach zwischen Helmut Schmidt und Siegfied Lenz, Günter Grass, Fritz J. Raddatz." *Die Zeit,* 22 August 1980, 29–31.

Dirks, Walter. "Das Abendland und der Sozialismus." *Frankfurter Hefte* 1:3 (1946): 67–78.

———. "Europa und die Neutralität." *Frankfurter Hefte* 6:5 (1951): 305–8.

Dohnanyi, Klaus von. "'Du verspielst jeden Respekt als Figur des öffentlichen Dialogs.'" In Negt, ed., *Der Fall Fonty,* 161–66.

Dohse, Rainer. *Der Dritte Weg: Neutralitätsbestrebungen in Westdeutschland zwischen 1945 und 1955.* Hamburg: Holsten Verlag, 1974.

Dorn, Thea. "Wie gefährlich ist der deutsche Staat?" *Die Welt,* 11 January 2006. http://www.welt.de/data/2006/01/11829523.html?prx=1. Consulted 11 January 2006.

Duve, Freimut, Heinrich Böll, and Klaus Staeck, eds. *Briefe zur Verteidigung der bürgerlichen Freiheit.* Reinbek: Rowohlt, 1978.

———. *Briefe zur Verteidigung der Republik.* Reinbek: Rowohlt, 1977.

Edschmid, Kasimir. "Aus meinem Notizbuch." In Weyrauch, *Ich lebe in der Bundesrepublik,* 50–59.

Eggebrecht, Axel. "Die Enkel der Hitlergeneration." In Duve, Böll, and Staeck, *Briefe zur Verteidigung der Republik,* 39–42.

———. "Soll die Ära der Heuchelei andauern?" In Walser, ed., *Die Alternative oder Brauchen wir eine neue Regierung?,* 25–35.

Eich, Günter. "Episode." In Wildemuth, *Heute — und die 30 Jahre davor,* 163.

———. "Inventur." http://www.dradio.de/dif/sendungen/buechermarkt/ 587156/. Consulted 28 April 2006.

"Ein Gespräch über die Zukunft mit Rudi Dutschke, Bernd Rabehl und Christian Semler." *Kursbuch 14* (1968): 146–74.

Ende, Michael. *Die unendliche Geschichte.* Stuttgart: Thienemanns Verlag, 1979.

Enzensberger, Hans Magnus. *Aussichten auf den Bürgerkrieg.* Frankfurt am Main: Suhrkamp, 1993.

———. "Berliner Gemeinplätze." *Kursbuch 11* (1968): 151–69.

———. "Beschwerde." In Wagenbach, *Vaterland, Muttersprache,* 181–82.

———. "Bürgerkrieg im Briefkasten." In Richter, *Die Mauer oder Der 13. August,* 175–77.

———. *Deutschland, Deutschland, unter anderem.* Frankfurt am Main: Suhrkamp, 1967, 7–13.

———. "Europäische Peripherie." *Kursbuch 2* (1965): 154–73.

———. "Gangarten." *Kursbuch 100* (1990): 1–9.

———. *Gedichte.* Frankfurt am Main: Suhrkamp, 1962.

———. "Gemeinplätze, die Neueste Literatur betreffend." *Kursbuch 15* (1968): 187–97.

———. *Die große Wanderung.* Frankfurt am Main: Suhrkamp, 1992.

———. "Hitlers Wiedergänger." In *Liebesgrüße aus Bagdad,* edited by Klaus Bittermann, 44–52. Berlin: Edition Tiamat, 1991.

———. "Ich will nicht der Lappen sein, mit dem man die Welt putzt." *Die Zeit,* 20 January 1995, 47–48.

———. "Ich wünsche nicht gefährlich zu leben." In Walser, *Die Alternative oder Brauchen wir eine neue Regierung?,* 61–66.

———. "Macht und Geist: ein deutsches Indianerspiel." In *Mittelmaß und Wahn.* Frankfurt am Main: Suhrkamp, 1991, 207–21.

———. "Notstand." In *Tintenfisch 2.* Berlin: Klaus Wagenbach Verlag, 1969, 19–20.

———. "Das Plebiszit der Verbraucher." In *Einzelheiten I.* Frankfurt am Main: Suhrkamp, 1964, 167–78.

———. "Schimpfend unter Palmen." In Weyrauch, *Ich lebe in der Bundesrepublik,* 24–31.

———. *Schreckens Männer: Versuch über den radikalen Verlierer.* Frankfurt am Main: Suhrkamp, 2006.

———. "Über die Schwierigkeit, Inländer zu sein." In *Deutschland, Deutschland, unter anderem,* 7–13.

———. "Versuch, von der deutschen Frage Abschied zu nehmen." In *Deutschland, Deutschland, unter anderem,* 37–48.

———. "Warum ich nicht in den USA bleibe." *Tagebuch,* März/April 1968, 12–13.

Eppler, Erhard, Michael Ende, and Hanne Tächl. *Phantasie, Kultur, Politik.* Stuttgart: Thienemanns Verlag, 1982.

Eyck, Herbert Adam von. "Der Hauptmann von Kapharnaum." In Schwarz, *Worte wider Waffen*, 95–99.

Fachdienst Germanistik 9:3 (1991): 1–2.

Franzen, Günter. "Links, wo kein Herz ist." *Der Spiegel*, 27 October 2003, 216–18.

Fried, Erich. "Englische Randglossen." In Richter, *Plädoyer für eine neue Regierung oder Keine Alternative*, 140–46.

Friedrich, Heinz. "Nationalismus und Nationalismus." In Schwab-Felisch, *Der Ruf*, 226–27.

Friedrich, Jörg. *Der Brand*. Munich: Propyläen Verlag, 2002.

Fries, Fritz Rudolf. "Braucht die neue Republik neue Autoren." In Naumann, *"Die Geschichte ist offen,"* 53–58.

Frisch, Max. "Drei Entwürfe zu einem Brief nach Deutschland." In *Bundesrepublikanisches Lesebuch*, edited by Hermann Glaser, 236–42. Frankfurt am Main: Fischer, 1980.

———. "Überfremdung I." In *Die Schweiz als Heimat*. Frankfurt am Main: Suhrkamp, 2nd ed., 1991, 219–21.

Fuchs, Jürgen. *Einmischung in eigene Angelegenheiten*. Reinbek: Rowohlt, 1984.

Fuchs, Käte, and Alfred Kantorowicz. "Suchende Jugend: Briefwechsel zwischen der Studentin Käte Fuchs und Alfred Kantorowicz." *Ost und West*, 2:2 (1948): 85–91.

Fuhr, Eckhard. "Der Geist und die Macht." *Die Welt*, 12 February 2005. http://www.welt.de/date/2005/02/12/461986.html?prx=1. Consulted 23 February 2005.

Gaitanides, Johannes. "Von der Ohnmacht unserer Literatur." In Weyrauch, *Ich lebe in der Bundesrepublik*, 10–23.

Gecay, Ayhan. "Ich bin gerne deutscher Bürger." *Die Zeit*, 6 December 2004, 14.

Geiger, Theodor. *Aufgaben und Stellung der Intellektuellen in der Gesellschaft*. Stuttgart: Ferdinand Enke, 1949.

"Gert Loschütz über Biermann und andere Dichter." *Deutschlandradio*, 22 January 2007. http://www.dradio.de/dkultur/sendungen/politischesfeuilleton/584711/. Consulted 2 October 2007.

Giordano, Ralph. "Menetekel Saddam Hussein." In *Liebesgrüße aus Bagdad*, edited by Klaus Bittermann. Berlin: Edition Tiamat, 1991, 74–85.

———. "Nein und dreimal nein." *FAZ Net*, 1 June 2007. http://www.faz.net/s/Rub594835B672714A1DB1A121534F010EE1/Doc~E87EE751. Consulted 2 June 2007.

———. "Über meine Unfähigkeit, konservativ zu wählen oder von Zwangsdemokraten und Gegenradikalen." In Gütt, *Wählen — aber wen?*, 25–40.

———. *Die zweite Schuld oder von der Schwierigkeit, Deutscher zu sein*. Munich: Knaur, 1990.

Giordano, Ralph, and Wolfgang Schäuble. "'Mir macht Angst, dass Sie so viel Verständnis haben.'" *Frankfurter Allgemeine Sonntagszeitung*, 2 March 2008, 7.

Glotz, Peter. "Freunde, es wird ernst." In Görtz, *Deutsche Literatur 1993*, 273–74.

Görner, Rüdiger, ed., *Politics in Literature*. Munich: iudicium, 2004.

Görtz, Franz Josef, Volker Hage, and Uwe Wittstock, eds. *Deutsche Literatur 1989*. Stuttgart: Reclam, 1990.

———. *Deutsche Literatur 1991*. Stuttgart: Reclam, 1992.

———. *Deutsche Literatur 1992*. Stuttgart: Reclam, 1993.

———. *Deutsche Literatur 1993*. Stuttgart: Reclam, 1994.

Grass, Günter. *Aus dem Tagebuch einer Schnecke*. Reinbek: Rowohlt, 1974.

———. *Beim Häuten der Zwiebel*. Göttingen: Steidl, 2006.

———. "Den Widerstand lernen, ihn leisten und zu ihm auffordern." In *Widerstand leisten*, 91–96.

———. "Des Kaisers neue Kleider." In *Über das Selbstverständliche*, 42–57.

———. "Ein Schnäppchen namens DDR." In *Ein Schnäppchen namens DDR*, 39–60.

———. *Ein weites Feld*. Göttingen: Steidl, 1995.

———. "Es steht zur Wahl." In *Über das Selbstverständliche*, 10–20.

———. "Geißlers Schüler." In *Vom Verlust der Scham und dem allmählichen Verschwinden der Demokratie*, edited by Heinz Ludwig Arnold, 159–61. Göttingen: Steidl, 1988.

———. "'Kein Kampf der Kulturen, sondern zweier Unkulturen.'" *Die Welt*, 10 February 2006. http://www.welt.de/data/2006/02/10/843397.html ? prx=1. Consulted 10 February 2006.

———. *Kopfgeburten oder Die Deutschen sterben aus*. Darmstadt and Neuwied: Luchterhand, 1980.

———. *Im Krebsgang*. Göttingen: Steidl, 2002.

———. "Kurze Rede eines vaterlandslosen Gesellen." In *Ein Schnäppchen namens DDR*. Frankfurt am Main: Luchterhand, 1990, 7–14.

———. "Lastenausgleich." in *Deutscher Lastenausgleich*. Frankfurt am Main: Luchterhand, 1990, 7–12.

———. "Loblied auf Willy." In *Über das Selbstverständliche*, 21–31.

———. "Offener Brief an die Abgeordneten des Deutschen Bundestags." In *Widerstand leisten*. Darmstadt and Neuwied: Luchterhand, 1984, 84–90.

———. "Offener Briefwechsel mit Willy Brandt." In *Über das Selbstverständliche*, 95–99.

———. "Rede über das Selbstverständliche." In *Über das Selbstverständliche*, 68–83.

———. *Rede vom Verlust*. Göttingen: Steidl, 1992.

———. "Selbstbildnisse eines Dichters." *Frankfurter Rundschau*, 4 October 2007. http://www.fr-online.de/top_news/?em_cnt=1219474. Consulted 4 October 2007.

———. *Über das Selbstverständliche*. Munich: DTV, 1969.

———. "Viel Gefühl, wenig Bewußtsein." In *Deutscher Lastenausgleich*, 13–25.

———. "Vom mangelnden Selstvertrauen der schreibenden Hofnarren unter Berücksichtigung nicht vorhandener Höfe." In *Über das Selbstverständliche*, 84–89.

———. "'Wir demontieren unsere Demokratie.'" *Der Tagespiegel*, 16 October 2007. http://www.tagesspiegel.de/kultur/Literatur-Guenter-Grass;art138, 2399916. Consulted 16 October 2007.

Graumann, Dieter. "Großartig, kleinmütig." *Frankfurter Rundschau*, 18 August 2006. http://www.fr-online.de/in_und_ausland/kultur_und_medien/ feuilleton/?em_cnt=950099. Consulted 18 August 2006.

Greiffenhagen, Martin and Silvia. *Ein schwieriges Vaterland*. Munich and Leipzig: List, 1993.

Greiner, Ulrich. "Die deutsche Gesinnungsästhetik." In Anz, *"Es geht nicht um Christa Wolf,"* 208–16.

———. "Es ist nun wirklich genug!" *Die Zeit*, 24 August 2006. http:// zeus.zeit.de/text/2006/35/L-Taeter. Consulted 25 August 2006.

———. "Mangel an Feingefühl." In Anz, *"Es geht nicht um Christa Wolf,"* 66–70.

———. "Der Seher auf dem Markt." *Die Zeit*, 25 April 1994, 53.

Grützbach, Frank, ed., *Freies Geleit fur Ulrike Meinhof: Ein Artikel und seine Folgen*. Cologne: Kiepenheuer und Witsch, 1972.

Güntner, Joachim. "Die deutsch-amerikanische Verständigung." *Neue Zürcher Zeitung*, 26 September 2002. http://www.nzz.ch/2002/09/26/fe/page-article8F9VE.html. Consulted 26 September 2002.

———. "Der Luftkrieg fand im Osten statt." In *Deutsche Literatur 1998*, edited by Volker Hage, Rainer Moritz, and Hubert Winkels, 271–75. Stuttgart: Reclam, 1999.

Gütt, Dieter, ed., *Wählen — aber wen?* Hamburg: Grüner & Jahr, 1987.

Habe, Hans. *Leben fur den Journalismus*. 3 vols. Munich, Zurich: Knaur, 1976.

Habermas Jürgen. "'Ein Abgrund von Trauer.'" *Der Spiegel*, 7 August 1995, 34.

———. "Die Moderne — ein unvollendetes Projekt." *Die Zeit,* 19 September 1980, 47–48.

———. "Der Zeigefinger. Die Deutschen und ihr Denkmal." *Die Zeit,* 31 March 1999, 42–44.

Hacks, Peter. "Brief an eine Dame in Paris über einen Ort namens Deutschland." In Barthélemy, *Mein Deutschland findet sich in keinem Atlas,* 29–30.

Härtling, Peter. "Eine natürliche Opposition." In Richter, *Plädoyer für eine neue Regierung oder Keine Alternative,* 177–81.

———. "In der Sprache bin ich zu Haus." In Barthélemy, *Mein Deutschland findet sich in keinem Atlas,* 20.

———. *Nachgetragene Liebe.* Darmstadt, Neuwied: Luchterhand, 1980.

Hage, Volker. "Kein Mord. Nirgends." In *Deutsche Literatur 1996,* edited by Franz Josef Görtz, Volker Hage, and Hubert Winkels, 268–73. Stuttgart: Reclam, 1997.

Hagelstange, Rudolf. "Endstation Kühlschrank. Maß und Vernunft frieren ein." *Die Kultur,* 16:112 (1958): 1–2.

Hamburger, Michael. *From Prophecy to Exorcism.* London: Longmans, 1965.

"Handke: Grass 'eine Schande furs Schriftstellertum.'" *FAZ.Net,* 13 September 2006. http://www.faz.net/IN/INtemplates/faznet/default.asp?tpl=common/ zwischenseite.asp&dox={B13E6D20-9263-F513-2451-EE466A862D56}&rub ={CF3AEB15-4CE6-4960-822F-A5429A182360}. Consulted 11 November 2006.

Handke, Peter. *Eine winterliche Reise zu den Flüssen Donau, Save, Morawa und Drina oder Gerechtigkeit für Serbien.* Frankfurt am Main: Suhrkamp, 1996.

———. "Ich komme aus dem Traum." *Die Zeit,* 6/11 February 2006. http:// zeus.zeit.de/text/2006/06/L-Handke-Interv_. Consulted 2. February 2006.

"Handkes Grass-Kritik: 'Schande für das Schriftstellertum." http://www. spiegel.de/kultur/literatur/0,1518,436864,00.html. Consulted 13 October 2008.

Harpprecht, Klaus. "Die SPD und ihre Intellektuellen." *Die neue Gesellschaft,* 18:11 (1971), 824–27.

Hartung, Klaus. "Die Linke und die RAF." In *Der blinde Fleck.* Frankfurt am Main: Verlag Neue Kritik, 1987, 148–59.

Havemann, Robert. "Nach zwanzig Jahren." In Richter, *Plädoyer für eine neue Regierung oder Keine Alternative,* 132–39.

Hein, Christoph. "Der alte Mann und die Straße. Ansprache zur Demonstration der Berliner Kulturschaffenden." In *Als Kind habe ich Stalin gesehen.* Berlin and Weimar: Aufbau, 1990, 175–77.

————."Die Zensur ist überlebt, nutzlos, paradox, menschenfeindlich, volks-feindlich, ungesetzlich und strafbar." In *Als Kind habe ich Stalin gesehen*. Berlin and Weimar: Aufbau, 1990, 77–104.

Heine, Heinrich, *Historisch-Kritische Gesamtausgabe der Werke*. Vol. 2. Ed. Manfred Windfuhr. Hamburg: Hoffman und Campe, 1983.

Heinrich Boll und sein Verlag Kiepenheuer und Witsch. City of Cologne, 1992.

Henscheid, Eckhard. "Nachwort." In Gerhard Henschel, *Das Blöken der Lämmer*. Berlin Tiamat, 1994, 149–61.

Hermand, Jost. "Streit in den fünfziger Jahren." In *Kontroversen, alte und neue: Akten des VII Germanistentages*, edited by Albrecht Schöne, 207–11. Tübingen: Max Niemeyer Verlag, 1986.

Heym, Stefan. "Auf Sand gebaut." In *Auf Sand gebaut*. Frankfurt am Main: Fischer, 1993, 26–36.

————. "Ich kann doch nicht mein ganzes Leben wegwerfen." *Die Zeit*, 6 December 1991, 64–65.

————. "Die Wunde der Teilung eitert weiter." *Der Spiegel*, 7 November 1983, 66.

Hochhuth, Rolf. "Klassenkampf." In Richter, *Plädoyer für eine neue Regierung oder Keine Alternative*, 65–87.

————. "Parteien und Autoren" in Duve, *Briefe zur Verteidigung der bürgerlichen Freiheit*, 180–96.

————. "Schwierigkeit, die wahre Geschichte zu erzählen." *Die Zeit*, 17 February 1978, 41.

————. "Die Sprache der Sozialdemokraten." in Wagenbach, ed., *Vaterland, Muttersprache*, 267–69.

————. *Wessis in Weimar*. Berlin Volk & Welt, 1993.

Höfer, Max A. *Meinungsführer, Denker und Visionäre*. Frankfurt am Main: Eichborn, 2005.

Hölderlin, Friedrich. *Werke und Briefe*. Ed. Friedrich Beißner and Jochen Schmidt. Frankfurt am Main: Insel, 1969.

Holink, Hein. *Westdeutsche Wiedervereinigungspolitik 1949–1961*. Meisenheim am Glen: Verlag Anton Hain, 1978.

Ich will reden von der Angst meines Herzens. Frankfurt am Main: Luchterhand, 1991.

igl, "Die Mauer, " *Frankfurter Allgemeine Zeitung*, 29 January 2007, 33.

Jacobsen, Hans-Adolf. "Vom Vergleich des Unvergleichbaren." *Die Zeit*, 9 December 1983, 51.

Jäger, Manfred. *Kultur und Politik in der DDR 1945–1990.* Cologne: Edition Deutschland Archiv, 1994.

Jahnn, Hans Henny. "Der Abgrund." In Wagenbach, *Vaterland, Muttersprache,* 147.

———. "Der Mensch im Atomzeitalter." In *Das Hans Henny Jahn Lesebuch,* edited by Uwe Schweikert, 69–83. Hamburg: Hoffmann und Campe, 1984.

Janka, Walter. *Schwierigkeiten mit der Wahrheit.* Reinbek: Rowohlt, 1989.

Jaspers, Karl. *Die Schuldfrage.* Munich, Zurich: Piper, 2nd ed., 1976.

Jens, Walter. "Isoliert die Desperados durch mehr Demokratie." In Duve, Böll, and Staeck, *Briefe zur Verteidigung der Republik,* 86–90.

———. "Widerruf in letzter Minute." In Cullen, *Das Holocaust-Mahnmal,* 206–10.

Jesse, Eckhard. "Die (Pseudo-)Aktualität der deutschen Frage — ein publizistisches, kein politisches Phänomen." In *Die deutsche Frage in der Weltpolitik,* edited by Wolfgang Michalka, 51–68. Wiesbaden: Steiner, 1986.

Kästner, Erich. "Offener Brief an Freiburger Studenten." In Wagenbach, *Vaterland, Muttersprache,* 110–11.

Kantorowicz, Alfred. "Einführung." *Ost und West* 1:1 (1947): 3–8.

Karsunke, Yaak. "Anachronistische Polemik." *Kursbuch 15* (1968): 165–68.

Kempowski, Walter. "Ich bin vergiftet worden." *Frankfurter Rundschau,* 4 August 2007. http://www.fr-online.de/top_news/?em_cnt=1185119. Consulted 15 August 2007.

Kirsch, Sarah. "Kleine Betrachtungen am Morgen des 17. November." In Naumann, *"Die Geschichte ist offen,"* 79–81.

Kleeberg, Michael. "Warum nicht wir." *Die Welt,* 19 March 2005. www.welt.de/data/2005/03/19/612334.html?prx=1. Consulted 19 March 2005.

Klotz, Johannes, and Gerd Wiegel, eds. *Geistige Brandstiftung? Die Walser-Bubis-Debatte.* Cologne: Papyrossa, 1999.

Knabe, Hubertus. "Die deutsche Oktoberrevolution." In *Aufbruch in eine andere DDR,* edited by Hubertus Knabe, 9–23. Reinbek: Rowohlt, 1989.

Knappstein, Karl Heinrich. "Die Stunde der Sozialreform." *Frankfurter Hefte* 1:3 (1946): 1–3.

Königsdorf, Helga. *1989 oder Ein Moment der Schönheit.* Berlin and Weimar: Aufbau, 1990.

Koeppen, Wolfgang. *Das Treibhaus.* Frankfurt am Main: Suhrkamp, 1982.

———. "Wahn." In Weyrauch, *Ich lebe in der Bundesrepublik,* 32–36.

Kogon, Eugen. "Gericht und Gewissen." *Frankfurter Hefte* 1:1 (1946): 25–37.

Konrád, György. "Abschied von der Chimäre." In Cullen, *Das Holocaust-Mahnmal,* 191–97.

Koopmann, Helmut. "Die Bundesrepublik Deutschland in der Literatur." *Zeitschrift für Politik* 26:2 (1979): 161–78.

Korn, Salomon. "Monströse Platte." In Cullen, *Das Holocaust-Mahnmal,* 36–41.

Krause, Tilman. "Christa steht auf Obstsalat." *Die Welt,* 16 July 2005. http://www.welt.de/print-welt/article682742/Christa_steht_auf_Obstsalat.html. Consulted 13 October 2008.

Kraushaar, Wolfgang. *Die Bombe im jüdischen Gemeindehaus.* Hamburg: Hamburger Edition, 2005.

Krüger, Horst, "Der Staat und die Intellektuellen." *Frankfurter Hefte,* 27:7 (1972): 488–95.

———. "Das Thema wird gestellt." In *Was ist heute links?,* 11–29.

———. "Was bleiben sollte." *Die Zeit,* 13 August 1971, 13.

———, ed. *Was ist heute links?* Munich: List, 1963.

Krüger, Ingrid, ed., *Mut zur Angst. Schriftsteller für den Frieden.* Darmstadt, Neuwied: Luchterhand, 1982.

Kuby, Erich. "Und ob wir eine neue Regierung brauchen." In Walser, *Die Alternative oder Brauchen wir eine neue Regierung?,* 146–54.

Kunert, Günter. "Was erwarten Sie von Deutschland? Was wünschen Sie dem vereinten Land?" *Die Zeit,* 5 January 1990, 52.

Kunze, Reiner. *Deckname "Lyrik."* Frankfurt am Main: Fischer, 1990.

———. *Die wunderbaren Jahre* Frankfurt am Main: Fischer, 1976.

Kuttenkeuler, Wolfgang, ed., *Poesie und Politik.* Stuttgart: Kohlhammer, 1973.

Lamprecht, Helmut, ed., *Politische Gedichte vom Vormärz bis zur Gegenwart.* Bremen: Carl Schünemann Verlag, 1969.

Lattmann, Dieter, ed., *Einigkeit der Einzelgänger.* Munich: Kindler, 1971.

———. *Die Einsamkeit des Politikers.* Frankfurt am Main: Fischer, 1982.

———. *Die lieblose Republik.* Frankfurt am Main: Fischer, 1984.

———. "Unsere real existierende Demokratie." In *Vom Verlust der Scham und dem allmählichen Verschwinden der Demokratie,* edited by Heinz Ludwig Arnold, 37–46. Göttingen: Steidl, 1988.

Lau, Jörg. "Schwellkörper Deutschland." In Negt, *Der Fall Fonty,* 141–47.

Leggewie, Claus, and Erik Meyer. *"Ein Ort, an den man gerne geht": Das Holocaust-Mahnmal und die deutsche Geschichtspolitik seit 1989.* Munich and Vienna: Hanser, 2005.

Lenz, Siegfried. "Das Dilemma der Außenseiter." In *Entwicklungsland Kultur*, edited by Dieter Lattmann, 64–68. Munich: Kindler, 1973.

———. "Die Politik der Entmutigung." In Walser, *Die Alternative oder Brauchen wir eine neue Regierung?*, 131–36.

———. "Das Wasser der Republik." In *Kämpfen für die sanfte Republik*, edited by Freimut Duve, Heinrich Böll, and Klaus Staeck, 88–93. Reinbek: Rowohlt, 1980.

Leonhard, Rudolf. "Unser Land." In Schwarz, *Wir heißen Euch hoffen*, 43.

Leonhard, Rudolf Walter. "Die deutschen Universitäten." In Richter, *Bestandsaufnahme*, 351–59.

Lestiboudois, Herbert. "Junge Generation." In *Der Anfang*, edited by Paul E. H. Luth, 46. Wiesbaden: Limes Verlag, 1947.

———. "Warum, wozu noch." In *Der Anfang*, edited by Paul E. H. Luth, 43–44. Wiesbaden: Limes Verlag, 1947.

Lettau, Reinhard. "It's time for a change." In Richter, *Plädoyer für eine neue Regierung oder Keine Alternative*, 129–31.

———, ed., *Die Gruppe 47. Bericht, Kritik, Polemik: Ein Handbuch*. Berlin: Luchterhand, 1967.

Lévy, Bernard-Henri. *Éloge des Intellectuels*. Paris: Grasset, 1987.

Loest, Erich. "Heute kommt Westbesuch." In *Von Abraham bis Zwerenz*, edited by Bundesministerium für Bildung, Wissenschaft, Forschung und Technologie, 1198–1206. Berlin Cornelsen, vol.2, 1995.

———. *Die Stasi war mein Eckermann*. Göttingen: Steidl, 1991.

Loth, Wilfried. *Stalins ungeliebtes Kind: Warum Moskau die DDR nicht wollte*. Berlin: Rowohlt, 1994.

Mann, Heinrich. "Dichtkunst und Politik." In *Essays*. Hamburg: Claasen, 1960, 299–315.

———. "Geist und Tat." In *Essays*, 7–14.

———. "Die Macht des Wortes." *Die neue Weltbühne* 4:10 (1935): 285–86.

Mann, Thomas. *Betrachtungen eines Unpolitischen*. Frankfurt am Main: Fischer, 2001.

———. *Germany and the Germans*. Washington, DC: Library of Congress, 1945.

———. "Offener Brief für Deutschland." In Wagenbach, *Vaterland, Muttersprache*, 47–48.

Mannheim, Karl. *Ideology and Utopia*. London: Routledge & Kegan Paul, 1968.

Maron, Monika. "Der Schriftsteller und das Volk." *Der Spiegel*, 12 February 1990, 68–70.

Mathenau, Jörg. *Martin Walser*. Reinbek: Rowohlt, 2005.

Meckel, Christoph. *Suchbild*. Düsseldorf: Claasen, 1980.

Meier, Christian. "Nicht Zerstörung, sondern neue Herausforderung der Vernunft." In *Intellektuellendämmerung*, edited by Martin Meyer, 77–95. Munich: Hanser, 1992.

Menasse, Eva, and Michael Kumpfmüller. "Wider die intellektuelle Gerontokratie." *Süddeutsche Zeitung*, 17 August 2006. Quoted from: Goethe-Institut Dossier: "Günter Grass in der Kritik — Ausgewählte Pressestimmen. http://www.goethe.de/kue/lit/dos/gra/pre/de1710133.htm. Consulted 30 October 2006.

Meyer, Martin. "Intellektuellendämmerung." In *Intellektuellendämmerung*. Munich: Hanser, 1992, 1–12.

Michael, Klaus. "Feindbild Literatur. Die Biermann-Affäre, Staatssicherheit und die Herausbildung einer Alternativkultur." *Aus Politik und Zeitgeschehen (Das Parlament)*, 28 May 1993, 23.

Michael, Klaus, and Peter Böthig, eds. *MachtSpiele*. Leipzig: Reclam, 1993.

Michel, Klaus Markus. "Ein Kranz für die Literatur." *Kursbuch 15* (1968): 169–86.

Mitscherlich, Alexander and Margarethe. *Die Unfähigkeit zu trauern*. Munich: Piper, 20.ed, 1988.

Mittenzwei, Werner. *Die Intellektuellen: Literatur und Politik in Ostdeutschland 1945–2000*. Leipzig: Faber & Faber, 2001.

Mohr, Reinhard. "Ostneid? Westneid? Es geht uns gut," *Die Welt*, 4 May 2007. http://www.welt.de/kultur/article850776/Ostneid_Westneid_Es_geht_uns_gut.html. Consulted 7 May 2007.

Molo, Walter von. "Ja, wir wollen uns retten." In Schwarz, *Wir heißen Euch hoffen*, 29–42.

Morshäuser, Bodo. *Hauptsache Deutsch*. Frankfurt am Main: Suhrkamp, 1992.

———. "Über das Risiko, von der Leiter zu fallen oder auf die Strahlung kommt es an." In Gütt, *Wählen — aber wen?*, 83–92.

Mosebach, Martin. *Ultima ratio regis*. Munich: Hanser, 2007.

Müller, Heiner. "Da trinke ich lieber Benzin zum Frühstück." In *"Zur Lage der Nation."* Berlin: Rotbuch, 45–58.

———."Dem Terrorismus die Utopie entreißen." In *"Zur Lage der Nation,"* 9–24.

Naumann, Michael, ed., *"Die Geschichte ist offen."* Reinbek: Rowohlt, 1990.

Negt, Oskar, ed., *Der Fall Fonty*. Göttingen: Steidl, 1996.

Neubert, Erhard. *Geschichte der Opposition in der DDR*. Bonn: Bundeszentrale für politische Bildung, 2nd ed., 1998.

Nickel, Günther. "Die medialen Kampagnen gegen Günter Grass, Martin Walser und Peter Handke." *titel-magazin* (2007). http://www.titel-magazin.de/print.php?sid=6282&POSTNUKESID=7cdd73c156f3bb. Consulted 5 October 2007.

Niven, William. "Bernhard Schlink's *Der Vorleser* and the Problem of Shame." *MLR* 98:2 (2003): 381–96.

Nohl, Hermann. "Die geistige Lage im gegenwärtigen Deutschland." In *Bundesrepublikanisches Lesebuch,* edited by Hermann Glaser, 150–54. Frankfurt am Main: Fischer, 1980.

Noll, Chaim. "Treue um Treue." In *Wir Kollaborateure,* edited by Cora Stephan, 90–106. Reinbek: Rowohlt, 1992.

Nossack, Hans Erich. "Unser Feind ist immer das Kleinbürgertum. An meinen in Brasilien lebenden Bruder." In Duve, Böll, and Staeck, *Briefe zur Verteidigung der Republik,* 124–25.

Nutt, Harry. "Ach, Walser!" *Frankfurter Rundschau,* 11 May 2006, 17.

Ortega y Gasset, José. "Der Intellektuelle und der Andere." in *Die Intellektuellen,* edited by Wolfgang Bergsdorf, 15–26. Pfullingen: Neske, 1982.

Orwell, George. "Why I Write." In *England Your England and Other Essays.* London: Secker and Warburg, 1954.

Parkes, K. Stuart. *Writers and Politics in West Germany.* Beckenham: Croom Helm, 1986.

Parkes, Stuart. "*Tod eines Kritikers:* Text and Context." In *Seelenarbeit an Deutschland: Martin Walser in Perspective,* edited by Stuart Parkes and Fritz Wefelmeyer, 447–68. Amsterdam and New York: Rodopi, 2004.

Peitsch, Helmut. "West German Reactions on the Role of the Writer in the Light of Reactions to 9 November 1989." In *German Literature at a Time of Change 1989–1990,* edited by Arthur Williams, Stuart Parkes, Roland Smith, 155–86. Bern: Peter Lang, 1991.

Peters, Peter. "'We are one Book.' Perspectives and Developments of an All-German Literature." In *The Individual, Identity and Innovation,* edited by Arthur Williams and Stuart Parkes, 297–314. Bern: Peter Lang, 1994.

Piwitt, Hermann Peter. "Einen Kranz niederlegen am Herrmannsdenkmal." In Buch, *Tintenfisch 15. Thema: Deutschland,* 17–24.

Plenzdorf, Ulrich. *Die neuen Leiden des jungen W.* Rostock: Hinstorff, 1973.

Preece, Julian. "Death and the Terrorist in Recent German Fiction." In Görner, *Politics in Literature,* 171–86.

Rada, Uwe. "Sonderwohlfahrtszone Ost." *die tageszeitung,* 24 September 2005. http://taz.de/pt/2005/09/24/a0202.nf/textdruck. Consulted 24 September 2005.

Raddatz, Fritz J. "Die Aufklärung entlässt ihre Kinder." *Die Zeit,* 27/29 June 1984, 9–10.

Reinecke, Stefan. "Ein Skandal, der gefällt." *die tageszeitung,* 10 May 2005. http://www.taz.de/pt/2005/05/10/a0170.nf/textdruck. Consulted 10 May 2005.

Richter, Hans Werner. "Die Alternative im Wechsel der Personen." In Richter, *Plädoyer für eine neue Regierung oder Keine Alternative,* 9–16.

———. "Beim Wiedersehen des 'Ruf.'" In Schwab-Felisch, ed., *Der Ruf,* 7–9.

———, ed., *Bestandsaufnahme.* Munich, Vienna, Basel: Kurt Desch, 1962.

———. "Deutschland — Brücke zwischen Ost und West." In Schwab-Felisch, *Der Ruf,* 46–49.

———. "In einem zweigeteilten Land." In Krüger, *Was ist heute links?,* 94–100.

———. *Die Geschlagenen.* Munich: DTV, 1969.

———, ed., *Die Mauer oder Der 13. August.* Reinbek: Rowohlt, 1961.

———. "Parteipolitik und Weltanschauung." In Schwab-Felisch, *Der Ruf,* 83–88.

———, ed., *Plädoyer für eine neue Regierung oder Keine Alternative.* Reinbek: Rowohlt, 1965.

———. "Von links in der Mitte." In Walser, *Die Alternative oder Brauchen wir eine neue Regierung?,* 115–24.

———. "Warum schweigt die junge Generation?" In Schwab-Felisch, ed., *Der Ruf,* 29–33.

Richter, Horst Eberhard. "Der Aufstand der Gefühle." *Die Zeit,* 26 June 1981, 52.

Rinser, Luise. "Für eine grüne ¨Politik oder Über den Mut zu denken." In Gütt, *Wählen — aber wen?,* 111–18.

Roßmann, Andreas. "Die Einheit — eine (literarische) Fiktion." *Deutschland Archiv,* 14:6 (1981): 568–69.

Rühmkorf, Peter. "Passionseinheit." In Walser, *Die Alternative oder Brauchen wir eine neue Regierung?,* 44–50.

Runge, Erika. *Bottroper Protokolle.* Frankfurt am Main: Suhrkamp, 1968.

Rutschy, Michael. "Warum uns die Bundestagswahl nicht interessiert." *Die Zeit,* 2 January 1987, 29.

Salmon, Christian. *Storytelling.* Paris: La Découverte, 2007.

Schacht, Ulrich. "Die Berliner Republik und das Grundgesetz." In *Für eine Berliner Republik,* edited by Heino Schwilk and Ulrich Schacht, 8–14. Munich: Langen-Müller, 1997.

———. "Das Maß der Erschütterung." In Schwilk, *Für eine Berliner Republik*, 47–60.

Schädlich, Hans Joachim. "Das Fähnlein der treu Enttäuschten." *Die Zeit*, 26 October 1990, 68.

———. "Traurige Freude." In Naumann, *"Die Geschichte ist offen,"* 159–64.

———. "Versuchte Nähe." In *Versuchte Nähe*. Reinbek: Rowohlt, 1980, 7–15.

Schäfer, Hans Dieter. "Zur Periodisierung der deutschen Literatur seit 1930." In *Das gespaltene Bewußtsein: Über deutsche Kultur und Lebenswirklichkeit.* Munich: Hanser, 1981, 55–71.

Schallück, Paul. "Von deutscher Resignation." In *Zum Beispiel*, 17–26.

———. "Von deutscher Tüchtigkeit." In *Zum Beispiel*, 7–11.

———. "Von deutscher Vergeßlichkeit." In *Zum Beispiel*, 12–16.

———. "Vorurteile und Tabus." In Richter, *Bestandsaufnahme*, 432–43.

———. *Zum Beispiel*. Frankfurt am Main: Europäische Verlagsanstalt, 1962.

Schedlinski, Rainer. "Gibt es die DDR überhaupt?" In *Aufbruch in eine andere DDR,* edited by Hubertus Knabe, 275–84. Reinbek: Rowohlt, 1989.

Schelsky, Helmut. *Die Arbeit tun die anderen*. Opladen: Westdeutscher Verlag, 1975.

Scheuch, Erwin K. "Die Arroganz der Ängstlichkeit." *Die Zeit*, 13 November 1981, 11.

Schirrmacher, Frank. "Dem Druck des härteren, strengeren Lebens standhalten." In Anz, *"Es geht nicht um Christa Wolf,"* 77–89.

———. "Vorbereitungsgesellschaft." *Frankfurter Allgemeine Zeitung*, 13 February 2006, 37.

Schlesinger, Klaus. "Am Ende der Jugend." In Wildemuth, *Heute — und die 30 Jahre davor*, 98–101.

———. "Sehnsucht nach der DDR?" In *Von der Schwierigkeit, Westler zu werden*. Berlin: Aufbau, 1998, 11–14.

Schmidt, Helmut. "'Fürchtet Euch nicht.'" *Die Zeit*, 23 December 1983, 1.

Schneider, Peter. "Bosnien — ein Kommunikationsfehler?" *Die Zeit*, 4 August 1995, 37–38.

———. *Deutsche Ängste*. Darmstadt and Neuwied: Luchterhand, 1988.

———. "'Erziehung zum Haß.'" *Die Welt*, 9 December 2005. http://welt.de/data2005/12/09/814871html?prx=1. Consulted 10 December 2005.

———. "Geschichte einer Trennung." In *Deutsche Ängste*, 19–29.

———. "Gibt es zwei deutsche Kulturen; Die Kühlschranktheorie und andere Vermutungen." In Schneider, *Extreme Mitellage*. Reinbek: Rowohlt, 1990, 120–57.

———. "Keine Lust aufs grüne Paradies." In *Deutsche Ängste*, 41–53.

———. *Lenz* Berlin Rotbuch, 1973.

———. *Der Mauerspringer*. Darmstadt and Neuwied: Luchterhand, 1984.

———. "Die Phantasie im Spätkapitalismus und die Kulturrevolution." *Kursbuch 15* (1968): 1–37.

———. "Plädoyer für einen Verräter." *Der Spiegel*, 13 February 1984, 66–69.

———. "Politische Dichtung. Ihre Grenzen und Möglichkeiten." In *Theorie der politischen Dichtung*, edited by Peter Stein, 141–55. Munich: Nymphenburger Verlagshandlung, 1973.

———. "PS zur Unterschrift der Professoren unter die Erklärung des Ministers Pestel." In *Nicht heimlich und nicht kühl*, edited by Heiner Boehncke and Dieter Richter, 28–29. Berlin Ästhetik und Kommunikation Verlag, 1977.

———. *Rebellion und Wahn*. Cologne: Kiepenheuer & Witsch, 2008.

———. "Der Ritt über den Balkan." *Der Spiegel*, 15 January 1996, 163–65.

———. . . . *schon bist du ein Verfassungsfeind*. Berlin: Rotbuch, 1975.

———. "Über das allmähliche Verschwinden einer Himmelsrichtung." In *Deutsche Ängste*, 54–65.

———. "Das Versprechen der Freiheit," *Der Tagesspiegel*, 23 February 2006. www.tagesspiegel.de/kultur/;art772,2180386. Consulted 23 February 2006.

———. "'Wir brauchen die Deutschen nicht.'" *Die Welt*, 8 December 2005. http://www.welt.de/data/2005/12/08/814524.html?prx=1. Consulted 10 December 2005.

Schneider, Reinhold. "Gedanken des Friedens." In *Schwert und Friede* Frankfurt am Main: Suhrkamp, 1987, 246–47.

———. "Das Schwert der Apostel." In Schwarz, *Worte wider Waffen*, 37–42.

Schneider, Rolf. "Die heilsame Entfremdung." *Der Spiegel*, 24 September 1990, 54.

Schnell, Ralf. *Geschichte der deutschsprachigen Literatur seit 1945*. Stuttgart: Metzler, 1993.

Schnurre, Wolfdietrich. "Von der Verantwortlichkeit des Schriftstellers." In Richter, *Die Mauer oder Der 13. August*, 116–19.

Schoenberner, Gerhard. "Zerstörung der Demokratie." In Walser, *Die Alternative oder Brauchen wir eine neue Regierung?*, 137–45.

Schonauer, Franz. "Das schmutzige Nest." In Walser, *Die Alternative oder Brauchen wir eine neue Regierung?*, 73–75.

Schreiber, Hermann. "Dabei sein ist out." *Der Spiegel,* 6 September 76, 46–52.

Schriftsteller Ja-Sager oder Nein-Sager: Das Hamburger Streitgespräch deutscher Autoren aus Ost und West. Hamburg: Rütten und Loening, 1961.

Schubert, Helga. "Etwas zu dem ich gehöre." In Barthélemy, *Mein Deutschland findet sich in keinem Atlas,* 26.

Schütte, Wolfram. "Katholik: 1x vom Teufel geritten." *titel-magazin.* http://www.titel-forum.de/modules/php?op=modload&name=News&file=article&sid=6370. Consulted 18 April 2008.

———. "Der Sommer des Ressentimentalisten." *titel-magazin.* http://www.titel-magazin.de/modules.php?op=modload&name=News&file=article&sid=672. Accessed 22 October 2008.

Schumpeter, Joseph A. *Capitalism, Socialism and Democracy.* London: Unwin, 1970.

Schwab-Felisch, Hans, ed. *Der Ruf. Eine deutsche Nachkriegszeitscrift.* Munich: DTV, 1962.

Schwarz, Georg, and Johannes von Tralow, eds. *Worte wider Waffen.* Munich: Willi Weismann Verlag, 1951.

Schwarz, Georg, and Carl August Weber, eds. *Wir heißen Euch hoffen.* Munich: Willi Weismann Verlag, 1951.

Schwilk, Heino, and Ulrich Schacht, eds., *Die selbstbewußte Nation: "Anschwellender Bocksgesang" und weitere Beiträge zu einer deutschen Debatte.* Frankfurt am Main: Ullstein, 1994.

Sebald, W. G. *Luftkrieg und Literatur.* Munich and Vienna: Hanser, 1999.

Seghers, Anna. "Appell an die deutschen Schriftsteller." In Wagenbach, *Vaterland, Muttersprache,* 122.

Seitz, Norbert. *Die Kanzler und die Künste: Die Geschichte einer schweren Beziehung.* Munich: Siedler, 2005.

Seligmann, Rafael. *Der Musterjude.* Munich: DTV, 2nd ed., 2002.

Şenocak, Zafer. "Dunkle deutsche Seele." *Die Welt,* 7 October 2005. http://www.welt.de/print-welt/article169207/Dunkle_deutsche_Seele.html. Consulted 18 October 2008.

———. "Eine ausweglose Ehehölle." *Die Tageszeitung,* 2 August 2005, 9.

———. "Krieg der Ignoranten — Gastkommentar." *Die Welt,* 10 February 2006. http://welt.de/data/2006/02/10/843575.html?prx=1. Consulted 11 February 2006.

———. "Der Terror kommt aus dem Herzen des Islam." *Die Welt.* http://www.welt.de/politik/article500196/Der Terror_kommt_aus_dem_Herzen des _Islam.html. Consulted 31 December 2007.

Shandley, Robert R., ed., *Unwilling Germans? The Goldhagen Debate*. Minneapolis: Univ. of Minnesota Press, 1998.

Sieburg, Friedrich. "Frieden mit Thomas Mann." *Die Gegenwart* 4:14 (1949): 14–16.

Siedler, Wolf Jobst. "Die Linke stirbt, doch sie ergibt sich nicht." In Richter, *Die Mauer oder Der 13. August*, 111–15.

Sonnemann, Ulrich. "Vom Preis des Unrechts und der Rentabilität des Rechts." In Richter, *Plädoyer für eine neue Regierung oder Keine Alternative*, 153–69.

Sontheimer, Kurt. *Das Elend unserer Intellektuellen*. Hamburg: Hoffmann und Campe, 1976.

———. *Zeitenwende?* Hamburg: Hoffmann und Campe, 1983.

Spinnen, Burkhard. "Bitte, seid behutsam. In jeder Beziehung." *Die Welt*, 14 August 2006. http://www.welt.de/print-welt/article235502/Bitte_seid_behutsam_In_jeder_Beziehung.html. Consulted 13 October 2008.

Steffen, Verena. *Häutungen*. Munich: Verlag Frauenoffensive, 1975.

Stephan, Cora. *Der Betroffenheitskult*. Berlin: Rowohlt, 1993.

———. "Vorwort." In *Wir Kollaborateure*, edited by Cora Stephan, 7–10. Reinbek: Rowohlt, 1992.

"'Stoppt den Bau dieser Moschee.'" *Kölner Stadt-Anzeiger*, 31 May 2007. http://www.ksta.de/servelet/OriginalContentServer?pagename=ksta/ksArtikel/Druckfas. Consulted 31 May 2007.

Strauß, Botho. "Anschwellender Bocksgesang." In *Der Aufstand gegen die sekundäre Welt*. Munich: Hanser, 1999, 55–78.

———. "Der Konflikt." *Der Spiegel*, 13 February 2006, 120–21.

Strauß, Franz Josef. "Die Zeit der Entscheidung ist da." In *Gegen den Terror*, edited by Walter Althammer, 22–30. Stuttgart: Verlag Bonn Aktuell, 1978.

Struck, Karin. "SPD wählen hieße, dem Chefarzt die Blumen zu bringen, nachdem Mutter und Hebamme ein Kind zur Welt gebracht haben." In Gütt, *Wählen — aber wen?*, 143–52.

Süskind, Patrick. "Deutschland, eine Midlife-Crisis." *Der Spiegel*, 17 September 1990, 116–25.

Syberberg, Rüdiger. "Gedanken zur Zeit." In Schwarz and von Tralow, *Worte wider Waffen*, 33–36.

Szczesny, Gerhard. "Humanistische Union." In Walser, *Die Alternative oder Brauchen wir eine neue Regierung?*, 36–43.

Taberner, Stuart. *German Literature of the 1990s and Beyond: Normalization and the Berlin Republic*. Rochester, NY: Camden House, 2005.

Tralow, Johannes von. "Nachwort." In Schwarz and von Tralow, *Worte wider Waffen*, 107–9.

Trauberg, Ursula. *Vorleben*. Frankfurt am Main: Suhrkamp, 1968.

Tucholsky, Kurt. *Ausgewählte Briefe*. Reinbek: Rowohlt, 1962.

Ullmaier, Johannes. *Von Acid nach Adlon und zurück*. Mainz: Ventil, 2001.

Verhandlungen des Deutschen Bundestags 8. Wahlperiode. Stenographische Berichte. Band 103, Bonn 1977.

Vinke, Hermann, ed., *Akteneinsicht Christa Wolf*. Hamburg: Luchterhand, 1993.

Wagenbach, Klaus. "Ernüchtert oder heimatlos." In Krüger, *Was ist heute links?*, 84–89.

———, ed., *Vaterland, Muttersprache*. Berlin: Klaus Wagenbach Verlag, 1979.

Wagner, Bernd. "Blitzschlag, Angst und Vaterlandsliebe." In Barthélemy, *Mein Deutschland findet sich in keinem Atlas*, 101–25.

———. "Kampf gegen die Menschenrechte." *Berliner Zeitung*. http://www.berlinonline.de/print.php.Berliner-zeitung/feuilleton/523452.html. Consulted 3 January 2008.

Wallraff, Günter. *13 unerwünschte Reportagen*. Cologne: Kiepenheuer und Witsch, 1969.

———. *Der Aufmacher*. Cologne: Kiepenheuer und Witsch, 1977.

———. "Autoren, Radikale im offentlichen Dienst." In *Phantasie und Verantwortung*, edited by Horst Bingel, 24–38. Frankfurt am Main: Fischer, 1975.

———. *Ganz unten*. Cologne: Kiepenheuer und Witsch, 1985.

———. "'Raus aus den Hinterhöfen.'" *Die Zeit*, 14/27 March 2008, 18.

Wallich, H. C. *Mainsprings of the German Revival*. New Haven: Yale University Press, 1955.

Walser, Martin. "11. November 1989." In *Über Deutschland reden*. Frankfurt am Main: Suhrkamp, new expanded edition, 1989.

———, ed., *Die Alternative oder Brauchen wir eine neue Regierung?* Reinbek: Rowohlt, 1961.

———. "An die Sozialdemokratische Partei Deutschlands." In Duve, Böll, and Staeck, *Briefe zur Verteidigung der Republik*, 156–59.

———. "Auskunft über den Protest." in *Heimatkunde*. Frankfurt am Main: Suhrkamp, 1968, 36–39.

———. "Auschwitz und kein Ende." In *Deutsche Sorgen*, 228–34.

———. *Deutsche Sorgen*. Frankfurt am Main: Suhrkamp, 1997.

———. "Deutsche Sorgen II." In *Deutsche Sorgen*, 453–67.

———. "Erfahrungen beim Verfassen einer Sonntagsrede." In *Die Walser-Bubis Debatte,* edited by Frank Schirrmacher, 7–17. Frankfurt am Main: Suhrkamp, 1999.

———. "Ein deutsches Mosaik." In *Erfahrungen und Leseerfahrungen.* Frankfurt am Main: Suhrkamp, 1965, 7–28.

———. "Engagement als Pflichtfach für Schriftsteller." In *Heimatkunde,* 103–26.

———. "Das Fremdwort der Saison." In *Die Alternative oder Brauchen wir eine neue Regierung?,* 124–30.

———. "Für eine IG-Kultur." In *Wie und wovon handelt Literatur.* Frankfurt am Main: Suhrkamp, 1973, 67–75.

———. "Händedruck mit Gespenstern." In *Stichworte zur "Geistigen Situation der Zeit,"* edited by Jürgen Habermas, vol.1, 39–51. Frankfurt am Main: Suhrkamp, 1979.

———. "Der hilfreiche Radfahrer oder Warum das Land gerettet ist." *Die Zeit,* 6 December 2004, 13.

———. *ohne einander.* Frankfurt am Main: Suhrkamp, 1993.

———. "Die Parolen und die Wirklichkeit." In *Heimatkunde,* 58–70.

———. "Praktiker, Weltfremde und Vietnam." *Kursbuch 9* (1967): 168–76.

———. "Das Prinzip Genauigkeit." In *Deutsche Sorgen,* 565–92.

———. "Skizze zu einem Vorwurf." In Weyrauch, *Ich lebe in der Bundesrepublik,* 110–14.

———. *Tod eines Kritikers.* Frankfurt am Main: Suhrkamp, 2002.

———. "Über den Leser — soviel man in einem Festzelt darüber sagen soll." In *Wer ist ein Schriftsteller?* Frankfurt am Main: Suhrkamp, 1979, 94–101.

———. "Über Deutschland reden." In *Deutsche Sorgen,* 406–27.

———. "Unser Auschwitz." In *Deutsche Sorgen,* 187–202.

———. "Wahlgedanken." In *Wie und wovon handelt Literatur,* 100–118.

———. "Wegschauen oder Hinschauen." *Der Spiegel,* 28 January 2008, 140–43.

Walther, Joachim. *Sicherungsbereich Literatur.* Berlin: Links, 1996.

Walther, Joachim, et al., eds. *Protokoll eines Tribunals.* Reinbek: Rowohlt, 1991.

Weber, Hermann, ed., *DDR: Dokumente zur Geschichte der Deutschen Demokratischen Republik 1945–1985.* Munich: DTV, 1986.

Weber, Max. *Politik als Beruf.* Stuttgart: Reclam, 1992.

Weidenfeld, Werner, ed., *Nachdenken über Dutschland.* Cologne: Verlag Wissenschaft und Politik, 1985.

Weisenborn, Günther. *Auf Sand gebaut.* Vienna, Munich, Basel: Desch, 1956.

————. "Wir bitten um Eure Rückkehr." In Wagenbach, *Vaterland, Mutter-sprache,* 43–45.

Weiss, Peter. "Unter dem Hirseberg." In Richter, *Plädoyer für eine neue Regierung oder Keine Alternative,* 147–49.

Weiss, Peter, and Hans Magnus Enzensberger. "Eine Kontroverse." *Kursbuch 6* (1966): 165–76.

Wellershoff, Dieter. "Deutschland ein Schwebezustand." In *Stichworte zur "Geistigen Situation der Zeit,"* edited by Jürgen Habermas, vol.1, 77–114. Frankfurt am Main: Suhrkamp, 1979.

————. "Fiktion und Praxis." In Kuttenkeuler, *Poesie und Politik,* 329–40.

Werner, Wolfgang. *Vom Waisenhaus ins Zuchthaus.* Frankfurt am Main: Suhrkamp, 1969.

Westphalen, Joseph von. "Fischer — der Roman." *die tageszeitung,* 10 April 2005, 13.

Weyrauch, Wolfgang, ed. "Bemerkungen des Herausgebers." In Weyrauch, *Ich lebe in der Bundesrepublik,* 7–9.

————. *Ich lebe in der Bundesrepublik.* Munich: List, [1961].

Wickert, Ulrich. *Vom Glück, Franzose zu sein.* Hamburg: Hoffmann und Campe, 1999.

Wiglaf, Droste, and Klaus Bittermann, eds. *Das Wörterbuch des Gutmenschen II.* Berlin: Tiamat, 1995.

Wildemuth, Rosemarie, ed. *Heute — und die 30 Jahre davor.* Munich: Ellermann, 3rd ed., 1979.

Williams, Arthur, Stuart Parkes, and Roland Smith, eds. *Literature on the Threshold.* Oxford: Berg, 1990.

Williams, Rhys W. "Inventing West German Literature: Alfred Andersch and the Gruppe 47." In *The Gruppe 47 Fifty Years on: A Re-appraisal of Its Literary and Political Significance,* edited by Stuart Parkes and John J. White, 69–88. Amsterdam and Atlanta: Rodopi, 1999.

Wolf, Christa. "Bei mir dauert alles sehr lange." *Die Zeit,* 7 October 2005. http://www.zeit.de/text/2005/40/Wolf-Interview. Consulted 1 October 2005.

————. "'Das haben wir nicht gelernt.'" In *Im Dialog,* 93–97.

————. *Im Dialog.* Frankfurt am Main: Luchterhand, 1990.

————. *Kassandra.* Darmstadt and Neuwied: Luchterhand, 1983.

————. *Medea: Stimmen.* Munich: Luchterhand, 1996.

————. "'Mitleidend bleibt das ewige Herz doch fest'": Zum 80. Geburtstag Heinrich Bölls." In *Hierzulande. Andernorts.* Munich: DTV, 2001, 175–94.

———. "Nirgends sein o Nirgends du mein Land." In Wolf, *Hierzulande. Andernorts.* Munich: DTV, 2001, 61–68.

———. "Sprache der Wende." In *Im Dialog*, 119–21.

———. *Störfall.* Darmstadt and Neuwied: Luchterhand, 1987.

———. "'Wider den Schlaf der Vernunft.'" In *Im Dialog*, 98–100.

Woods, Roger. *Germany's New Right as Culture and Politics.* Basingstoke: Palgrave, 2007.

Zahl, Peter Paul. "Die andauernde Ausbürgerung." In Buch, *Tintenfisch 15: Thema: Deutschland*, 95–104.

Zaimoğlu, Feridun. "'Liebe ist reaktionär.'" *SPIEGEL ONLINE*, 13 March 2008. http://www.spiegel.de/kultur/literatur/0,1518,druck-541282,00.html. Consulted 14 March 2008.

Zeller, Bernhard, ed. *Als der Krieg zu Ende war.* Munich: Kosel Verlag, 1973.

Zimmer, Dieter E. "Deine Angst und meine Angst." *Die Zeit*, 13 November 1981, 10–12.

———. "Ein Kapitel Geist und Macht." *Die Zeit*, 17 May 1974, 13–14.

Zimmermann, Hans Dieter. *Der Wahnsinn des Jahrhunderts.* Stuttgart, Berlin, Cologne: Kohlammer, 1992.

Zweite Berliner Begegnung: Den Frieden erklären. Darmstadt and Neuwied: Luchterhand, 1983.

Zwerenz, Gerhard. "Deutschland, automatisiertes Schlachtfeld." *die tageszeitung*, 22 April 1983, 10.

Index